# SHORT LESSONS *in*
# U.S. HISTORY

( a revised edition of
*How Our Nation Became Great)*

E. Richard Churchill
Linda R. Churchill

J. WESTON
**WALCH**
**PUBLISHER**
Portland, Maine

Photos on the following pages appear courtesy of
AP/WIDE WORLD Photos:

163, 170, 175, 183, 186

Photos and art on the following pages appear courtesy of
Dover Pubications:

6, 8, 13, 34, 35, 36, 43, 52, 53, 56, 58, 66, 70, 82, 88, 91,
93, 98, 100, 101, 104, 111, 115, 117, 132, 136, 140, 143, 147

This is a revised edition of a book
previously titled *How Our Nation Became Great.*

1     2     3     4     5     6     7     8     9     10

ISBN 0-8251-3940-6

# CONTENTS

# INTRODUCTION

Many thousands of copies of this book have found their way into students' hands since the first edition was published. And, many thousands of students have benefited. This book does what it is designed to do: It helps learners understand the basics of United States history through easy-to-manage, high-interest lessons.

This new edition for the turn of the millennium includes a new chapter carrying the reader through the Clinton presidency and the final years of the twentieth century. Some of the special features included in this new edition are mini-biographies with a multicultural view, critical-thinking questions called "Think About It," and detailed time lines covering key events in United States history from 1492 to 1999.

We hope you will appreciate both the down-to-earth style of this book and the stories it tells. Perhaps *Short Lessons in U.S. History* will provide you with a springboard to further study of the complex, diverse history of the United States.

# MAPS HELP US UNDERSTAND UNITED STATES HISTORY

## Introduction

The history of our nation takes us back many years. When we study something that happened long ago, we need special tools to help with our learning.

Maps are one of the most useful tools in the study of United States history. They give us a picture of where events took place. By using a map, we can get a good idea where states and important places are located.

## Finding Locations on the Map

Our earth is a huge *sphere*, or ball. About one fourth of the surface of the earth is covered by land. Water covers the other three fourths of the earth.

Sometimes we use a *globe*, which is a model of the earth, when we want to see where a city or nation is located. At other times we use *maps*, or flat pictures of the earth's surface.

The earth is about 8,000 miles across. This means the earth has millions of square miles of surface. In order to find exactly where something is on that surface, we need some guides.

A major guideline is known as the *equator*. This line runs east and west around the very center of the earth. The equator divides the earth into two halves, or *hemispheres:* the Northern Hemisphere and the Southern Hemisphere.

At the very northern point on the earth is the *North Pole.* The *South Pole* is at the most southern point on the earth. It is quite easy for us to locate something on or near the equator or either of the poles. But what about places in between?

Every circle contains 360 degrees. A *degree* is a way of measuring distance around a circle or sphere. Since the earth is a sphere, it contains 360 degrees. The distance from the North Pole to the South Pole is halfway around the earth. Therefore, there are 180 degrees between the North Pole and the South Pole. Another way of looking at this is to see that there are 180 degrees from the equator over a pole and back to the equator.

To locate places between the equator and the poles, it helps to know how many degrees north or south of the equator those places are. The equator is the starting point for counting degrees north and south. The poles are 90 degrees north or south of the equator. Their location is usually written as 90°.

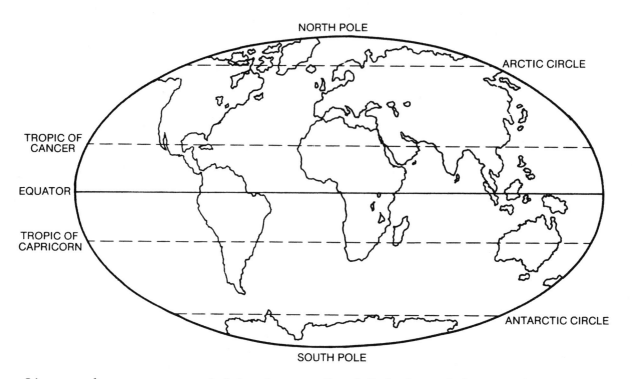

NORTH POLE

ARCTIC CIRCLE

TROPIC OF
CANCER

EQUATOR

TROPIC OF
CAPRICORN

ANTARCTIC CIRCLE

SOUTH POLE

Lines are drawn on maps and globes that are parallel to the equator. The lines are called lines of *latitude*. They are also known as *parallels of latitude*. These lines are one degree apart north and south of the equator.

Locations for places north or south of the equator are given in degrees of latitude. Cairo, Egypt, for example, is 30° north latitude. This means that Cairo is 30 degrees north of the equator.

The *Tropic of Cancer* and the *Tropic of Capricorn* are special parallels of latitude $23\frac{1}{2}°$ north and south of the equator. Two other special parallels are $66\frac{1}{2}°$ north and south of the equator. They are the *Arctic Circle* and the *Antarctic Circle*.

Parallels or lines of latitude are fine for locating places north or south of the equator. But what about finding our way east and west around the earth?

The earth is divided into an eastern and a western half, or hemisphere. The *Prime Meridian* runs from the North Pole to the South Pole through Greenwich, England. It is used as the starting point for measuring east and west around the globe.

All meridian lines run from the North Pole to the South Pole. They are usually called lines of *longitude*. These lines are located one degree apart from each other all the way around the globe.

There are 180 lines or degrees of longitude to the east of the Prime Meridian. Naturally, there are another 180 lines or degrees of longitude west of the Prime Meridian.

We can locate cities and nations by the number of degrees they are east or west of the Prime Meridian. Denver, Colorado, for example, is 105° west of the Prime Meridian.

The lines of latitude and longitude form what we call a *grid*. Once we know the number of degrees a place is north or south of the equator and east or west of the Prime Meridian, we can locate that place on a map or globe.

## More Information About Maps

To understand the information shown on a map, we need to know several things. One of the very important things we have to know is *direction*. It doesn't do much good to look at a map and have no idea whether one city is north or south of another. For this reason, maps sometimes have an arrow or *compass* telling the map user which direction is north. Unless a map's arrow tells you otherwise, north is always located at the top of a map.

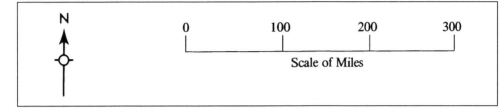

In order to know just how large a section of the earth a map shows, we need a *scale of distance*. A scale of distance is a line that looks like a little ruler. Each section on the scale of distance stands for a certain number of miles or kilometers on the earth's surface.

The earth is about 25,000 miles around at the equator. Maps may be a few feet across or even only inches across. Therefore, an inch on a map may stand for hundreds or even thousands of miles on earth.

A small map that shows one entire hemisphere might have a scale of distance in which one inch stands for several thousand miles. A map the same size that shows a small nation might use a scale in which one inch represents ten or twenty miles.

At times, the scale of distance is written out in words rather than shown as a line divided into sections. Such a written scale might say: "One inch equals one hundred miles."

Maps often show *time zones*. By dividing the 360 degrees in a circle into the 24 hours in a day, we learn that an hour is 15 degrees. In other words, every 15 degrees from east to west on the earth, the time changes by 1 hour.

Sometimes, the time zones have little clock faces at the top of the map. These clocks point to different times in different zones. Their purpose is to help the map user compare the time in one place with the time in another.

Maps that show national *borders* are called *political* maps. These maps often include important cities as well. Political maps often use color or shading to help the map user tell one nation or region from another.

Some maps show *physical features*. Mountain ranges, rivers, deserts, and lakes are common physical features. Some of these features may also appear on political maps.

Special maps may tell how much rainfall, or *precipitation*, an area gets each year. Other special maps show average temperatures. *Population density* maps give the user an idea how close people live to each other.

Still other maps tell what crops are grown or what languages are spoken in nations or regions.

The more you use maps, the easier they are to understand. Maps are a big help in learning about the history of our nation.

# A Quick Review

Read each statement in this quick review of what you have learned about maps. Decide whether the statement is true or false. Write "true" or "false" in the space before each statement.

1. _____ Our earth is a sphere.

2. _____ The equator divides the earth into east and west hemispheres.

3. _____ Lines of latitude are parallel to the equator.

4. _____ The Arctic Circle is south of the equator.

5. _____ The Prime Meridian runs through Denver, Colorado.

6. _____ Maps are usually drawn with north at the top.

7. _____ A scale of distance is always shown in kilometers.

8. _____ Political maps often use color or shading to show borders.

9. _____ Mountains and rivers are physical features.

10. _____ The world has 26 time zones.

# A NEW LAND IS REACHED AND SETTLED (1003–1733)

## Time Line

| EVENTS ELSEWHERE | DATE | EVENTS IN AMERICA |
| --- | --- | --- |
| | 1492 | Columbus was first European to arrive in West Indies |
| | 1498 | Cabot claimed East Coast for England |
| | 1513 | Ponce de León claimed Florida for Spain |
| *Reformation began* | 1517 | |
| *Cortés conquered Mexico* *Magellan began his sail around the world* | 1519 | |
| | 1534 | Cartier explored St. Lawrence River |
| | 1540–41 | Coronado explored the Southwest De Soto was first European to reach the Mississippi River |
| | 1565 | St. Augustine established |
| *England defeated Spanish Armada* | 1588 | |
| *Elizabeth I died* | 1603 | Champlain began exploration of Quebec |
| | 1607 | Jamestown, first English colony, established |
| | 1609 | Santa Fe established |
| | 1619 | English women and slaves came to Virginia People voted for representatives |
| | 1620 | Plymouth established |
| | 1623 | Dutch settled New Amsterdam |
| | 1630 | Massachusetts Bay established |
| | 1664 | English took New Amsterdam |
| | 1681 | Pennsylvania established |

## Introduction

About 1,000 years ago, the first European sailors, Norsemen, explored the coast of what is now Newfoundland. They stayed only a short while. For the next 500 years, Europeans did not return to North America. Then on October 12, 1492, Christopher Columbus landed in the West Indies. This was a world new to Europeans.

During the 250 years that followed, explorers and settlers from many European nations came to this new world. Most of them came looking for freedom or wealth—or both. Some found what they were hunting for. Many failed. Some went home to Europe. Many died in the wild new land. A great many people stayed on and made their homes in the new land.

## The Explorers Begin to Arrive

Over a thousand years ago, a Viking ship sailed from Iceland toward Greenland. Due to fog and a change in wind, the Vikings missed Greenland. Instead, they reached the part of North America now known as Newfoundland. Seventeen years later, *Leif the Lucky* sailed from Greenland in search of the land his friends had seen earlier. It was the year 1003 when Leif and 35 other men and women stepped off their ship. Within a short time, scouts had found good fishing, tall grass, and wild grapevines. The Vikings were so pleased with the new land that they built houses and stayed for the winter. When spring came, they sailed back to Greenland.

The next European visitor arrived in North America almost 500 years later. That visitor, *Christopher Columbus*, was not expecting to sight land when he did. Even after he and his crew landed, he had no real idea where they were. He thought they were in India. It is likely Columbus had never heard of the strange new land Leif the Lucky had discovered. The Vikings' explorations were unknown to most of the world.

In order to understand the great interest in exploration at the time of Columbus, we need to know a few things about Europe in 1492.

## Astrolabe and Magnetic Compass

Early European explorers depended on two devices to help them navigate across uncharted seas. These aids were the astrolabe and the magnetic compass.

The Chinese may have been the first people to use the *magnetic compass*. By the 1100's, it was being used by sailors in the Mediterranean Sea as well as by Chinese navigators.

The first magnetic compasses were simple but effective. They were just pieces of magnetized iron that were placed on a layer of cork. The cork floated on a bowl of water.

By the time of Columbus, the use of the magnetic compass had improved. Sailors knew that magnetic north was not true north and were able to adjust for the difference. They also used the compass card, which gave 32 directions or points of the compass. For instance, the compass card used north, north by east, north-northeast, northeast by north, northeast, northeast by east, and so on around the 360 degrees of the compass.

The *astrolabe* was an instrument used by ancient astronomers. Sailors took up its use when they realized it would help them navigate. The astrolabe was used to measure the angle of stars above the horizon.

The astrolabe was a metal disk that hung from a frame so the disk was always upright or vertical. It had sights through which the navigator looked at a star. A series of markings helped measure the star's elevation.

Using the compass for direction and the astrolabe for location, sailors had a good idea how far they had traveled and where they were.

In Europe, the Renaissance was just beginning. The people of Europe were trading with the people of China and the Indies. Europeans were beginning to wonder about the rest of the world.

Traders from cities along the Mediterranean Sea traveled to the eastern edge of the Mediterranean. There, they met *caravans* that had carried spices, fine cloth, and rare jewels all the way from the Indian Ocean. The traders loaded these things onto their ships and brought them back home.

Cities in Italy such as *Venice* and *Genoa* were becoming rich because of all this trading. Naturally, other nations were jealous and wanted some of the business for themselves. For this reason, both Spain and Portugal became interested in finding a fast and easy way to sail to China and the Indies.

---

### Prince Henry's Navigation School

*Prince Henry* of Portugal wanted his nation to make money from trading with China and other Asian nations. At the time most of this trade was controlled by cities in Italy.

In order to give Portuguese sailors an advantage, Prince Henry set up a school where ships' *navigators* would be trained. He felt that learning navigation and geography would enable them to locate new routes to the Far East.

It was Prince Henry's idea that ships could sail south around Africa. He got the best books and maps available and began to train his navigators and sea captains. Henry's sailors went farther and farther south along the African coast. By the time Prince Henry died in 1460, his ships had sailed south of the equator.

---

In 1487, a sailor from Portugal named *Bartholomeu Dias* sailed around the southern tip of Africa. Eleven years later, *Vasco da Gama* followed the path of Dias but continued across the Indian Ocean and reached India. Portugal then had a way to reach India and China by water. This made the shipping of goods much cheaper than the old way of first using a ship, then a caravan, and then a ship again to reach Europe.

### Think About It:

Caravans brought goods from China and Southeast Asia to the Mediterranean Sea. Why did European nations want to find all-water routes to the East?

But back to Columbus. In 1492, Queen Isabella and King Ferdinand of Spain had just been married. Their marriage helped join all of Spain into one nation. When Columbus arrived with his idea of reaching the Indies by sailing west, he came at the right time. Italy was getting rich, and Portugal was close to being a big trading nation. Spain wanted a share in the trade as well, so Columbus was given three ships, and his historic voyage began.

On August 3, 1492, the three tiny ships left Palos, Spain. Using only a compass and the stars as a guide, Columbus sailed west. As the ships sailed farther and farther from land, the crew liked the voyage less and less. Huge ocean waves seemed ready to swallow the small ships. But finally, on October 12, land was sighted.

The land was not the Indies, as Columbus had hoped, and he did not return to Spain with great riches. Even though he made three more trips and started a settlement, he never did find spices, precious jewels, or other fine things. But he did encounter a world unknown to Europe, and he did claim a large amount of land for Spain.

Christopher Columbus

Columbus's great voyage was as fantastic to the people of his time as space travel is to us today. Actually, Columbus's voyage was far more daring than today's moon shots. Columbus had no team of scientists to help him on his way. He was truly on his own.

---

**Think About It:**

If you had lived during the time of Columbus, would you have been willing to go with him on his first voyage? Give several reasons why you would or would not have wanted to sail with him.

---

After Columbus, Europeans knew the New World was there. People from many nations were willing to explore it, and they claimed land for their home countries in Europe.

## Other Explorers Follow Columbus

In 1497, *John Cabot* left Bristol, England. His voyage took him along the eastern coast of Canada and past New England. He claimed all the land he sailed past for England. Cabot made a second voyage the following year, but he never returned to England. Perhaps a storm at sea sank his ship, or maybe he got off course and struck an iceberg. Nobody knows.

*Ponce de León* was the governor of the island of Puerto Rico when he heard about the land to the north. When he sailed north in 1513, he discovered what is now known as Florida. It is said he was looking for a fountain whose waters would make him young again. Whether that is true or not, he did explore much of the land around Florida. Everything he explored he claimed for Spain. In 1521, a Native American arrow ended Ponce de León's exploring and his life.

There was no question that a new world had been found. Strangely enough, many explorers spent their time trying to find their way around this new land instead of exploring it. In 1519, *Ferdinand Magellan* sailed around South America and across the Pacific. Then came a number of explorers trying to sail around North America to get to China. They were hunting for the *Northwest Passage*, which they thought went through North America. This would connect the Atlantic Ocean to the Pacific Ocean and make it easier to get to China.

*Jacques Cartier* left France in 1534 to sail to the New World. When he discovered the great *St. Lawrence River*, he thought he had found the Northwest Passage. It was not until he had sailed up the river for many days that he realized he had found a river, not an ocean passage. His voyages led France to claim land in what is now Canada.

Six years later, in 1540, a Spaniard named *Francisco Coronado* left the great Spanish settlement at Mexico City. He and his huge group of men marched north looking for the Seven Cities of Gold. They never found the golden cities, of course. All they found were Native American *pueblos* and hot, burning desert. They also found death from the desert and from angry Native Americans. Their great march gave Spain claim to all of the present-day southwestern United States.

While Coronado was tramping across the western deserts, another Spanish explorer was wandering along the mighty *Mississippi River*. He was *Hernando de Soto*. His fleet of ships had left Havana, Cuba, in 1539. He landed in Florida and marched westward. By 1541, he had found the Mississippi. Like Coronado, these people found no gold. They found Native Americans, whom they mistreated, and a fever called "malaria," which killed many of the Spaniards. When de Soto died, his men buried him in the Mississippi so the Native Americans would not know their leader had died. In 1543, the few remaining members of the expedition reached Mexico and safety. They had claimed more land for Spain, but it meant little to the 300 dead men who were left behind.

---

### Drake and the Sea Dogs

*Francis Drake* was the boldest and best known of the English *sea dogs*. These English sailors raided Spanish settlements and treasure ships. The voyage that made Drake famous began in England in 1577.

Drake and five ships crossed the Atlantic Ocean and sailed south around South America. Only one ship, the *Golden Hind*, made it through the Strait of Magellan. This ship, with Drake in command, sailed up the western coast of South America and Central America, and as far north as California.

One at a time the English captured Spanish treasure ships. With Drake's own ship full of gold and silver, it was time to sail home. Instead of risking fights with Spanish warships, Drake sailed west across the Pacific Ocean. He then crossed the Indian Ocean, sailed around Africa, and returned north to England.

Drake's voyage gave England claim to the west coast of North America because Drake landed there to repair his ship.

The king of Spain was furious and demanded Drake's head. Instead, Queen Elizabeth I made Drake a knight, so history remembers him as Sir Francis Drake.

---

*Samuel de Champlain* left France in 1603 and spent years exploring the area along the St. Lawrence and the Great Lakes. He started a settlement at Quebec, which was the first lasting French settlement in North America. Then he started another settlement at *Montreal*. His journeys gave more land to France.

It was in 1609 that *Henry Hudson* left Holland. He was looking for China but discovered what is known as the *Hudson River* in New York instead. Not willing to let well enough alone, Hudson set out the next year in an English ship. This time he sailed farther north looking for the Northwest Passage. Winter caught his ship in *Hudson Bay*. By spring, food was scarce and the crew frightened. The crew put Hudson, his son, and a few crewmen in a small boat in the icy sea. The boy and men in the small boat were never heard from again. The land around Hudson Bay now belonged to England, but no one really seemed to care.

A French priest, *Father Marquette*, and a French explorer, *Louis Joliet*, left Lake Michigan in canoes in 1673 looking for a passage to Asia. Instead they located the Mississippi River. When they realized they were in a river and not on their way to Asia, they turned back and went home. Of course they claimed the land they explored for France.

Nine years later **Robert La Salle** traveled through the Great Lakes and then down the Mississippi River to the Gulf of Mexico. La Salle was interested in finding an easy way for French traders to get into the middle of North America. Once he realized the Mississippi River would serve his purpose, he claimed it for France.

**Think About It:**

Remember that de Soto claimed the Mississippi River area for Spain. Then Marquette, Joliet, and La Salle claimed the same land for France. What do you suppose might happen when two strong nations both claim the same land?

In less than 200 years, most of North America had been claimed by nations of Europe. Settlements had begun. More and more people were coming to this wild new land. Soon it would begin to show signs of European-style civilization.

**Think About It:**

All of the European explorers claimed the land they crossed or sailed past. What gave them the right to claim this land in the New World?

## Exploration Puzzle Quiz

**Directions:** Explorers used every clue to help them in their search. Follow each clue and try to unscramble the letters after the clue to spell something about exploration.

1. This Portuguese sailor reached India by sailing around Africa.

   g a d m a a  _____

2. These sailors were often called "Norsemen." They saw the New World long before Columbus did.

   i k g v n i s _____

3. Many explorers hunted for this route to China.

   w o r n t e s t h   a p e g s s a

   _____

4. This sailor claimed much land for England.

   b a t o c  _____

5. This Spanish explorer discovered the Mississippi River.

   s e d t o o  _____

6. This Spaniard looked for the Seven Cities of Gold but did not find them.

   r a d o o n o c

   _____

7. This explorer was left with his son in a small boat.

   s u d h o n _____

8. This Frenchman discovered the St. Lawrence River.

   t e r r i a c  _____

9. This priest did a lot of exploring for France.

   t e r q e t m u a

   _____

10. The Mississippi River was claimed for France by this man.

    s a l e a l l  _____

## Exploration

We have tried to show how Spain, England, France, and Holland got their claims to North America. All the explorers who traveled for a country are grouped together on the key to the map at the lower left of page 12. For example, several explorers sailed for France, but some of these made their trips more than 100 years apart. Study both the map and its key. Then write the proper answers after each of the following statements.

1. Explorers from this country traveled only in the southern part of North America.
   _____

2. This country claimed land in the far north of North America.
   _____

3. Explorers for this country traveled down the Mississippi, claiming all that land for their country. _____

4. Columbus was the first to explore for this nation. _____
   _____

5. Cabot gave this country claim to most of the east coast of North America.
   _____

6. La Salle explored for this country and eventually died in the exploration of North America. _____

7. Coronado explored the southwestern part of North America for this country.
   _____

8. This is the only explorer shown on the map who explored for two nations—England and Holland. _____
   _____

9. This explorer started from Mexico City. _____
   _____

10. This explorer claimed the mouth of the Mississippi River for Spain. _____
    _____

11. This English explorer died in a large bay which is now named for him. _____
    _____

12. This explorer, and not Columbus, was actually the first of the group on the map to see North America, since Columbus explored islands off the coast of North America.
    _____

13. To get to the New World, explorers had to travel across this ocean. _____
    _____

14. The coast of Greenland was explored for England by this man. _____
    _____

15. This was the last explorer shown on the map to explore North America. _____
    _____

## Exploration of the New World: 1492–1609

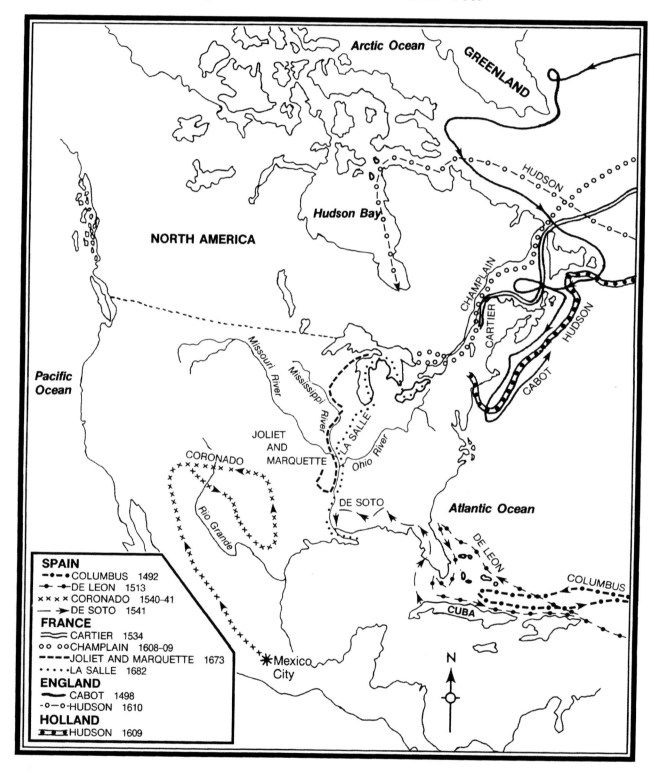

SPAIN
- –•–•–COLUMBUS  1492
- –•––•–DE LEON  1513
- ××××CORONADO  1540-41
- ———➤ DE SOTO  1541

FRANCE
- ≈≈≈≈CARTIER  1534
- ∘∘∘∘∘CHAMPLAIN  1608-09
- – – – – JOLIET AND MARQUETTE  1673
- • • • • LA SALLE  1682

ENGLAND
- —— CABOT  1498
- –∘–∘–HUDSON  1610

HOLLAND
- ▮▮▮HUDSON  1609

## *Elizabeth I (1533–1603)*

By the time she died in 1603, **Queen Elizabeth I** had helped make England richer and more powerful than ever before.

Elizabeth had to be strong herself to survive. It was natural that she wanted her nation to be strong.

Her sister, Mary, was queen of England before Elizabeth. Mary hated Elizabeth and probably wanted to kill her. Instead, when Elizabeth was twenty years old, Mary had her imprisoned in the Tower of London. Later, Elizabeth was released and sent to Hatfield House, which was north of London. There she lived for five years until her sister died.

Once Elizabeth I became ruler of England, her troubles were just beginning. Her cousin Mary, Queen of Scots, ruled Scotland. Many felt Mary of Scotland should rule England as well. Eventually Elizabeth had her cousin captured and put into prison. Twenty years later, when a new plot was discovered to make Mary the queen, Elizabeth ordered her cousin's head cut off.

As bold as Elizabeth was, it is no wonder she sent sailors such as Drake out to raid Spanish ships and settlements. But Elizabeth wanted to settle new lands to expand her empire. Therefore, she sent sailors such as Sir Walter Raleigh to the New World to start English colonies.

When Spain began to resent and fear Elizabeth's growing power, **King Philip II** decided to conquer England. He ordered a mighty fleet of warships to be built. By 1588, Spain's mighty **Armada** was ready to sail to England and attack.

Elizabeth knew the attack was coming. She ordered a series of brush piles built on hilltops. When the Spanish Armada was sighted, the brush piles were set on fire as a signal. The smaller, faster English ships put out to sea.

The small English ships daringly sailed in under the Spanish guns and attacked. After hours of fighting, a storm came up, and destroyed even more Spanish ships. The battle was over. The Armada was beaten. England and Queen Elizabeth I ruled the seas!

Elizabeth realized the value of foreign trade and setting up colonies in newly discovered lands. To encourage trade, the East India Company was formed. This company was responsible for helping England grow rich.

For 45 years Elizabeth ruled England. By the time of her death, the nation was the most powerful in the world. Under Elizabeth's reign, the **British Empire** began, grew, and prospered.

## Explorers Who Came to Stay

We have already mentioned the French settlements of Quebec and Montreal. These towns were used mainly as trading centers. The French in the New World most often made a living as fur traders. The Native Americans brought furs to the French, who traded with guns, ammunition, knives, and other items. The French then sold the furs for money with which they bought more trade goods. The Native Americans got what they wanted, and the French got the furs.

Even the French *missionaries* got along well with the Native Americans. These priests usually lived with them and taught Christianity without force.

But what about the settlements on lands claimed by the other nations of Europe?

In 1565, Spaniards built a fort at *St. Augustine, Florida*. It had a great wall around it and a moat dug around the wall. St. Augustine is the oldest city in North America.

In northern New Mexico in 1609, the Spanish had a city called *Santa Fe*. This city was the capital of northern Mexico. Today it is the capital of the state of New Mexico.

The English did not do quite so well at first. *Walter Raleigh* started a settlement on *Roanoke Island* in 1585. The Roanoke Colony was near what is now North Carolina. It ran into trouble from the beginning; food ran low and the Native Americans fought the colonists. When other colonists arrived, things seemed a bit better. *Virginia Dare*, the first English child born in the New World, was born at Roanoke. By 1591, the colony had vanished. When an English ship stopped to visit the colony, no one was there. The only clue was the word "CROATOAN" carved on a tree. No trace was ever found of the missing people of Roanoke.

In 1607, the English made another try at starting a colony in the New World. This time settlers landed along the James River in what is now Virginia. Again they got off to a poor start. *Jamestown* was built on low, marshy land. Mosquitoes bothered the settlers and carried disease. Many settlers spent their time hunting for gold instead of helping build the town and plant the fields. A Native American battle added to the troubles. By the end of the first year, 67 out of the 105 colonists had died. If some of the Native Americans had not given the settlers food, more Englishmen would have starved.

---

**Think About It:**

Columbus reached the New World in 1492. Jamestown was begun in 1607. Why did it take so long for English colonization to begin?

---

*John Smith* became the leader of the group during that first year. He established the rule that men who did not work would not eat. All supplies were put in a storehouse, and each worker got the same amount to use. Jamestown could be called America's first experiment in communism!

During the following years, the colony became stronger. A Native American, *Pocahontas*, married a settler, *John Rolfe*. This brought peace between the Native Americans and English for a time. Rolfe and other colonists began growing tobacco to ship to England. Tobacco was soon so important it grew even in the streets of Jamestown. So began the idea of growing only one cash crop. Farmers in the South followed that idea for many years and often ruined their land because of it.

## Pocahontas (1595–1617)

Pocahontas was the younger daughter of Powhatan, leader of a group of Algonquin tribes living in Virginia. Her real name was Matoaka. Pocahontas means "playful one." She helped establish peace between her people and the white settlers. She brought food to the settlers when they were nearly starving. She met and married an English settler, John Rolfe. One year later, they had a son. They traveled to England, where she was treated as a princess by the King and Queen of England. In 1617, she died of smallpox and was buried in England, far from her people.

In 1619, three things happened that changed life in Jamestown. A Dutch ship came to Jamestown with a cargo of African *slaves*. The slaves were sold to colonists to work in the fields. With slave labor, a farmer could raise more crops and make more money. No one bothered to ask the slaves what they thought of the idea.

Also in 1619, a shipload of unmarried women came from England. They became wives for the men of Jamestown. Families were started, and Jamestown became a real town.

The third important event of 1619 was a new kind of government. The people of the colony were allowed to elect *representatives* to help the English governor make laws. This was the beginning of self-government for the European people of the New World.

A year later, in 1620, the *Mayflower* arrived at what was later named *Plymouth Colony*. The people in charge of the voyage were called *Pilgrims*, which meant "travelers." These people had moved from place to place in Europe because their religion made them unpopular. The move to *New England* was their last hope.

### The Mayflower Compact

When the *Mayflower* finally reached land, it had been blown far off course by strong winds. The charter granted to the Pilgrims entitled them to settle in Virginia. Instead, they landed far to the north in what is now Massachusetts.

The leaders felt their charter was not valid, or good, outside of Virginia. Before going ashore, the Pilgrims held a meeting and drew up a new charter they called the *Mayflower Compact*. The men signed the paper, which stated that they agreed all would take part in making laws for the new settlement. The Compact also stated that the members of the group agreed to obey these laws.

A part of the Mayflower Compact reads, " . . . do enact, constitute, and frame such just and equal laws, ordinances, acts, constitutions, and offices, from time to time, as shall be thought most meet and convenient for the general good of the colony."

Thus in 1620, Plymouth Colony took a step toward its own self-government.

The unlucky Pilgrims landed farther north than they had planned. It was December, and the weather was terrible. They lived on the tiny ship while homes were built. Over half of the people in the new colony died that first winter.

The next spring, friendly Native Americans taught the settlers about growing corn and helped them get farms started. The following fall, the settlers had a good harvest and their little colony was saved. They invited the Native Americans to a feast and celebrated the first Thanksgiving.

### Samoset

Samoset first met English settlers when he was fishing. This Native American learned words in English and aided the Plymouth colonists. He helped the Native Americans and the colonists to better understand one another. He was the first Native American to deed land to English colonists.

Another religious group arrived in 1630. About a thousand **Puritans** settled around **Boston**, Massachusetts. This rich colony was called **Massachusetts Bay Colony** and grew quickly.

Beginning in 1623, the Dutch built a trading city called **New Amsterdam**, where New York is now. A Dutchman gave the Native Americans $24 worth of goods for Manhattan Island, which is now downtown New York City.

By now, people from many nations were coming to North America. People came for many reasons. Some found what they wanted, others did not.

## Later English Colonies

Jamestown was the beginning of the colony of Virginia. Plymouth and Massachusetts Bay Colonies became the colony of Massachusetts. But what about the other English colonies?

Four years after the Puritans arrived, the English colony of **Maryland** was begun. It was started by Lord **Baltimore**, a member of the **Calvert** family. The Calverts were Catholics. In 1634, only Protestants were really welcome in England. The Calverts settled the city of Baltimore and allowed people of any religion to join them. This was the first colony to allow complete **religious freedom**.

Religion was an important part of most of the New England colonies. Some people could not get along with the Puritans of Massachusetts Bay. One of these people was a preacher named **Roger Williams**. He felt everyone should have religious freedom. He also thought the Puritans should treat the Native Americans better. The Puritan leaders did not like his ideas and sent him away from their colony. He traveled southwest and started his own settlement called **Providence** in 1636. Williams paid the Native Americans for the land and soon had a successful colony. After a time, his little colony was called **Rhode Island**.

The same year Williams moved to Providence, another minister left Massachusetts Bay. **Thomas Hooker** and his friends moved to the rich land along the Connecticut River. These pioneer people were the first of many people to move west. Even though they did not travel far, they started the movement toward the west that lasted for 200 years. The people who settled **Connecticut** wrote a plan for the government of their colony. This was the first **written constitution** in the New World.

During the next 30 years or so, English settlers arrived faster and faster. In 1664, the English decided there was no reason to let the Dutch control New Amsterdam any longer. An English fleet sailed into the harbor and ordered the Dutch to surrender. Even though the Dutch governor was furious, he had little choice. The English flag was raised, and New Amsterdam became *New York*. The Dutch people were allowed to stay, but England now ruled the colony.

It is likely that many Swedish people laughed at the Dutch. Several years earlier the Dutch had taken *Delaware* away from the Swedes. When the English took New York, they also got Delaware. The English got something more than land from the Swedes. They also learned how to build log cabins, such as were later used by men like Daniel Boone.

**Think About It:**

The Dutch took Delaware from the Swedes. England took New York and Delaware from the Dutch. Why could one country take land already claimed by another nation?

In 1681, a member of the *Quaker* religion started a new colony. *William Penn* was given a great amount of land in the New World in payment for a debt. He called his colony *Pennsylvania*, which means "Penn's Woods." Penn got along well with the Native Americans and allowed people of all religions to come to his colony.

Beginning with Jamestown, Virginia, the English settled twelve colonies during the 1600's. We have mentioned eight of them. The final English colony was not founded until 1733. It was started as a home for prisoners.

In England, a person who could not pay his or her debts was often sent to prison until the debt was paid. Of course, a poor person could not raise money while in prison and usually ended up staying in prison. A rich man, *James Oglethorpe*, felt this was wrong. He asked the king of England for permission to take some of the prisoners to the New World and start a colony. King George II liked the idea. These people who owed money could work in the new colony and earn money to pay their debts. Also, this new colony would protect the Carolinas and Virginia from the Spaniards, who had settled Florida. Even though the prisoners ran the risk of Native American or Spanish attack, it was better than prison. Due to poor land and raids from Native Americans and Spaniards, *Georgia* did not do as well as Oglethorpe had hoped. It did survive, however, and became the final English colony in what is now the United States.

**Think About It:**

It was common for new towns, rivers, or colonies to be named after English rulers. Who do you suppose ruled England when the following towns and colonies were named?

| | |
|---|---|
| Charlestown | Maryland |
| Jamestown | Georgia |

# New World Settlements

The map on page 19 shows the English colonies in the New World. It also shows part of the French and Spanish territory. For each question below, look at the map to determine the correct answer. In each case, underline the correct one.

1. The eastern boundary for the English colonies is
   (a) where their land borders the French territory    (b) the Atlantic Ocean
   (c) the Mississippi River    (d) where Georgia touches Spanish territory

   **Our map divides the English colonies into three groups because of different conditions found there. Check the key on your map to answer some of these questions.**

2. There are four New England colonies. Which of these colonies is *not* a New England colony?  (a) Rhode Island   (b) New Hampshire   (c) New York   (d) Connecticut

3. The smallest of the thirteen English colonies is
   (a) Rhode Island    (b) South Carolina    (c) Delaware    (d) Connecticut

4. The Hudson River was very important to
   (a) Massachusetts    (b) Virginia    (c) Maryland    (d) New York

5. The unsuccessful settlement of Roanoke, which disappeared, could be hunted for in
   (a) Virginia    (b) Georgia    (c) North Carolina    (d) Delaware

6. The first permanent English settlement in the New World was Jamestown. This settlement is located in the colony of
   (a) North Carolina    (b) Massachusetts    (c) New Jersey    (d) Virginia

7. The smallest of the Middle colonies is
   (a) Rhode Island    (b) Delaware    (c) Maryland    (d) Georgia

8. The only settlement in Spanish territory shown on your map is
   (a) Quebec    (b) Roanoke    (c) St. Augustine    (d) New York City

9. Land west of the Mississippi was claimed by  (a) France  (b) England  (c) Spain  (d) Sweden

10. Plymouth settlement is located in
    (a) Rhode Island    (b) Virginia    (c) Massachusetts    (d) Connecticut

11. Quebec was one trading city started on the St. Lawrence River. The other trading city on the St. Lawrence was    (a) New York    (b) Roanoke    (c) St. Augustine    (d) Montreal

12. The river separating the colonies of Maryland and Virginia is the
    (a) Potomac    (b) Hudson    (c) Ohio    (d) Mississippi

13. There are more Southern colonies than New England or Middle colonies. How many Southern colonies are there?    (a) one    (b) three    (c) five    (d) seven

14. The territory along the Ohio River was claimed by
    (a) France    (b) England    (c) Spain    (d) Holland

15. The only English colony to touch Spanish territory is
    (a) Massachusetts    (b) Georgia    (c) South Carolina    (d) Pennsylvania

# Map of English Colonies: 1750

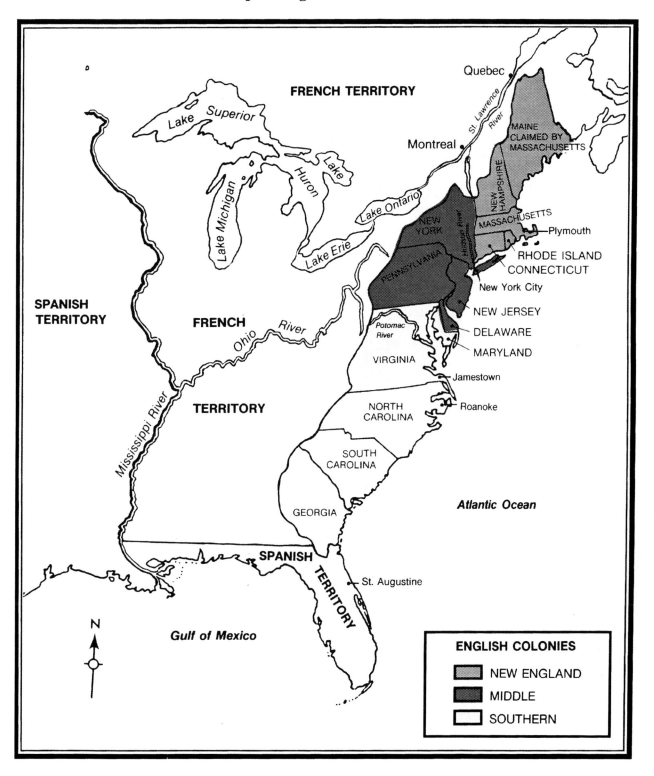

# Settlers

**Directions:** Match each clue with a word or name from the stories you have just read about early settlements in the New World. Write the answers in the numbered spaces.

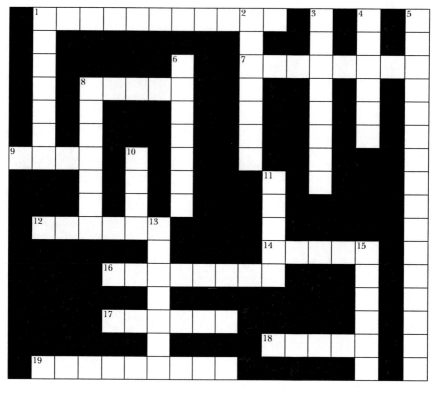

## Across

1. Oldest city in the United States
7. Roger _____ was told to leave Massachusetts Bay.
8. John _____ married Pocahontas.
9. William _____ founded a colony especially for Quakers.
12. Oldest French city in the New World
14. People who started New Amsterdam
16. Colony started by the Swedes but taken over by the Dutch
17. People who lived in Quebec and Montreal
18. Kind of worker brought to Jamestown in 1619
19. The first English settlement in the New World to survive

## Down

1. Capital of northern Mexico, settled in 1609
2. English name for New Amsterdam
3. People who settled Plymouth Colony
4. Religion of early settlers of Pennsylvania
5. Colony begun by the Puritans
6. Colony settled by English prisoners
8. Name of lost English colony
10. Virginia _____ was the first English child born in North America.
11. _____ Island was founded by Roger Williams.
13. Family that started a colony where Catholics would be safe
15. Thomas _____ began settlement of Connecticut.

# THIRTEEN COLONIES BECOME A NATION (1636–1781)

3

## Time Line

| EVENTS ELSEWHERE | DATE | EVENTS IN AMERICA |
|---|---|---|
| | 1754 | French and Indian War began |
| | 1755 | General Braddock killed |
| | 1759 | English captured Quebec |
| | 1763 | Peace treaty signed; Pontiac Rebellion |
| | 1765 | Stamp Act passed |
| | 1766 | Stamp Act repealed |
| | 1767 | Townshend Acts |
| *James Cook explored New Zealand and Australian coasts* | 1770 | Boston Massacre |
| | 1773 | Boston Tea Party |
| | 1774 | First Continental Congress |
| | 1775 | Paul Revere's Ride; Battle of Lexington and Concord |
| *France and Spain agreed to help Americans* | 1776 | Declaration of Independence; Battle of Trenton |
| *Lafayette helped Americans* | 1777 | Battle of Saratoga; winter at Valley Forge |
| *French fleet sent to help Americans* | 1778 | |
| | 1780 | Treason by Benedict Arnold |
| | 1781 | Cornwallis surrendered at Yorktown |
| | 1783 | Peace treaty signed |

## Introduction

In the years following the settlement of the English colonies, many people came to the new land. Life in the New England colonies was very different from life in the Southern colonies. For that matter, life in the French or Spanish colonies was different from life in the English colonies. These differences finally led to war between the French and English settlers.

The English colonists also had troubles with England. These troubles seemed small at first, but they grew quickly into serious problems. Finally, in 1775, the colonists began to fight the soldiers of England. The Revolutionary War was fought and won by the colonists. From that victory came a new nation. That nation is the United States of America.

## Life in the Colonies

Life in the Spanish colonies of the new land was entirely different from life in the other colonies. Usually the land in the Spanish colonies was owned by large landholders. These *rancheros* of the Southwest owned huge areas of land. Much of the work was done by Native American workers, who were actually slaves to the Spaniards.

The Catholic Church played an important part in the lives of the Spanish colonists. All too often, the Church itself was guilty of treating American Indians badly. The Church became a partner in the hunt for gold and silver. Because of the Spanish greed for gold, many Native Americans died in the mines trying to bring the precious metal out from under the earth.

### *Junípero Serra (1713–1784)*

Junípero Serra was a Spanish *missionary* (Christian teacher) who came to Mexico City. He learned the languages of the native people and taught them about farming. From him they learned how to raise sheep and weave cloth from the wool. He traveled to California in 1769, where he started a series of missions. In California, Serra continued to teach the Native Americans about farming and living peacefully. He became a saint of the Catholic Church in 1988.

The French got along well with the Native Americans. Their settlements were built because of trade, usually along rivers. In addition to the cities and trading posts along the St. Lawrence River and the Great Lakes, the French began to settle along the Mississippi River. Such cities as New Orleans and St. Louis began as trading cities. Also, these cities gave the French control of the river.

### Think About It:

The cities of New Orleans and St. Louis gave the French control of the Mississippi River. How did cities give a nation control of a river? Why was controlling rivers important?

The English colonists were unlike either the French or the Spanish. The English treated the Native Americans far better than the Spaniards did. However, the English did not get along with the Native Americans as well as the French did. In general, the English wanted land for farms. They cleared the forests and planted crops. The French usually did little farming.

Life in the English colonies was different from colony to colony. In the South, the plantation system developed. Plantations were huge farms of up to several thousand acres. The owner used slaves to do the farming on the plantation. Usually only one crop was grown on the plantation. For years that crop was tobacco, which was shipped to Europe. Some plantations grew rice, and later cotton became the most important crop. Since raising only one crop wore out the soil, plantation owners needed increasing amounts of land.

The plantation was usually along a river. This helped in the shipping of crops. A boat came right to the plantation to collect the crop. Roads were so poor it was impossible to ship tons of tobacco or cotton by wagon.

Life for the plantation owners was interesting. The people dressed well, visited friends at other plantations, and gave parties.

Boys were educated by teachers who came to live at the plantations. When a boy was ready for college, he was often sent to England. Girls did not attend college.

Religion was not nearly as important to the Southerners as it was to the people of New England. Churches were not very strong in the Southern colonies.

Not everyone in the Southern colonies lived on plantations. Many small farmers barely made a living and owned no slaves. Then, as now, there were more poor people than rich.

---

### Indentured Servants

Many of those who wished to come to the New World were too poor to pay for their passage aboard ship. One way some of these poor people managed to come to America was to become *indentured servants*.

An *indenture* was a written agreement that the person signed. It said that person would work for another person who paid for his or her fare to the colonies. The servant worked for three to seven years without pay in return for transportation to the colonies. During this time the servant received food, clothing, and shelter, but no pay.

Indentured servants worked on farms, in shops, or at whatever their employer wanted them to do. At the end of the indentured time, the person became free to go where he or she wanted. Some employers gave their freed servants a gun, clothing, and even a few acres of land.

Many of the indentured servants went on to become successful merchants, business owners, or farmers.

---

North of Maryland were the Middle colonies. Farms here were smaller than Southern plantations, and very few slaves were used. Most people made a living from trading and shipping goods or some other business. Quakers and Catholics mixed with people of other religions.

The Middle colonies were in between the Southern and New England ways of life. School was more important than in the South, but not as important as in New England. Life was harder than in the South, but not as harsh as in New England.

The New England farms were often poor, so the people had to find other ways of

making a living. Tall forests were used for shipbuilding. Ships meant fishing and trading. Many New Englanders lived as fishermen or sailors.

The clothing of the people of New England told much about their lives. Black and gray were common colors.

Religion was important to the New England colonies. The Puritans had the strictest religion. Church attendance was required of everyone. A person who did not belong to the Puritan religion was not allowed to live in many Puritan towns. Remember that this was the reason that the colonies of Rhode Island and Connecticut had been started.

The minister was the most important person in town. His word was law, and only a few daring people ever argued with him.

Every child went to school to learn to read the **Bible**. Other things were taught, but reading the Bible was the main point of Puritan education. Teachers used a stick to settle any problems in school. By 1636, Massachusetts had a college. It was called Harvard.

---

**Think About It:**

The New England and Southern colonies were quite different. Their approaches to farming, education, and religion were among the differences. What caused these major variations?

---

## Puritan Sunday

The **Puritans** of New England were extremely strict and very religious. Sunday was devoted entirely to religion. No work was done on Sunday, and every member of the family was expected to go to church.

The churches had no heat and were terribly uncomfortable during the harsh New England winters. Members sat on hard wooden benches with men on one side of the church and women and girls on the other. Boys sat in the balcony and were expected to be silent. Noisy boys were punished for not keeping quiet.

The sermons were extremely long. Puritan ministers preached two sermons each Sunday. Everyone attended both services. All members of the church were expected to think and read only about religion on Sunday.

Such things as card playing and dancing were strictly forbidden on Sunday. In fact, no pleasures were allowed on Sunday at all.

The Puritans felt God would punish them for doing wrong, and especially for not attending to religion on Sunday.

---

An interesting thing about the Puritan towns of New England was the punishment given to people who did wrong. Who has not talked about someone else to a friend? This is **gossip**. Gossip was likely to be punished by the **ducking stool**: a chair on the end of a long pole was ducked into a pool of water. The person guilty of gossiping was tied to the chair.

People who broke laws might have to spend the day standing at a **pillory**. The head and hands of the lawbreaker were locked in a wooden board. To add to the punishment, the lawbreaker often had to stand on tiptoe to keep from choking.

Other lawbreakers might sit with hands and feet locked in **stocks**. Sometimes such a person sat on the edge of a board. To make the seat less comfortable, the edge was often sharpened.

Anyone passing a person in either pillory or stocks was allowed to tease the lawbreaker. If some mud was handy, it was all right to throw it at the person. Some people even carried rotten eggs or ripe tomatoes to throw at those being punished.

Other punishments were much harsher. Some towns had a whipping post where lawbreakers were lashed with a long whip. A thief might have a red-hot branding iron used to burn the letter *T* on his or her forehead. People who swore might have a hole burned through their tongues. Liars were sometimes punished by having their tongues cut out.

Probably the worst of all Puritan punishments happened in the town of *Salem* in 1692. Some teenage girls claimed they had been bewitched by an old woman. The old woman was found guilty of being a *witch* and hanged. The girls accused many other people of being witches. Before long, nineteen innocent people had been hanged and one old man pressed to death with huge rocks.

> **Think About It:**
> The Puritans were deeply religious. They believed in education. How did they allow themselves to kill people accused of witchcraft?

# Colonial Life

**Directions:** Each clue below should help you think of a word about life in colonial times. The blanks above the clues show how many letters are in each answer. The answers are in the material you just read.

1.      C _ _ _ _ _ _ _
2.      _ O _ _ _ _ _ _
3.    _ _ L _ _ _ _ _
4.    _ _ O _ _ _ _
5.      N _ _ _ _ _   _ _ _ _ _ _ _ _ _
6.    _ I _ _ _
7.    _ _ A _ _ _ _ _
8.    _ _ L _ _

9.    _ L _ _ _ _ _ _ _ _
10.   _ I _ _ _ _
11.    F _ _ _ _ _
12.    E _ _ _ _ _ _ _ _

## Clues

1. Done to forest land in order to have farms

2. Important crop in the Southern colonies

3. Very important thing in Puritan life

4. Wooden frames used to punish lawbreakers

5. People treated as slaves in many Spanish colonies

6. Book all Puritans were supposed to read

7. Severe punishment used by Puritans for stealing

8. Town where witch trials were held in 1692

9. Huge farm in the Southern colonies

10. Used for transportation instead of roads by early colonists

11. People who got along best with the Native Americans

12. More important in New England than in Southern colonies

## Frontier Life and War with the French

Some settlers did not want to live in the settled colonies. These men and women pushed west into the unexplored forests. Some of them were looking for cheap land where they could begin farming without much money. Others wanted to trap animals for furs. Many of these early *frontiersmen* just liked the adventure of new places and did not like living near people.

More and more people moved into the lands west of the English colonies. Some used rivers for travel; others followed valleys through the mountains.

When a group of frontier settlers found a place they liked, they would build a fort or stockade for shelter and protection. With the stockade as a community center, cabins were built around it and lands cleared for farming.

Perhaps the most famous of the early frontiersmen was *Daniel Boone*. His settlement of Boonesborough in Kentucky was one of the first settlements west of the *Appalachian Mountains*.

The Native Americans felt threatened by the people who moved into their forests and took their lands. Life on the early frontier was never safe from Indian attack.

Another danger on the frontier was the French. This danger increased with each new settlement. La Salle had claimed for France all of the land drained by the Mississippi River. This included all the land between the Appalachian Mountains and the Rocky Mountains. The French were afraid the English settlers would ruin their land for hunting and trapping.

> **Think About It:**
>
> Can you think why the English cutting down trees and making farms would ruin hunting areas for the Native Americans and the French?

For about 100 years, France and England had fought each other in war after war. Any time these nations fought in Europe, their colonies fought in the New World. For this reason, the French and English colonists did not trust each other.

The French saw increasing numbers of English colonists coming into the *Ohio River Valley*, so they began to build forts to defend their land. The English felt the French had no right to build these forts. The English said their colonies reached from ocean to ocean.

In 1753, the governor of Virginia sent a messenger to warn the French to leave the land along the Ohio River. That messenger was a young man named *George Washington*. The French paid no attention to the warning. The next year Washington was sent with some soldiers to capture a French fort. They failed to take the fort and had to surrender to the French. The French sent the soldiers back to Virginia. This was the beginning of the *French and Indian War*.

In 1755, a British general named *Braddock* was sent to capture *Fort Duquesne*, the French fort Washington had failed to capture. Braddock's soldiers built a road for the small army to travel on. Washington, who was with Braddock, warned the general that the French and Native Americans fought from behind trees instead of marching into battle as Braddock was used to doing. Braddock paid no attention. Because of this, his army was surprised and Braddock was killed. The English soldiers and Virginia colonists returned to Virginia in defeat. The French had beaten the English.

---

**Think About It:**

General Braddock lost his life and a battle because he would not listen to Washington. Why might an English leader not listen to a colonist?

---

During the next two years, the French won battle after battle. England did not send enough soldiers to fight a war. The colonists were slow getting their own armies organized. Finally, the English sent *General Wolfe* to lead the colonial armies. Almost at once the English began to win battles. Fort Duquesne was captured at last and renamed Fort Pitt. Today it is called Pittsburgh.

By 1759, the English army was strong enough to attack Quebec, Canada. This French city was built on a high cliff above a river. It was easy for the French to defend their city. The English fired cannons at the city week after week without doing much damage. Then one night General Wolfe sent his soldiers to climb the cliffs. The next morning, French General *Montcalm* woke up to see English soldiers outside the city walls. Montcalm had his soldiers attack the English troops. In the battle that followed, many men died. Both generals, Wolfe and Montcalm, were killed in the fight. The French lost the battle, however.

With the defeat of Quebec, the French lost the war. The *peace treaty* was finally signed in 1763. The French had to give up all the land east of the Mississippi River. They were allowed to keep the city of New Orleans. England gained control of half of Canada and almost half of what is now the United States.

Since Spain had helped France in the war, the English took Florida away from Spain as punishment. France then gave New Orleans and the land west of the Mississippi to Spain. After the Revolutionary War, Spain regained Florida for a short while. Spain also secretly returned New Orleans and millions of acres west of the Mississippi to France.

---

**Think About It:**

Can you think of any reason Spain might have been willing to help France fight the English? Do you suppose Spain hoped to gain land if France won the war?

---

## Colonial Land Claims

The map on page 30 shows the parts of North America east of the Mississippi held by England, France, and Spain about the time of the French and Indian War. Where land claimed by one country touched another country's claim, there was always trouble. Some of this trouble was solved with the French and Indian War, which ended in 1763.

Match the correct country with each statement below. Be sure to check the map on the next page before you answer.

1. The Ohio River Valley in 1750 belonged to this nation. _____

2. The land east of the Appalachian Mountains belonged to this country.

   _____

3. South of the colony of Georgia was land controlled by this country.

   _____

4. The St. Lawrence River was claimed by this country. _____


Now look at how much changed after the French and Indian War.

5. England, because it won, was given the Ohio River Valley along with the area around the Great Lakes. England gained this land from what country?

   _____

6. This country, because it had helped France in the war, lost Florida to England.

   _____

7. Most of the rivers shown on this map start in the
   (a) Atlantic Ocean    (b) Appalachian Mountains    (c) Great Lakes

8. The settlers moved into the Ohio River Valley through passes in the Appalachian Mountains. One pass shown is called the
   (a) Appalachian Pass    (b) Cumberland Gap    (c) Duquesne Gap    (d) Ohio River

9. The settlement that is shown south of the Ohio River in what is now Kentucky was called    (a) Cumberland    (b) Pitt    (c) Duquesne    (d) Boonesborough

# The Colonies to 1763

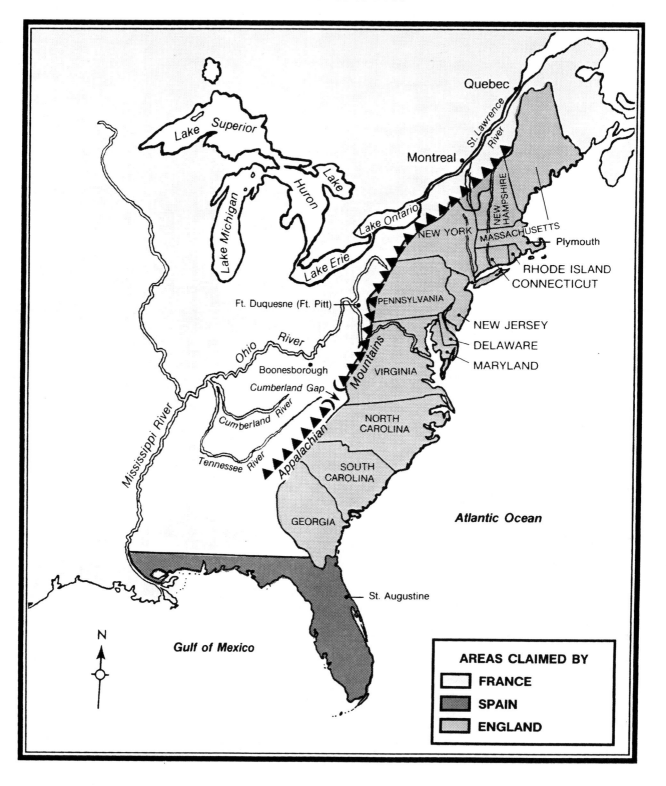

AREAS CLAIMED BY

FRANCE

SPAIN

ENGLAND

## The Colonists Have Trouble with England

After the end of the French and Indian War, the English colonists were allowed to vote for the people who would govern them. They could also own land and were free to live as they pleased. This was far better than the French colonists, who lived the way the government told them, or the Spanish colonists, who had to do what the large landowners said. The English colonists should have been happy, but they were not.

For one thing, many of the colonial governors were chosen by the king of England, This gave the king a lot of power over the colonists. Even though the colonists voted for their own *representatives* to make laws, the governor was very powerful.

There were different ideas about the reasons for having colonies. The colonists felt the colony was for their own good; England felt the colonies were for the good of England. In order to make sure the colonists traded only with England, the *Navigation Acts* were passed by the English *Parliament* (lawmakers). The Acts said all goods being shipped to the colonies had to be English or to be shipped from England. Also, all ships coming to the colonies had to be English or colonial ships with English or colonial crews. If Holland wanted to send tea to Massachusetts, it first had to send the tea to England, where it was unloaded, put onto English ships, and then brought to Massachusetts. Holland, of course, had to pay for unloading the ships and for the use of the English ships.

This was added to the price the colonists paid for the tea.

The English also said the colonists could make, or *manufacture*, only certain things. For example, the colonists could not manufacture things to sell to France. Nor could they manufacture things English business owners were making for sale. This forced the colonists to depend on England for many things they needed. Many colonists paid no attention to the English laws. Colonial ships often traded with nations other than England. This unlawful trade—*smuggling*—helped many colonists grow rich, but it also made the English angry.

At the end of the French and Indian War, the English made several changes in the way they ruled the colonies. The English said that since England had sent soldiers to protect the colonies, the people of the colonies must pay for the soldiers. Also, the king of England said English soldiers would have to stay in the colonies to protect the colonists from Native Americans. When a Native American chief named *Pontiac* led a great uprising against the colonists in 1763, the English government was certain the colonists needed the English soldiers. It was decided that 10,000 English soldiers would be sent to protect the colonists. The colonists would have to pay a tax to support the soldiers and pay for the cost of the French and Indian War. In addition, the colonists could no longer settle land west of the Appalachians. Worse, any colonists already living west of the mountains had to leave their homes and come back to the colonies. The colonists were angry about this.

## Pontiac (1720–1769)

Pontiac was a chief of the Ottawa, living in the Ohio territory. He was a brilliant man who grew to distrust and then hate the settlers. He told other Native Americans not to trust the colonists who were taking their lands. He brought many Native Americans together to stop the colonists. In 1763, Pontiac led them against frontier forts and killed settlers and soldiers.But after some early victories, Pontiac's Conspiracy was stopped. Native Americans did not unite again. He was killed by another Native American, which caused a bitter war among the tribes.

Then, in 1765, the English government passed the *Stamp Act.* This law said that tax stamps must be placed on all legal papers, books, newspapers, and other items. The colonists claimed the tax was not legal, since they had no representation in Parliament. "Taxation without representation" became a common complaint.

**Think About It:**

"No taxation without representation" was a colonial justification for not paying taxes. Would two or three colonial representatives in Parliament have really made any difference in which laws were passed?

Tax collectors hired to sell the tax stamps were treated badly by the colonists. Some stamp sellers were chased out of town. Others were placed on fence rails and carried out of town. Many were covered with hot tar and then coated with feathers. This was enough to discourage most tax collectors.

The colonists refused to buy British goods. When the English merchants began to complain about bad business, Parliament *repealed* the Stamp Act in 1766. The colonists had won a victory.

The victory did not last long. The next year, the *Townshend Acts* were passed in England. These Acts allowed British soldiers to search any house, building, or ship for smuggled goods. The Acts also placed a tax on such things as lead, paint, paper, glass, and tea. All these things were shipped from England. The money raised from these taxes would pay British officials in America. Also, the *New York Assembly*, a group of colonial lawmakers, was no longer allowed to meet.

Again, the colonists got angry. People began to talk against England. Many colonial merchants stopped buying English products. Tempers got shorter. Then trouble sprang up in Boston.

During the evening of March 5, 1770, a group of boys in Boston began throwing snowballs at some British soldiers. A crowd gathered. The angry, frightened soldiers fired into the crowd. Five people were killed, including *Crispus Attucks*, an African American. News of the *Boston Massacre* spread rapidly through the colonies. Every time the story was told, the number of dead colonists grew. Perhaps the only thing that kept the peace was that Parliament decided to repeal the Townshend taxes. Only the tax on tea was kept to show the colonists that England still had the right to tax them.

For the next three years, relations between England and the colonists were pretty smooth. Then, in 1773, trouble over the tea tax began again. England let the tea leave Europe without paying a tax. This made the tea cheaper than ever before, even after the tax in the colonies still being charged. The colonists thought there was a trick. The smugglers were very unhappy, because tea from England now sold more cheaply than smuggled tea.

**Think About It:**

Colonists depended upon England for many things. They openly broke British laws. They complained about British rule. In what ways were colonists better off than many people living in England?

On the night of December 16, 1773, a group of colonists dressed as Native Americans climbed aboard a British ship in Boston Harbor. By morning, the entire shipment of tea had been dumped into the harbor. The **Boston Tea Party** was the last straw for the British.

British lawmakers passed laws to punish Boston. The harbor was closed, so no ships could enter or leave. The Massachusetts lawmakers could no longer meet. More British soldiers were sent to Boston. Citizens of Boston had to allow the soldiers to live in their houses. They had to feed the soldiers as well.

In September of 1774, **delegates** from 12 colonies met at the **First Continental Congress**. They discussed what should be done to make England understand that the colonists had rights. The Congress protested the taxes to England. The delegates also planned to stop buying British goods. Also, they decided to meet again in May 1775.

**Think About It:**

Was the British government right in taxing the colonists? Before you answer, think about the way we pay taxes today.

## Committees of Correspondence

Colonial leaders realized they needed some way for people living in one colony to keep in touch with those living other places. **Samuel Adams** came up with a way to do this. He set up a **committee of correspondence** in Boston. Members of the group wrote letters to people living in other towns in Massachusetts. In these letters they told what was happening and what the British were doing.

Those who received letters wrote back to share the news about what was taking place in their town. The idea spread throughout Massachusetts and to towns and cities all over New England. Virginia joined in. After the Boston Tea Party, committees of correspondence were in place throughout all 13 colonies.

In addition to writing the news in letters, members of some committees printed leaflets that gave readers reasons why the British should not be allowed to control them. In a time when newspapers were unavailable to most and there was no other form of communication, these committees helped keep colonists informed and alert.

## The Colonies Break with England

Most people knew trouble was coming. Many colonists began to store arms and ammunition, even though it was against the law. On the night of April 18, 1775, British **General Gage** sent soldiers from Boston to capture **Samuel Adams** and **John Hancock**, who were helping buy weapons. The colonists were told the soldiers were coming when **Paul Revere**, **William Dawes**, and **Samuel Prescott** rode to warn the colonists. Colonists known as **Minutemen** gathered to meet the soldiers. Minutemen and soldiers met at **Lexington**, and several **patriots** were killed. More minutemen met the British at a bridge near **Concord**.

From there, until the soldiers got back to Boston, the Minutemen followed the British, shooting at them from behind fences and trees, a tactic learned from the French and Indian War.

Paul Revere

The next battle came on June 17. Over a thousand colonists climbed **Breed's Hill** above Boston on the night of June 16. The next morning, the British found the colonists ready for a fight. Twice the British charged the hill shoulder to shoulder. Twice the colonists drove the British back. On the third attack, the colonists ran out of ammunition and had to retreat. The English took the hill, but they lost more men than the colonists lost. The battle of Breed's Hill is remembered wrongly as the **Battle of Bunker Hill**, a hill nearby where today there is a monument.

The Lexington monument

It was not until March of the next year that the British were finally driven out of Boston. By then the colonial troops had captured a cannon at a British fort and were able to fire down on the British from a hill near town.

From the battles at Lexington and Concord until the summer of 1776, many small battles took place. Often the colonists won, but not always. In spite of the fighting, most colonists hoped to settle their problems with England without going to war.

**King George III** of England would not listen to colonial requests to change the laws. Instead, he had stricter laws passed and began hiring German troops called **Hessians** to fight the colonists.

---

### Think About It:

England had a powerful army. Even so, German troops were hired to help fight the colonists. Why might the English have hired these German soldiers?

---

The **Second Continental Congress** met and, after much talking, wrote the **Declaration of Independence**. The Declaration said the colonies were forming a new nation and were now free of English rule. On July 4, 1776, Congress **adopted** the Declaration. The United States of America became a nation.

Not everyone thought this was a good idea. Many people called **Tories** or **Loyalists** were still loyal to King George. These people often fought the patriots or else moved to Canada to stay out of the fighting that was sure to come.

## The American Revolution

Few people in Europe thought the Americans had a chance against the English. The English had a powerful navy and a trained army. They had weapons and money to buy supplies. The Americans had few weapons, no navy, no army, no money, and no real government.

The Americans did have several things in their favor. The patriots were fighting for something they felt was right. Many British soldiers did not want to fight the colonists. The British were a long way from home and had to get their supplies from across the ocean. Partway through the war, the nations of France and Spain began to help the Americans. They both hated England and were glad to attack English ships and send supplies and men to help the Americans.

American colonists fighting

A final thing favoring the Americans was the way the British fought. The red-coated soldiers were used to marching into battle side by side across open fields. This did not work in the American forests. The colonials fought like Native Americans, from behind trees and rocks. General George Washington commanded the entire colonial or **Continental Army.** His courage and ability helped the colonists stay strong and brave, even when things looked bad.

Soon after the war really began, the Americans lost New York City to the British. It was in New York that a young teacher named **Nathan Hale** was captured by the British when he was trying to find out the enemy plans for General Washington. Hale's famous words

before he was hanged were: "I only regret that I have but one life to lose for my country." With patriots like Hale fighting for America, it is easy to see why the British were finally defeated.

> **Think About It:**
>
> British soldiers and sailors were as brave as the colonists. For what reasons might British troops be unwilling to kill colonial soldiers and sailors?

For quite a while, however, it seemed as though the Americans would surely lose. The British slowly drove Washington's tiny army across New Jersey and into Pennsylvania. Many colonists gave up and went home when Washington needed them most. On Christmas night 1776, Washington and his men won their first big victory. On that night they crossed the Delaware River and surprised the Hessian soldiers at Trenton, New Jersey. The **Battle of Trenton** was over almost before it started.

Washington crossing the Delaware

## Francis Marion (1732–1795)

*Francis Marion* was born in 1732 in South Carolina. His parents had come from France seeking religious freedom. An older brother raised Francis after their father died.

As a boy Marion learned how to live and survive in the swamps near his brother's plantation. When he was fifteen Marion went to sea as a cabin boy. The ship wrecked and he survived for many days in a lifeboat without food and water. That ended his desire to go to sea.

Years later Marion owned his own plantation. He was also a part-time soldier who in 1761 fought Cherokee Indians.

During the following years, Marion watched as the colonists and England began to disagree. He was elected to the South Carolina legislature as a representative who felt colonists should govern themselves.

When war with England began in 1775, Marion joined the army and was soon promoted to major. The next year, the British sailed toward Charleston, South Carolina. Marion and his men built a fort to defend the city. It was constructed of two walls of palm logs with the space between filled with sand.

The British arrived with fifty ships to fight Marion and his three hundred soldiers. To the surprise of the British, the log and sand fort was impossible for their cannon to destroy. After an all-day battle, the British sailed away with many ships damaged and the fort still standing.

For the next four years the war went badly for the colonists. In 1780 the British captured Charleston. Marion and others escaped into the swamps.

When they heard that General Gates was in North Carolina, the ragged men rode to join him. Gates sent them to Williamsburg, where they formed *Marion's Brigade* of guerrilla troops.

Hiding in the swamps between battles, the men lived on captured British supplies. They made swords out of saw blades and melted pewter dishes for bullets. Marion's horse Ball became famous for its courage. Ball feared no river or swamp. Where Ball led, the others' horses followed.

Marion and his troops fought by any means to defeat the British. In 1781, they cut and notched logs which they carried to Fort Watson. At night they fitted the logs into a tower. In the morning they fired into the fort from the high tower and quickly defeated the British.

At Fort Motte, which was a fort built around a house, Marion's troops fired flaming arrows onto the roof to drive the British out. After Marion's forces captured the British, men from both sides helped put out the fire.

In 1782, Marion's Brigade fought its last battle. The long war ended, and in December British soldiers left Charleston. Marion's Brigade was not part of the victory parade. The city officials did not want Marion's ragged soldiers on display.

Marion married after the war and lived on his own plantation. He died in 1795, knowing he had done much to make America free. His fellow Americans remembered him as the *Swamp Fox.*

When the British tried to catch the Americans after Trenton, they got a surprise. Washington had marched off and was beginning the **Battle of Princeton**, which he also won. Things were looking up for the Americans!

The turning point in the war came in October 1777. The English planned to crush the American army at **Saratoga**. Things went wrong for the British, and the Americans won a great victory.

Even though a terrible winter at **Valley Forge**, Pennsylvania, followed, the Americans were on their way to victory. Though many American soldiers left the army and many others died during the winter, Washington's men were ready for more fighting when spring came.

West of Washington's battles, another part of the war was going on. **George Rogers Clark** was attacking the British forts along the frontier. He and his small army captured fort after fort until they had control of the **Northwest** from the Great Lakes to the Ohio and Mississippi rivers.

Meanwhile, American ships were beginning to attack British vessels. Many British supply ships were captured by the American **privateers**.

The most famous American sailor was **John Paul Jones**, who attacked British ships whenever he saw them. In his most famous fight, his ship, *Bonhomme Richard*, was so badly damaged it was sinking. Jones sailed close beside the British ship, *Serapis*, which was defeating him. When asked to surrender, he replied, "I have not yet begun to fight!" and opened fire at a distance of a few feet. Soon he captured the larger *Serapis*, which he sailed home.

In the South, the British were very successful. They won battle after battle. It was not until 1780, at **King's Mountain** and later at **Cowpens**, that the Americans were able to defeat the English.

Also in 1780, a famous American general tried to betray America. **Benedict Arnold**, who had helped the Americans win at Saratoga, became unhappy and planned to turn the fort at **West Point** over to the British. He was found out, however. Arnold managed to escape and joined the British army. Today, the words "Benedict Arnold" mean "traitor" whenever they are used.

On October 19, 1781, the war came to an end. Washington, with the help of a large fleet of French ships, trapped **Lord Cornwallis** and his entire army at **Yorktown** in Virginia. After six years of fighting, the war was over. The United States was a free and independent nation!

## American Revolution

Below are ten statements dealing with the map on the American Revolution. They should be quite easy to answer if you check the map on page 40 first. Write the correct answer after each statement.

1. George Rogers Clark sailed down the Ohio to capture this fort from the British.

   _____

2. With the capture of the fort on the Wabash River, the land between the Great Lakes and the Ohio River was American. This land was called

   _____ .

3. Two rivers in the east join to form the Ohio River. These two rivers meet at

   _____ .

4. This battle in South Carolina helped the Americans beat the British.

   _____

5. This was General Washington's winter headquarters in Pennsylvania.

   _____

6. The American Revolution came to an end when Cornwallis surrendered to George

   Washington here in Virginia. _____

7. American General Benedict Arnold tried to give this fort on the Hudson River to the

   British. _____

8. This town on the upper Hudson River was called the "Turning Point of the Revolution" because the Americans defeated the British here.

   _____

9. This city at the mouth of the Hudson River was captured by the British, who held it

   during the whole war. _____

10. Both Princeton and Trenton, victories for Washington, were in this colony.

    _____

## Where Am I?

In the last two units you have heard about many places in the New England area. After each statement below are several choices. See if you can remember "where you are." If you need to, check the past units for the answers. Underline each correct answer. Use the maps on pages 40 and 41 to help you.

1. I attended a tea party here:
   (a) Providence   (b) Boston   (c) Concord   (d) Saratoga

2. While I was here, people were worried about witches bothering two girls:
   (a) West Point   (b) Boston   (c) Salem   (d) Concord

3. The first shots of the Revolution were fired here:
   (a) Lexington   (b) Providence   (c) Saratoga   (d) Plymouth

4. The first colony established in the New England area was here:
   (a) Boston   (b) Plymouth   (c) Salem   (d) Lexington

5. When I visited this town, I was told the battle that took place here was called the "Turning Point of the American Revolution."
   (a) Providence   (b) Boston   (c) West Point   (d) Saratoga

6. This body of water lies between Long Island and Connecticut:
   (a) Atlantic Ocean   (b) Lake Champlain   (c) Long Island Sound   (d) Cape Cod

7. Thomas Hooker left Massachusetts Bay Colony, moved west, and started this colony:
   (a) Connecticut   (b) Rhode Island   (c) New Hampshire   (d) New York

8. This body of water was named for a famous French explorer:
   (a) Cape Cod   (b) Lake Champlain   (c) Hudson River   (d) Long Island Sound

9. While I was visiting this city, a number of colonists were massacred:
   (a) Salem   (b) Lexington   (c) Boston   (d) Providence

10. This was named for a famous explorer who sailed for both England and Holland:
    (a) Hudson River   (b) Lake Champlain   (c) Long Island
    (d) both the Connecticut River and the colony of Connecticut

# American Revolution

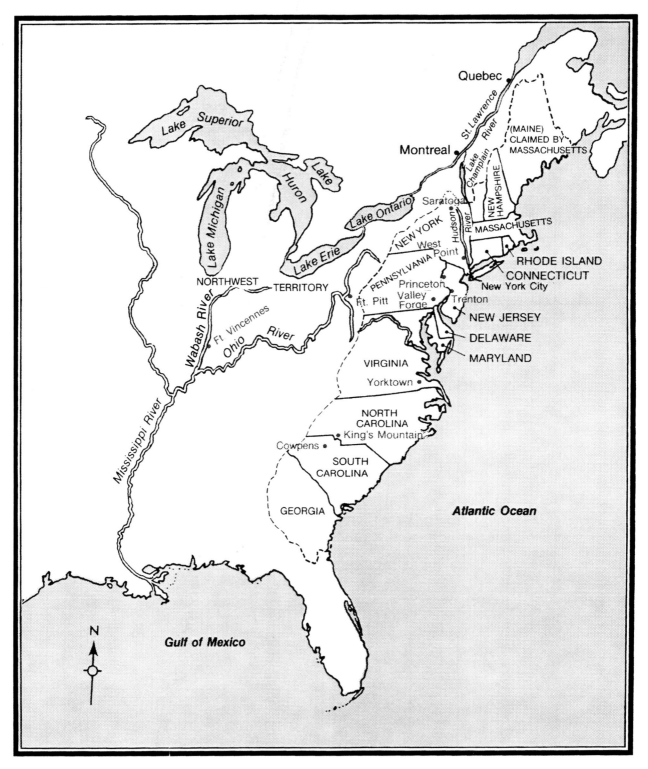

## New England States: 1700–1783

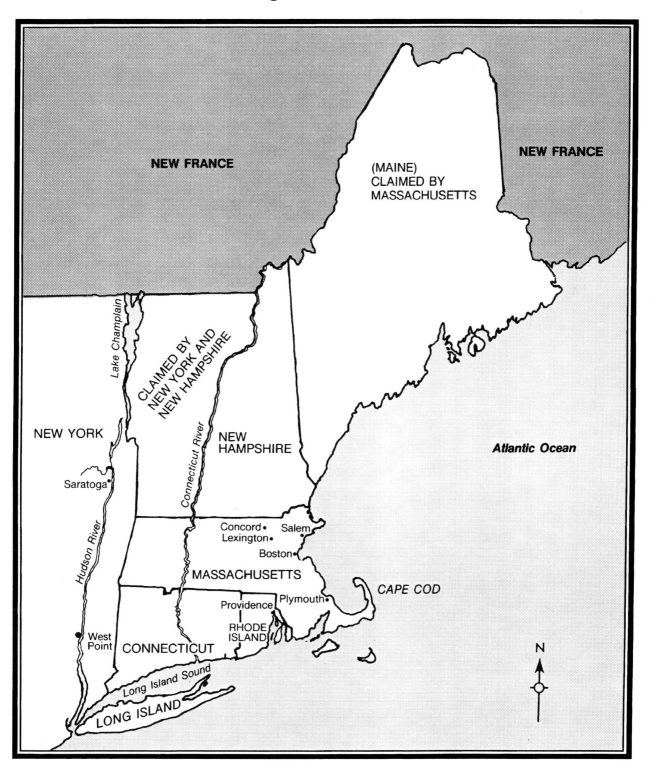

# THE NEW NATION (1781–1823)

## Time Line

| EVENTS ELSEWHERE | DATE | EVENTS IN AMERICA |
|---|---|---|
| | 1781 | Articles of Confederation |
| | 1783 | Treaty ending Revolution signed |
| | 1785 | Ordinance of 1785 |
| | 1787 | Northwest Territory organized |
| | 1789 | Constitution approved; Washington first president |
| *Declaration of Rights of Man; French Revolution began* | 1791 | Bill of Rights added to Constitution |
| | 1794 | Whiskey Rebellion |
| | 1801 | U.S. fought Barbary pirates |
| *French Revolution ended* | 1802 | |
| | 1803 | Louisiana Purchase |
| *Napoleon led France* | 1804 | Lewis and Clark expedition began |
| | 1806 | Lewis and Clark returned |
| | 1807 | Zebulon Pike explored Southwest |
| | 1811 | Tecumseh and Battle of Tippecanoe |
| | 1812 | Madison declared war on England |
| | 1814 | End of War of 1812 |
| *Napoleon defeated at Waterloo* | 1815 | Jackson fought Battle of New Orleans |
| | 1819 | U.S. acquired Florida |
| *Britain annexed Australia* | 1820 | |
| | 1823 | Monroe Doctrine |

## Introduction

The war with England was over. A new nation, the United States of America, had been formed. What kind of government would it have? How were the people going to pay the nation's debts for the war they just concluded? What about the frontier to the west? What could be done to protect the rights of the people? How would the new nation get along with the other nations of the world?

Americans faced these and other questions. It seemed as though all the problems needed to be solved at once.

## How Did Our Constitution Come to Be?

The Second Continental Congress met in 1775. It went on meeting until March 1, 1781. For six years it was all the government the United States had. In 1781, a plan for government was put into use. The plan was called the *Articles of Confederation.*

The Articles gave the new government power to have an army and navy, to declare war, to deal with the Native Americans, to start a mail service, to borrow money, and to ask states for money to run the government. The states, which used to be colonies, would send representatives to *Congress.* Each state had one vote in Congress.

The new plan for government started in 1781 and ran into trouble right away. The new government had no power to tax people to raise money. If states did not want to pay their share of the cost of government, they did not have to. The government had neither the power to settle arguments between states nor the strength to control trade among the states. The larger states became angry because smaller states had as much power in Congress as the bigger states. Something needed to be done, or the new nation would fall apart before it even got started.

In June 1787, a group of men met in Philadelphia. George Washington headed the meeting. Important men, such as *Benjamin Franklin* and *James Madison,* were there. At the start, the men planned just to improve the Articles of Confederation. They soon decided that something completely new was needed, so they set to work to write a plan for a better government.

Virginia had an idea for the new government. Why not divide the government into three parts? One part could make laws; a second part could be sure the laws were obeyed; and a third part could see that the laws were proper and just.

Benjamin Franklin

Virginia wanted the law-making part, called *Congress,* to have two parts. One part would have representatives elected by the people. Large states would have many members and small states only one or two members each. The second part of Congress would be elected by the first part.

New Jersey and other small states wanted each state to have the same number of representatives in Congress. This would keep the bigger states from running the government by themselves.

After a long discussion, a *compromise* was reached. Virginia and New Jersey both gave in on some ideas. Congress would have two parts, or *houses.* The *Senate* would have two members from each state. The *House of Representatives* would have a few members from small states and more members from larger states. Both houses of Congress must agree upon a matter before it could become law.

It was decided that Congress would have the power to control trade with foreign nations and among states. However, Congress could not control the slave trade until 20 years later.

---

**Think About It:**

Congress was given the power to tax and to control foreign trade. How did these two powers help make the new government strong?

---

The *president* and *vice president* were to be chosen by electors from each state. A state got as many electors as it had senators and representatives. We still have this system today.

A *Supreme Court* was set up to settle problems among states. Less powerful courts would handle problems of justice throughout the nation.

Finally, on September 17, 1787, the *Constitution of the United States* was finished. In it was the plan for government we still use today.

But many people were afraid of the new Constitution. They thought it made the government too strong. *Thomas Jefferson* suggested adding the *Bill of Rights* to the Constitution. The changes, or *amendments*, to the Constitution helped protect the rights of Americans. The Bill of Rights, containing

the first ten amendments, was added to the Constitution in 1791. They gave protections such as these:

1. Americans may worship as they please.

2. Americans have freedom of speech and of the press.

3. Americans accused of a crime may have a trial by jury and cannot be punished cruelly.

4. Soldiers cannot be put into an American's house without permission.

5. A person's house cannot be searched without proper court orders.

By 1789, the 13 states had approved the new Constitution. It became the law of the land. The United States is still governed by this plan of government. In all the years since the Constitution was adopted, only 26 changes, or amendments, have been made. Ten of these changes were in the Bill of Rights.

---

## *Benjamin Banneker (1731–1806)*

Benjamin Banneker was the son of a slave. He was also a genius who excelled in math and astronomy. He built the first clock in America out of wood. When Thomas Jefferson heard of him, Jefferson appointed Banneker to help survey and plan the District of Columbia. Banneker memorized the architect's plans. When the architect was fired, Banneker was able to supervise the construction of Washington, DC. Banneker wrote an almanac that predicted weather, tides, and other valuable information. Entirely self-taught in astronomy, he correctly predicted a 1789 solar eclipse.

---

## How Did the New Government Work?

On April 30, 1789, George Washington became the first president of the United States. As president of the new nation, he had great power, but not nearly as much power as a king.

The Constitution had given each part or **branch** of government power to curb the other branches. For example, both houses of Congress had to approve a law. In addition, the president usually had to agree to the law before it could become a real law. If the Supreme Court thought a law went against the Constitution, it could say the law was **unconstitutional**. This meant the law could no longer be a law.

The idea of one branch of government being able to limit the power of the rest of the government is called a system of **checks and balances**. In this way, no one part of the government can become too strong.

Another way the Constitution protected the people was in the election of the members of Congress and the president. Senators are elected every six years. Representatives must be voted on every two years. The president is elected every four years. The **justices (judges)** of the Supreme Court are appointed for life.

If the people of a state become unhappy with the laws passed by Congress, they can elect different people to represent them. If the people of the nation do not like the job done by the president, they can elect a new one the next time. Why then are Supreme Court judges not elected? Since these judges have such an important job protecting the rights of the people, it was decided they should never have to be elected. In this way, they are able to make law decisions they feel are right without having to worry about being

reelected in four or six years. This makes the Court stronger and lets the judges act without fear.

**Think About It:**

Presidents try to influence the way this nation is run. The greatest influence any president can have comes from the judges that president appoints. Why is this true?

After a description of the form the new government took, it is important to consider how it worked.

One of the first things President Washington did was choose some men to advise him. These men were called his **cabinet** and were in charge of departments of government set up by Congress. That first cabinet had a **secretary of state**, to handle our problems with other nations; a **secretary of war**, to take care of military matters; a **secretary of the treasury**, to take charge of raising money for the government and other money matters; and an **attorney general**, to advise the government on matters of law. Over the years, more departments have been added and the cabinet has grown. The one thing that has not changed is that the president chooses his or her own cabinet.

**Alexander Hamilton** was in charge of the Treasury. It was Hamilton's job to raise enough money to keep the government going. The ideas he used were much the same as our government uses today to pay the cost of government. When the new government borrowed money, a **bond** was issued. This bond was a promise by the government to repay the borrowed money by a certain date. In addition, the person who loaned the money was paid **interest**. This means that for every dollar loaned to the government, the person was paid several cents a year for the use of the money. This, too, is still done today. Hamilton also started the **Bank of the United States**, which was used by the government.

The government collected a tax on all goods *imported* or brought into the country. Such a tax is called a *tariff*. Today, the government still collects tariffs on many imported products.

Hamilton suggested another tax called an *excise* tax. This was a tax on things made and sold in America.

> **Think About It:**
>
> What are some of the things the government taxes today?

The first thing Hamilton taxed was whiskey made and sold in the United States. Farmers in western Pennsylvania refused to pay the tax on the whiskey they made. This was called the *Whiskey Rebellion*. It was the first problem of this sort to challenge President Washington. Washington knew no nation can become great unless its laws are obeyed. Because of this, President Washington sent an army of 15,000 men to Pennsylvania. The farmers paid the tax.

> **Think About It:**
>
> One of the arguments the colonists had with England was over taxation. Was Washington right or wrong when he sent troops to collect taxes? Why?

Washington was president for two terms. In 1796, he said no one should be president more than twice. John Adams was elected president, and Washington retired to his home at Mount Vernon.

---

## A New Government

**Directions:** Answer each of the following questions by placing one letter in each blank. Whenever a letter has a number under it, write that letter in the corresponding numbered blank at the end of the exercise.

1.  An early plan for our government was the _ _ _ _ _ _ _ _ of Confederation.
                                                                           2

2.  _ _ _ _ _ _ Washington was chairman of the group that met in Philadelphia
     13     5
    in 1787 to plan a new government.

3.  When each side gives in a little bit, the agreement is called a
    _ _ _ _ _ _ _ _ _ _.
       3

4.  Large states have more representatives than small states in the _ _ _ _ _ _ of
    Representatives.                              6

5.  Small states have as many members in the _ _ _ _ _ _ _ as do large states.
                                                 16

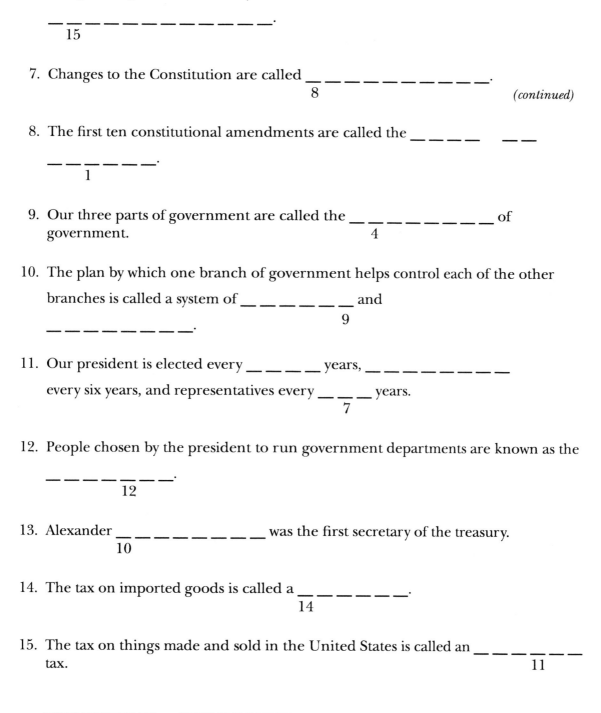

6. The plan of government finally decided on for the United States is written in the

_ _ _ _ _ _ _ _ _ _ _ _.
  15

7. Changes to the Constitution are called _ _ _ _ _ _ _ _ _ _ _.
                              8                               *(continued)*

8. The first ten constitutional amendments are called the _ _ _ _ _ _ _

_ _ _ _ _ _.
  1

9. Our three parts of government are called the _ _ _ _ _ _ _ _ _ of
government.                            4

10. The plan by which one branch of government helps control each of the other

branches is called a system of _ _ _ _ _ _ _ and
                               9

_ _ _ _ _ _ _ _ _.

11. Our president is elected every _ _ _ _ years, _ _ _ _ _ _ _ _ _

every six years, and representatives every _ _ _ years.
                                            7

12. People chosen by the president to run government departments are known as the

_ _ _ _ _ _ _ _.
    12

13. Alexander _ _ _ _ _ _ _ _ _ was the first secretary of the treasury.
       10

14. The tax on imported goods is called a _ _ _ _ _ _ _.
                           14

15. The tax on things made and sold in the United States is called an _ _ _ _ _ _ _
tax.                                                     11

_ _ _ _ _ _    _ _ _ _ _ _ _ _ _ _
1 2 3 4 5 6    7 8 9 10 11 12 13 14 15 16

# The United States in 1783

The map on page 49 shows what the United States looked like after the American Revolution. The 13 infant states gradually grew to 16 states.

Check the map for the answers to the following statements. Underline each correct answer.

1. The east coast of the young nation was the
   (a) Mississippi River   (b) Great Lakes   (c) Atlantic Ocean   (d) Gulf of Mexico

2. Pennsylvania spread westward so it would border this Great Lake:
   (a) Lake Huron   (b) Lake Erie   (c) Lake Michigan   (d) Lake Ontario

3. North of the United States is Canada, which was controlled by the
   (a) Spanish   (b) United States   (c) British   (d) French

4. When the fourteenth state was created, both New York and New Hampshire gave up their land claims. This new state was
   (a) Kentucky   (b) Vermont   (c) Tennessee   (d) Florida

5. Cape Hatteras is a piece of land jutting out into the Atlantic Ocean. It is in
   (a) North Carolina   (b) Georgia   (c) Florida   (d) Delaware

6. Another of the 13 original states has a cape. This state is
   (a) New York   (b) Maryland   (c) New Jersey   (d) Massachusetts

7. Many travelers moved west along the Wilderness Road. The start of this road is in
   (a) Maryland   (b) Pennsylvania   (c) Rhode Island   (d) Connecticut

8. The fifteenth state borders Virginia on the west. It is
   (a) Tennessee   (b) Kentucky   (c) Georgia   (d) Florida

9. The northern border for the new state of Kentucky was
   (a) a boundary line with Tennessee   (b) the Mississippi River   (c) the Ohio River
   (d) the Great Lakes

10. The land west of the Mississippi was claimed by the
    (a) British   (b) Spanish   (c) United States   (d) Native American tribes

11. The sixteenth state of the United States was
    (a) Tennessee   (b) Florida   (c) Ohio   (d) Maine

12. Chesapeake Bay is bordered by Virginia and
    (a) Delaware   (b) Pennsylvania   (c) Maryland   (d) New Jersey

13. Lake Ontario is bordered by Canada and
    (a) Pennsylvania   (b) Vermont   (c) New Hampshire   (d) New York

14. If you traveled the Wilderness Road into Kentucky, you would go through the mountain pass called the
    (a) Wilderness Pass   (b) Cumberland Gap   (c) Tennessee Pass   (d) Appalachian Gap

15. The western border of the United States in 1783 was the
    (a) Mississippi River   (b) Great Lakes   (c) Gulf of Mexico   (d) Atlantic Ocean

# The United States: 1783

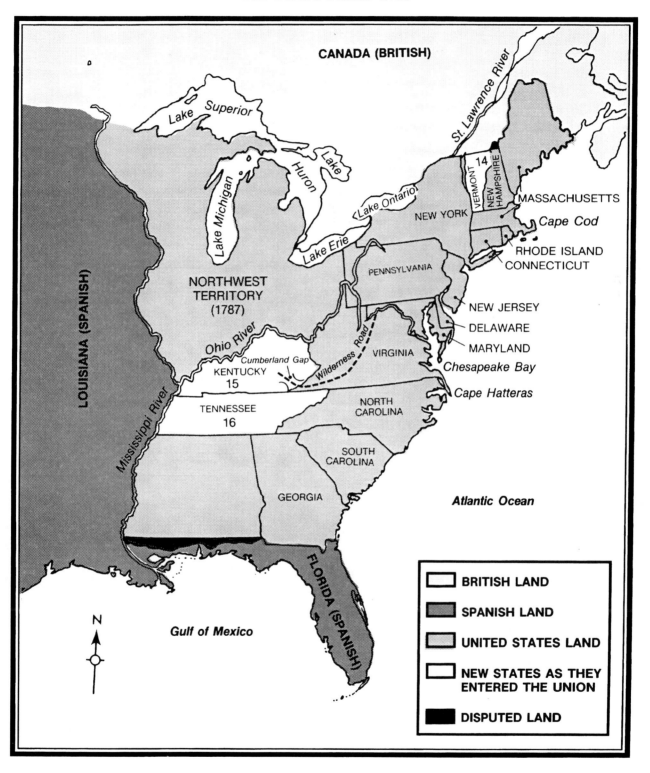

CANADA (BRITISH)

St. Lawrence River

Lake Superior

Lake Huron

Lake Michigan

Lake Ontario

Lake Erie

14

VERMONT

NEW HAMPSHIRE

MASSACHUSETTS

*Cape Cod*

NEW YORK

RHODE ISLAND

CONNECTICUT

NORTHWEST TERRITORY (1787)

PENNSYLVANIA

NEW JERSEY

DELAWARE

MARYLAND

*Chesapeake Bay*

LOUISIANA (SPANISH)

Ohio River

Cumberland Gap

Wilderness Road

VIRGINIA

KENTUCKY 15

*Cape Hatteras*

TENNESSEE 16

NORTH CAROLINA

Mississippi River

SOUTH CAROLINA

GEORGIA

*Atlantic Ocean*

FLORIDA (SPANISH)

N

*Gulf of Mexico*

| | BRITISH LAND |
| | SPANISH LAND |
| | UNITED STATES LAND |
| | NEW STATES AS THEY ENTERED THE UNION |
| | DISPUTED LAND |

## The United States Grows

Even before the Revolutionary War, many settlers had moved west from the Atlantic Ocean. After the war, the lands won from the English by George Rogers Clark were opened to settlement. The *Ordinance of 1785* set up a system of surveying, or measuring land. Land was divided into *townships* of 36 *sections*. A section was one mile square and contained 640 *acres*. This kind of land measurement is still used in much of the United States.

The land north of the Ohio River was surveyed and then sold by sections. The cost was $1 per acre. Some of that land is worth $1,000 or more per acre today. In 1787, this land was organized into the *Northwest Territory*. The word "territory" meant the land belonged to the United States but was not yet divided into states.

The *Northwest Ordinance* said that when 5,000 adult men lived in a new territory, that area could elect its own lawmakers. When 60,000 free people lived in a territory, it could become a state. The people had the same freedoms as others living in states. Slavery was not allowed in the Northwest Territory.

People began to go to the Northwest Territory. They came on horseback and by wagons. The rivers carried them on rafts and huge flatboats. As might be expected, the Native Americans were not happy. President Washington sent several military forces out to fight them. The Native Americans defeated the first two groups. Finally, *Anthony Wayne*, a famous Revolutionary War general, took an army to fight the Native Americans. He beat them so badly they agreed to leave the settlers alone.

---

### Flatboats on the Ohio

We usually think of settlers traveling west by covered wagons. However, many families traveled down the Ohio River on flatboats. A common flatboat journey was from Pittsburgh to the new lands in Kentucky.

A *flatboat* was a huge raft made of heavy planks. A room of rough lumber was built on the raft's deck. On each side of the raft was one huge oar attached to the side of the raft. These oars were used to help propel the flatboat down the river. At the rear, or stern, another huge oar was attached to steer the clumsy flatboat.

All the family's possessions were loaded onto the flatboat. This included their farm animals, which were tied at the rear of the craft.

The huge flatboat floated down the river. When sandbars or submerged rocks and logs were sighted, the boat was steered around them. At such times the oars on both sides helped control the craft.

At night the flatboat was tied up to the shore while the family slept. Whenever possible, the boat tied up near a settlement in order to be safe from Indian attack. Food for the livestock was purchased along the way, as were supplies the family needed.

Once the long journey ended, the boat was taken apart, and the lumber used to build a home for the family.

Between 1791 and 1796, the United States added three more stars to its flag: Vermont, Kentucky and Tennessee became states. The new nation was growing.

---

**Think About It:**

People living in a territory had the same freedoms as those living in states. Why might people want their territory to become a state?

---

## Land Measurement

One of the most important items in the Ordinance of 1785 was the method of measuring land. This method was used to tell one piece of land from another.

Each township was given a number. The township was six miles long by six miles wide. This was too large for the average farmer, so each township was divided into chunks one mile by one mile. These chunks of land are called "sections." Each township was to have 36 sections in it.

### Township

| 6 | 5 | 4 | 3 | 2 | 1 |
|---|---|---|---|---|---|
| 7 | 8 | 9 | 10 | 11 | 12 |
| 18 | 17 | 16 | 15 | 14 | 13 |
| 19 | 20 | 21 | 22 | 23 | 24 |
| 30 | 29 | 28 | 27 | 26 | 25 |
| 31 | 32 | 33 | 34 | 35 | 36 |

6 Miles

————— 6 Miles —————

Each section was given a number. The Ordinance said one section in each township was to be kept for schools. Even then, schools were important.

Many farmers did not want a whole section of 640 acres. They could buy instead a half-section of 320 acres or even a quarter-section.

The deed to a piece of property might read: "Township 81, Section 13, northwest ¼." This means the property can be found in Township 81. The section number is 13. But the property does not include all of Section 13, only the northwest one fourth, or 160 acres.

If you live in what was the Northwest Territory or west of the Mississippi River, your property was first measured using this method. Even if you have only a small house with very little land, it stands on a section in a township.

**1 Mile**

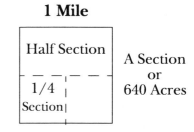

## The Biggest Real Estate Deal in History

Soon after Washington became president, the French people began their own revolution. The United States had promised to help France in case of war. Soon the war spread to include England and other nations of Europe. The United States was too small and weak to go to war, so our country decided to stay **neutral** and not take sides.

The Americans decided to go on trading with the warring nations. That is when trouble began. English warships stopped American ships sailing toward France. The English took the ships and **impressed** the sailors. This meant that American sailors were forced to become part of the British navy.

This made the Americans very angry. It looked as though another war would break out with England. In 1794, a **treaty**, or agreement, was signed with England. England agreed to take its soldiers away from the northwestern edge of the United States. England did not agree to stop searching our ships, however. The treaty was not liked by most Americans, but war did not break out between the two countries.

Meanwhile, the French began capturing American ships trying to trade with England. The United States started attacking French ships, and it looked as though war would come. Before war actually happened, we signed a treaty with France. Ships of the two nations stopped fighting each other.

More and more, the United States realized it would have to be strong to get along in the world.

Our next problem came on the Mississippi River. Settlers in the Northwest Territory used the Ohio and Mississippi rivers to get their farm goods to market. The rivers were the only way the farmers could move their crops. The roads were useless for heavy loads, or else they did not exist. People using the Mississippi River came to **New Orleans** and loaded their goods onto ocean ships. In 1802, Americans were told they could no longer use the port of New Orleans. France once again owned New Orleans and the millions of acres of land west of the Mississippi known as **Louisiana**. Spain had secretly given this area back to France.

President Jefferson sent men to offer to buy New Orleans from France. The French leader **Napoleon** was preparing for another war and needed money. He offered to sell New Orleans and the entire territory of Louisiana for $15 million. Jefferson closed the deal at once and, in 1803, the United States became the owner of over 500 million acres

of land. The cost per acre was about three cents! The **Louisiana Purchase** was a real bargain.

Napoleon

**Think About It:**

Three cents per acre made the Louisiana Purchase a bargain. Napoleon needed money to pay for another war. What other reasons may he have had to sell all that land?

Strangely enough, President Jefferson did not actually know what he had purchased. In order to find out, he sent **Meriwether Lewis** and **William Clark** to explore the new land. They began exploring in 1804 and returned two years and four months later in 1806. They had traveled up the Missouri River to its beginning, its **source**. They had crossed the Rocky Mountains to the Pacific Ocean and back again. On this trip the famous Native American woman **Sacajawea** helped Lewis and Clark find their way. When Lewis and Clark finally arrived home, they had a wonderful story to tell. The United States had nearly doubled its size.

famous 14,110-foot-tall Pike's Peak is named for Zebulon Pike, who discovered it in 1807.

## Sacajawea (1786–1812)

Sacajawea was kidnapped from her tribe, the Shoshone, as a child. She was taken by other Native Americans and sold to a French-Canadian trader. She, her husband, and their baby boy joined the Lewis and Clark Expedition, where she became the major guide. Sacajawea got help for Lewis and Clark because other tribes liked her. Also, her brother was chief of the Shoshone. The expedition would have been harder or impossible without her.

***Zebulon M. Pike*** was another explorer sent out to look at the new purchase. On one trip he went to the source of the Mississippi River. On a second trip he explored what is now Colorado and New Mexico. Colorado's

Zebulon Pike

## Exploring the Louisiana Purchase: 1803–1807

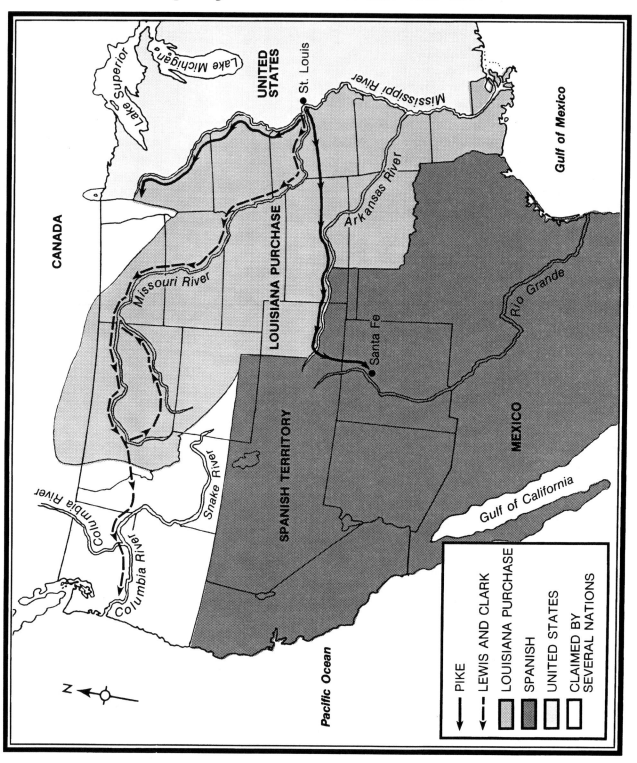

## Louisiana Purchase

The map on page 54 shows the large amount of land that was purchased by the United States in 1802. In addition to the Louisiana Purchase area, the routes of three famous exploration parties are shown. By using the map and thinking carefully, you can answer the statements below. Write your answers after each statement.

1. The western boundary for the United States before the Louisiana Purchase was the

   _____ .

2. How many states (part or whole) were made from the Louisiana Purchase area?

   _____

3. This exploration party explored the Missouri River and went to the Pacific Ocean.

   _____

4. This explorer was sent to find where the Mississippi River started.

   _____

5. Name the explorer who explored along the Arkansas River until he got into Spanish territory, where he was captured as a spy. _____

6. Both Pike and Lewis and Clark started their exploring from this city.

   _____

7. This river starts in Canada and flows through the northwestern part of the United States. This river was explored by Lewis and Clark. _____

8. The Mississippi River empties into this body of water. _____

9. The city of St. Louis is located where these two rivers meet. Name both rivers:

   _____ and _____ .

## War with Pirates and the War of 1812

For many years a group of pirates lived in northern Africa beside the Mediterranean Sea. The British had paid money to the pirates so they would not attack British ships. The United States did the same thing for several years. Then, in 1801, the pirates declared war on the United States. President Jefferson sent warships to fight the *Barbary pirates*. After several battles at sea, the United States set up a *blockade* around the harbor at *Tripoli*. The pirates soon agreed to let the United States ships use the Mediterranean in safety.

## Tecumseh (1768–1813)

**Tecumseh**, who was born in Ohio in 1768, may have been the greatest Native American leader of all time. He and his twin brother were members of the Shawnee tribe. Tecumseh became a war chief. His brother was a medicine man called **The Prophet**.

The Prophet got his name for predicting the future. One of the brothers learned from colonists that an eclipse of the sun was due. The Prophet gathered the tribe and told them he would darken the sun. The eclipse came and the earth grew dark. The Prophet worked his magic and the sun reappeared.

The two brothers planned to drive the colonists from their lands. Tecumseh traveled from tribe to tribe to unite the Native Americans into one great federation. This federation would cover all the land east of the Mississippi River.

Tecumseh was certain the colonists would fight the British again. When the next war came, he planned to join with Britain. Then he felt the colonists could be defeated.

Since Tecumseh was a fine speaker, many tribes joined with him. One that did not was the Creek tribe. In his anger at the Creeks, Tecumseh said that when he got to Detroit he would stamp his foot on the ground. The Creek Indians would feel the earth shake when he did.

Soon after that, on December 16, 1811, a great earthquake occurred. The Creeks were terrified. They were certain Tecumseh had great power.

While Tecumseh was traveling, his brother was in charge of their people. They were camped along the Tippecanoe River in Indiana. General **William Henry Harrison** of the U.S. Army camped near them on November 6, 1811. He had with him a thousand soldiers.

Tecumseh had ordered The Prophet not to fight until Tecumseh was ready. However, The Prophet attacked Harrison's forces on

November 7. The Native Americans were defeated. Harrison destroyed their village. Tecumseh was furious with his brother. The **Battle of Tippecanoe** was a blow to his plans.

Six months later, the colonists were fighting the British in the War of 1812. Tecumseh joined the British. He was made a general and given a uniform. However, **Colonel Procter** was really in command.

Tecumseh and his warriors fought better than the British. Everyone knew Tecumseh was a better commander than Procter. Procter allowed Native Americans to torture prisoners. Tecumseh ordered this stopped. When Procter said the warriors were out of his control, Tecumseh told Procter to get out of his way.

Procter kept retreating before General Harrison's troops. Tecumseh forced Procter to stand and fight along the Thames River in Canada. Knowing he could not win, Tecumseh prepared for battle on October 5, 1813. He dressed as a Native American and prepared to meet his death.

The Americans won the battle. Procter ran and his troops surrendered. Chief Tecumseh and his warriors fought to the death. His dreams of a Native American federation died with him. Had Tecumseh's plan worked, the Americans might well have lost the War of 1812.

Almost at the same time that the Barbary pirates stopped causing trouble, England and France began fighting again. They began capturing American ships once more. Once again the English were *impressing* American sailors into the British navy. The United States refused to trade with both nations, but this did not change the situation. It hurt the United States more than it hurt England or France. Besides, many American shipowners refused to obey the no-trading law because they were losing money.

Americans were angry about other things. A Native American chief named Tecumseh led his people north of the Ohio River in a war in 1811. The settlers claimed the British in Canada had helped Tecumseh. Many Americans were looking for any excuse to try to gain more land. The *War Hawks* (Americans who wanted to go to war) felt that if the United States fought and won a war, more land might be gained from England and Spain.

In June 1812, President Madison declared war on England. It was a war for which we were not ready and a war most Americans did not want. Many battles were fought along the border between Canada and the United States. Neither side was able to *invade* the other. In 1814, the British did burn some American towns along the Atlantic coast. They even sailed up Chesapeake Bay to Washington and burned the Capitol and White House. British ships attacked *Fort McHenry* at Baltimore but were unable to defeat it. It was at that battle that *Francis Scott Key* wrote *"The Star-Spangled Banner."* He was on a British ship and watched the entire battle. Even though he wrote the famous song in 1814, it did not become the national anthem until 1931.

At sea, the United States had better luck than on land. Most of the sea battles were actually fought on Lake Erie and Lake Champlain. Commodore *Oliver Hazard Perry* fought and won a great battle on Lake Erie. The Americans also won a battle on Lake Champlain. However, the British navy was in control of the Atlantic Ocean. Few American ships were able to leave harbor.

---

### Old Ironsides

During the War of 1812, the **Constitution** with its 44 guns was the pride of the American fleet. When the *Constitution* met the British ship *Guerrière*, none of the British expected to lose. But lose they did, to the surprise of people the world over. No one expected the British navy to lose a sea battle.

It was in a later battle that the *Constitution* earned its famous nickname. The American ship met the *Java* off the coast of Brazil. During a furious battle, the *Constitution* had its wheel shot away. To steer the ship, seamen below deck pulled the rudder cables when commands were shouted down to them.

Despite its damaged steering, the *Constitution* continued to fight. When its crew shot away the main mast of the *Java*, the battle turned in favor of the Americans. The *Constitution* fired broadside after broadside into the British ship, while Americans on deck shot at the British crew. By the end of the day, the battle was won, and the *Constitution* got a new nickname. From then on, it was called **Old Ironsides**.

These victories at sea did not win the War of 1812. They did give Americans hope, however. Old Ironsides became a symbol for that hope and did a lot to keep spirits high.

Old Ironsides is still afloat in Boston Harbor, as impressive today as it was during the War of 1812.

---

On Christmas Eve 1814, a peace treaty was signed. The war was over. Neither side could claim victory.

However, word of the treaty was slow in reaching everyone. On January 8, 1815, the final battle of the war was fought at *New*

*Orleans.* General ***Andrew Jackson*** had his 4,500 men dig *trenches* and wait for the 5,300 British soldiers. The red-coated English marched side by side toward the Americans. Many of the Americans were armed with long squirrel rifles. These Kentucky and Tennessee riflemen were crack shots from their years of hunting for a living. In half an hour, the battle was over. The British lost over 2,000 men; the Americans lost 8. The only major land battle the Americans won in the War of 1812 was fought *after* the war had ended!

Andrew Jackson

**Think About It:**

In the Battle of New Orleans, the British marched side by side toward the Americans—the same way they fought unsuccessfully during the Revolution. Why were the British still fighting in such an old-fashioned manner?

Another interesting thing about the Battle of New Orleans was that a French pirate, Jean Lafitte, helped the Americans against the British.

Four years after the Battle of New Orleans, President Monroe was having trouble with natives of ***Florida.*** Florida had first been claimed by Spain. In the French and Indian War, it was given to Great Britain. Florida became Spanish again after the American Revolution. Spain had become a weak nation and was not really interested in settling Florida. The Native Americans in Florida would move north to steal from and destroy settlements in Georgia, returning to Florida to hide. President Monroe asked Spain to stop them. When Spain did nothing, President Monroe asked General Jackson to put a stop to the Native American raids. Jackson and his men followed the Native Americans from Georgia into Florida. Before President Monroe knew what had happened, Jackson had captured Florida! In order to save trouble, the United States paid off $5 million worth of debts the Spaniards owed to Americans, and Spain gave Florida to the United States.

### Sequoya (1760–1843)

This member of the Cherokee tribe was fascinated by General Andrew Jackson's writing. White men could communicate through "talking leaves," which were sheets of paper with writing on them. Sequoya developed an alphabet for the Cherokees. Soon a printing press was printing their own newspaper in their own language! This helped unite the entire Cherokee nation by teaching them to read and write their own language.

By now the nations of Europe were beginning to respect the United States. In 1823, President Monroe made it clear that Europe and the Americas were separate, and were to stay that way. The President told the rest of the world that the United States would not interfere in European affairs. He also said that Europe should not interfere in the affairs of any countries in either North or South America. This came to be known as the ***Monroe Doctrine.***

# War of 1812

**Directions:** Each clue below will help you think of the word or words needed to fill a space in the puzzle on page 60. You can find the answers on the map on page 61.

## Across

1. This battle occurred after the War of 1812 was over. It is the southernmost battle site shown on the map (two words).

4. This city on Lake Ontario was the scene of a battle in Canada.

7. Our capital, _____ , DC, was burned by the British.

8. This state borders only New York and Pennsylvania (two words).

9. The British crossed this water to get to Washington and Baltimore (two words).

11. When the British ships would not let American ships out to sea, it was called a _____.

15. This is the only state shown on the map that has land both east and west of the Mississippi River.

17. West from the state of Ohio is the _____ Territory.

18. The words "North" and "South" are the only things different about the names of these two states. What name do these two states share?

19. This city in Maryland was attacked by the British.

20. South of Georgia is _____ _____ (two words).

## Down

2. The United States won many sea battles on this Great Lake.

3. This is the only state that touches Lake Ontario (two words).

5. This state is north of the Mississippi Territory.

6. Many farmers used this river to get to the Mississippi River.

9. This lake borders New York and Vermont.

10. The British blockade was set up in this ocean.

12. This battle was named for a city between Lake Huron and Lake Erie.

13. These people controlled Canada.

14. A battle in New York took place near this lake.

16. This country is north of the United States.

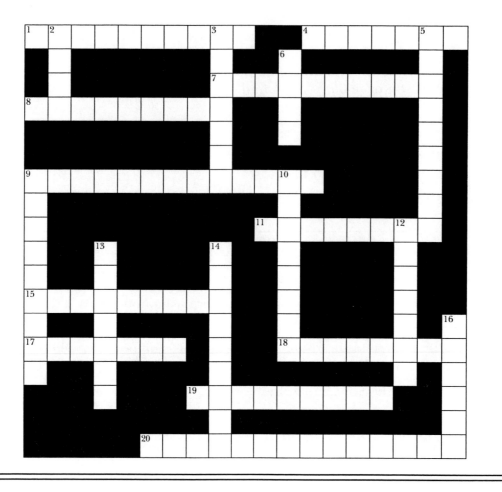

# War of 1812

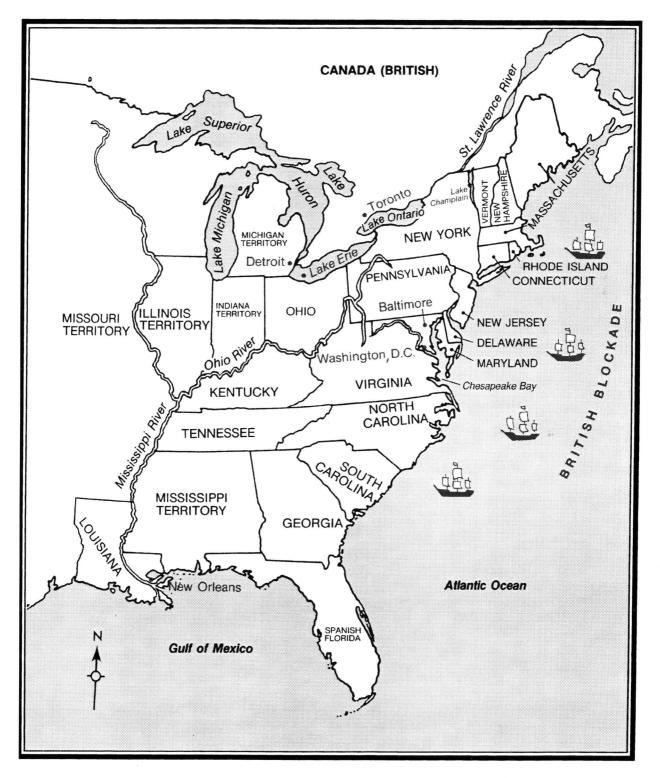

CANADA (BRITISH)

Lake Superior

Lake Michigan

Lake Huron

Lake Erie

St. Lawrence River

Toronto

Lake Ontario

Lake Champlain

MICHIGAN TERRITORY

Detroit

MISSOURI TERRITORY

ILLINOIS TERRITORY

INDIANA TERRITORY

OHIO

Ohio River

Mississippi River

KENTUCKY

TENNESSEE

MISSISSIPPI TERRITORY

LOUISIANA

New Orleans

GEORGIA

SOUTH CAROLINA

NORTH CAROLINA

VIRGINIA

Washington, D.C.

PENNSYLVANIA

Baltimore

NEW YORK

VERMONT

NEW HAMPSHIRE

MASSACHUSETTS

RHODE ISLAND

CONNECTICUT

NEW JERSEY

DELAWARE

MARYLAND

Chesapeake Bay

BRITISH BLOCKADE

Atlantic Ocean

Gulf of Mexico

SPANISH FLORIDA

N

# THE NATION KEEPS GROWING (1793–1874)

5

## Time Line

| Events Elsewhere | Date | Events in America |
|---|---|---|
| | 1793 | Whitney invented cotton gin |
| | 1803 | Louisiana Purchase |
| | 1807 | Fulton used steam to power *Clermont* |
| | 1812–14 | War of 1812 |
| *Napoleon defeated at Waterloo* | 1815 | |
| | 1818 | National Road |
| *Mexico gained freedom from Spain* | 1821 | |
| | 1822 | Austin guided Americans into Texas |
| | 1825 | Erie Canal completed |
| | 1828 | Andrew Jackson elected president |
| | 1830 | Cooper developed steam locomotive |
| *Slavery abolished in Britain* | 1833 | |
| | 1836 | Texas free from Mexico; Battle of Alamo; Whitman's mission in Oregon |
| | 1840 | McKay's clipper ship |
| | 1844 | Morse developed telegraph |
| | 1845 | Howe invented sewing machine; Texas became a state |
| | 1846 | Mexican War began; U.S. acquired Oregon Country |
| | 1848 | End of Mexican War; gold discovered in California |
| | 1849 | California gold rush |
| | 1850 | California became a state |
| | 1853 | Gadsden Purchase |
| | 1860 | Pony Express began |

## Introduction

The United States had grown from 13 colonies into a nation that was able to stand up to the rest of the world. Within a few years' time, it had doubled the land it owned.

In the years following Jackson's victory at New Orleans, the nation changed in many ways. The way of life in the South continued to be unlike that in the New England area. New inventions changed the way of living for many people in all parts of the nation. Better roads and new canals helped people and goods move from one part of the country to another. It was during this time, too, that the West and its people began to be important in the affairs of the nation.

## Transportation and Communication Improve

In order for a nation to be united and strong, people, goods, and ideas must be able to move from one part of the country to another quickly and easily. Five things helped bring the parts of the nation closer together by speeding transportation and communication. These things were roads, canals, steamships, railroads, and telegraph lines.

Early roads were narrow, full of holes, and muddy when it rained. Just before the beginning of the War of 1812, the government started building the *National Road*. When it was finally finished, it ran from western Maryland to central Illinois. It was the finest road in America at the time.

People traveling on the road bought supplies in towns along the way. Merchants in these towns made money, and quite often the towns grew in size.

The government did not go into the road-building business fast enough to supply all the roads needed. For this reason, private individuals and companies built roads. In order to use such a road, a fee or *toll* was paid. A pole or pike was placed across the road. After the toll was paid, the pike was turned to let the traveler onto the road. From this came the word *turnpike*. The idea of toll roads has stayed with us, but it takes the money of an entire state to build a toll road today.

A great step forward in transportation was the building of *canals*. Canals were dug to join lakes and river or to go where no natural waterways went. Horses or mules walking on land pulled canal boats or barges through the water. Such travel was slow but cheap.

The governor of New York, De Witt Clinton, realized how valuable this cheap transportation could be for his state. It was his idea to build the *Erie Canal*. This canal would connect Albany with Buffalo, New York. When the 363-mile-long canal was finished in 1825, it was possible to go by boat from New York City to the Great Lakes. The trip took about ten days.

The Erie Canal was a great undertaking. The cost of moving goods between Buffalo and New York City dropped to $10 a ton, instead of the old cost of $100 a ton. Goods moved more than twice as fast as before. Nearly everything going to the area around the Great Lakes was carried on the Erie Canal. Such cities as New York, Albany, and Buffalo grew rapidly. Canals, like roads, were good for cities.

---

**Think About It:**

Why did cities grow once canals or roads were built?

---

Until 1807, the only way to move a boat upriver or against the current was by using oars, poles, or tow ropes. The muscle power might come from men or mules.

About the time of the American Revolution, Britisher *James Watt* invented a new kind of power. It was the *steam engine*. Wood or coal heated water hot enough to make steam. The steam was used to turn factory machines. Watt's invention began a completely new age in manufacturing. His invention started the *machine age*, or the *Industrial Revolution*.

An American named *Robert Fulton* decided that a steam engine could be used to power a ship. While Fulton worked, people laughed. His first ship, the **Clermont**, was called "Fulton's Folly" by people who thought it would not work. Then one day in 1807, the *Clermont's* huge paddle wheel began to turn, driving the ship up the Hudson River. On that historic voyage, Fulton's ship traveled 300 miles in just over 60 hours. The age of steam transportation had begun.

Steamship

Soon after Fulton's ship sailed, the United States began building **railroads**. The early railroads were little more than stagecoach bodies pulled by horses over wooden rails. It was not until 1830 that **Peter Cooper** built a steam-powered locomotive. His first locomotive burned wood and was just a steam engine on wheels. When this tiny locomotive, called *Tom Thumb*, raced a horse-pulled train, the horse won.

However, the horse-drawn train was soon out of business. In 1830, *Tom Thumb* had only 30 miles of track on which to run. By 1850, trains had about 9,000 miles of track, and more tracks were being put down every year.

Why did railroads become so popular so fast? First, trains were able to carry heavy loads. Second, travel by rail was faster than either road or water. And third, railroads could be built to go almost anywhere.

So far we have discussed moving people and goods. What about ideas? **Samuel F.B. Morse** had a plan that he hoped would speed communication. In May 1844, his idea was tested. A **telegraph** wire was strung between Baltimore, Maryland, and Washington, DC, 40 miles away. Using **Morse code**, Samuel Morse sent a message over that 40-mile wire. It was received in seconds! Telegraph was the fastest known means of sending words or ideas.

Telegraph

---

**Think About It:**

How did improved travel and communication help the nation to grow?

---

### Lyceums and Chautauqua

From colonial times on, people wanted to learn. In 1826, Josiah Holbrook started a new kind of group in Massachusetts. He called this a **lyceum**. People went to a lyceum to learn by listening to speeches and debates. Within ten years there were 3,000 lyceum groups in the nation.

Lyceums were important social and educational groups for nearly 40 years. Speakers such as Ralph Waldo Emerson and Henry Ward Beecher were popular in their day. The grand thing about lyceums was that people listened and learned. Even those who had never attended school could enjoy the program.

In 1874, a new form of learning and entertainment began at Chautauqua Lake, New York. Similar to the lyceum, the **Chautauqua meetings** were devoted to talks and discussions on interesting subjects. Towns would set up their own Chautauqua, which enabled people to become better informed while enjoying the company of friends and neighbors.

Discussion groups, which many cities and towns have today, grew out of the idea of the Chautauqua.

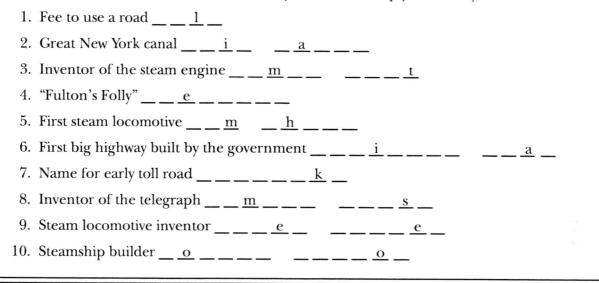

## Puzzle Quiz

**Directions:** Use words from the pages you just read to fill in the blanks following the clues. Each set of blanks has one letter already filled in to help you check your answers.

1. Fee to use a road _ _ l _

2. Great New York canal _ _ i _ _ a _ _ _ _

3. Inventor of the steam engine _ _ m _ _ _ _ _ _ t

4. "Fulton's Folly" _ _ e _ _ _ _ _ _

5. First steam locomotive _ _ m _ h _ _ _ _

6. First big highway built by the government _ _ _ i _ _ _ _ _ _ _ a _

7. Name for early toll road _ _ _ _ _ _ k _

8. Inventor of the telegraph _ _ m _ _ _ _ _ _ _ s _

9. Steam locomotive inventor _ _ _ e _ _ _ _ _ _ e _

10. Steamship builder _ o _ _ _ _ _ _ _ _ o _

## The Cotton Kingdom

Southern plantation owners needed lots of land because their one-crop farming wore out the land so rapidly. Tobacco had been the main crop in the South for many years. Some cotton had been raised, but it was harder to get ready to sell than tobacco. Then an inventor named *Eli Whitney* made his first *cotton gin* in 1793. This machine removed the seeds from cotton. It was now possible to get cotton ready to sell quickly and easily. Once Whitney's machine became well known and widely used, Southern plantation owners quickly changed to cotton raising.

Since the Southerners needed more land, they moved into what are now the states of Alabama, Mississippi, and Louisiana. More slaves were needed to clear the new land and raise cotton. Some *planters*, or plantation owners, moved as far west as Texas looking for land that could grow cotton.

Even though most people in the South were not plantation owners, the rich planters ran the government in the South. They were the people elected to Congress. They wanted laws passed to help the slave owners.

African American field hands who worked in the cotton fields cost as much as $2,000. A planter who owned 100 slaves had $200,000 invested in slaves alone.

Many slaves worked as cooks and servants in the big plantation homes. Some were blacksmiths, carpenters, and other special workers on the plantation. A great many were field hands who worked hard from dawn to dark in the fields. The slaves lived in tiny cabins on the plantation. Usually, each one-room cabin was built of logs. Cooking and heating were done with a fireplace. The owner gave the slaves pork, cornmeal, and molasses. Some slaves had small gardens that they worked after their other jobs were done.

The lives of the Southern "poor white" farmers were little better than the lives of plantation slaves. Many of those poor farmers hoped one day to be plantation owners themselves. They worked their entire lives in the cotton fields trying to make enough money to become wealthy planters.

## The North Manufactures and Trades

While the South depended more and more on farming and cotton growing, the North farmed less and less. Instead, the North was becoming a trading and manufacturing area.

> **Think About It:**
>
> Land in the South was better for farming than in the North. How did this limit the economy in the South?

Some of the finest ships in the world were built in New England. Port cities such as New York and Boston were growing rapidly. The United States was beginning to trade with nations as far away as China.

Many New England sailors made a living fishing. Other New Englanders sailed with whaling ships on voyages that sometimes lasted two years. The oil from the whale's body was used as fuel for lamps.

By the middle of the 1840's, **Donald McKay** had perfected a new kind of sailing ship. It was called the **clipper ship**. Clippers were the finest ships in the world at that time. The *Flying Cloud*, one of the most famous of all clipper ships, could sail as much as 375 miles in a day. This is faster than many American cargo ships sailed in 1940, a hundred years later.

The days of the clipper ships did not last long. Steamships began to appear on the ocean. Though the clippers were more beautiful and even faster, the steamships became increasingly popular. The steamships could carry more cargo and did not have to depend on the wind for speed.

Clipper ship

In addition to building great ships, the Northerners were manufacturing (making) things. The Industrial Revolution was changing the way goods were made. Already, in England, great factories were using new machines to manufacture things faster than ever before. The United States needed these same machines to keep up with England.

The question was: How could the Americans get the plans to the modern English machines? England would not allow any machines or plans for the machines to leave the country. Finally, **Samuel Slater** solved the problem. He had worked in an English cloth factory, and he remembered how the machines worked. In less than a year, he built America's first **spinning machine**. Almost at once cotton mills sprang up all over New England. America was on its way to becoming a great manufacturing nation.

*Textile*, or cloth, mills were the beginning of New England manufacturing. Rivers provided power for the new factories. Many people were glad to leave their poor, rocky farms to work in the factories.

*Elias Howe* invented the *sewing machine* in 1845. Clothing could now be made cheaply and quickly. Shoe-making factories were started in New England and became larger year by year. Pennsylvania used its vast amounts of coal and iron ore to build a huge iron industry. Almost overnight, it seemed, America had become an important *industrial*, or manufacturing, nation.

In order to help the Northern manufacturers, the government placed *tariffs*, or taxes, on foreign goods. This made foreign goods cost more and let American manufacturers make more products because they were sure of being able to sell them.

However, problems went with manufacturing. Workers were poorly paid, and working conditions were terrible. Factories were cold in the winter and hot in the summer. Women and children worked long hours. Men worked 12 hours a day for $5 a week. Women got paid $2 for the same amount of work, and children got only $1. Many Southerners claimed that the Northern factory workers were treated worse than Southern slaves. This was often true. For many years, factory workers were little better than slaves to their jobs.

All this manufacturing brought changes to the cities of the North. As people left farms to work in factories, the cities grew. Factory workers began to buy things they used to raise or make for themselves. This gave jobs to storekeepers and other workers. People became *specialized*, or used to doing only one job.

As the North became industrial with railroads, shipping, and factories, the South remained a farming region. Slaves were necessary to life in the South. The North set its slaves free. Factories provided jobs in the North. The people of the North wanted to see high taxes placed on English goods. The people of the South wanted to sell their cotton to England and buy things in return without the high tax. The two parts of the nation were drifting apart in their thinking. This would soon lead to trouble.

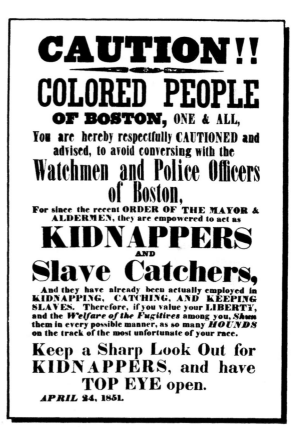

**Think About It:**

Southerners often said Northern factory workers were worse off than slaves. Give some reasons why this statement was true. Then give some reasons why the factory workers were better off than slaves.

## North and South

**Directions:** Read each statement below. If it tells only about the South, place a *1* after it. If it describes the North, write a *2* after it. Place a *3* after any statements that tell about *both* North and South.

1. Wealthy planters owned huge plantations. _____

2. The cotton gin made cotton growing important. _____

3. Textile mills hired many workers. _____

4. Clipper ships sailed to all parts of the world. _____

5. People who worked for others had no chance to become rich. _____

6. Manufacturing was more important than farming. _____

7. Factory owners wanted tariffs on goods from other countries. _____

8. Cities grew quickly and became important. _____

9. Three new states were settled by people needing more land for their huge plantations. _____

10. Whaling and shipbuilding provided jobs for many people. _____

Now check your answers. Do you have twice as many 2's as 1's? Add all your 1's, 2's, and 3's together. Is your total 18? It should be!

## The West Elects a President

As more and more people settled the West, these people asked for more things from the government. They wanted good transportation so they could get their products to market. They wanted cheap land so new settlers could start farms of their own. And they wanted a say in their government.

In 1828, the first westerner, Andrew Jackson from Tennessee, was elected president. People all over the nation admired Jackson, but he was especially popular in the West.

One of the things President Jackson believed in was the *spoils system.* This meant that a government leader should give good jobs to his friends and the people who worked to elect him. The spoils system is not a good system. Government workers should be chosen for what they can do, not whom they know or how hard they worked to elect someone. This is why many government jobs today are *civil service* jobs in which a person keeps his or her job even when a new boss takes over.

It was during Jackson's term as president that South Carolina became terribly unhappy about tariff laws. The South did not like the tariffs the North demanded. When a new tariff was passed, South Carolina threatened to *secede*, or withdraw from the United States. This made President Jackson so angry he threatened to send troops to South Carolina to collect the tax. South Carolina stayed in the United States.

Do you remember that Alexander Hamilton began a National Bank? Andrew Jackson ended it. He felt the bank had too much power over the country, so he had the secretary of the treasury begin to use state banks for government funds.

## Americans Have More Privileges

About this time, changes were made that gave many Americans better opportunities.

*Voting* is a right that helps a person have some say about the government. During the 1800's, more and more people were allowed to vote. By 1860, any free man (but not woman) over the age of 21 could vote. Before that, many states had said a person had to own property in order to vote.

People began to have *political conventions*, or meetings, to decide who should run for government office. The convention system lets more people have a say in who might run for office.

By the time Jackson was president, many Northerners had started trying to outlaw, or *abolish*, slavery. Many of these antislavery people were ministers who felt it was wrong for one person to own another. One way these people tried to abolish slavery was to vote for people who were against slavery.

Many people became interested in trying to have better prisons built. They thought criminals should be helped rather than just being locked up. Better treatment for insane people was also demanded.

Still other people demanded *free public education*. Under this system, children of rich and poor alike could go to school. Taxes were used to pay for the schools so every American could become educated.

Not all changes asked for came about, however. Many people felt the use of alcohol was bad, and they wanted liquor outlawed. Except for a few states, their efforts failed.

Women began demanding equal rights, equal pay, and the right to vote. The right to vote was a long time in coming. Equal rights and equal pay are still vital issues for many women.

---

**Think About It:**

Citizens demanded improvements in many areas. What can happen when government does not provide what people want?

## Susan B. Anthony (1820–1906)

*Susan B. Anthony* was the second of three girls in a Quaker family. There was never any singing in her home because Susan's father thought singing might turn the children's minds from God.

When Susan was 17, her father's business failed. Everything was sold to pay the bills. The girls no longer went to school because they could not pay for it. The family moved and started over.

When she was 19, Anthony got a teaching job in a Quaker school for girls. At the school, Anthony heard speeches on the evils of slavery and alcohol. Speakers also talked about the need for changes in labor laws and for political rights for women.

Anthony began to talk at school against drinking and slavery. When the term ended, she returned home, where things were not going well. Her father's business again failed. After he let some young people have a dance in his home, the Quakers read him out of the Church in a meeting.

The family moved to Rochester, New York, when Anthony was 25. She took a job in an academy and joined the Daughters of Temperance to fight liquor. She made her first speech before this group.

Anthony was elected to attend Temperance conventions throughout the East. At one of them she met *Elizabeth Cady Stanton*, who worked for women's rights. Women's rights and getting women the right to vote became important in Anthony's life.

In 1856, William Lloyd Garrison asked Anthony to join the Anti-Slavery Society. She joined and gave many speeches. At times she was pelted with rotten eggs, was booed, and had her words drowned out by stamping feet.

When the Civil War broke out, Anthony returned to her home. When the war ended, Anthony and Stanton again went to work to

gain women's *suffrage*, or the right to vote. They did not have much success until George Francis Train became their manager. Their speaking tours became successful. They started a weekly newspaper, the *Revolution*.

Then their success faded and Train resigned. Anthony was $10,000 in debt and had to stop printing the newspaper. Both Anthony and Stanton toured the nation speaking and raising money to pay their debts.

In 1872, Anthony joined the Republican party. She went home to Rochester. While there, she registered and voted. She was arrested and had to appear before the state circuit court. The judge ordered the jury to find her guilty and fined her $100. Money poured in from all over New York to pay her fine.

Anthony was asked to speak on women's suffrage in Europe. When she returned home, she was elected president of the National American Woman Suffrage Association.

Success came slowly. Wyoming, Colorado, Utah, and Idaho gave women the right to vote.

When Susan B. Anthony died in 1906, she had given much of her life to women's rights.

## America Moves Toward the Pacific Ocean

In 1821, Mexico became a nation instead of just another Spanish possession. All of Spain's land west of the Mississippi River then became the property of Mexico. The next year, *Stephen F. Austin* led some American families into *Texas* to settle. The Mexican government let him have a huge piece of land. In return, the settlers promised to obey the laws of Mexico and go to the Catholic Church.

---

### The Santa Fe Trail and Trade

In 1821, Missouri merchant William Becknell and friends found themselves in northern New Mexico. Mexican soldiers captured them and took them to *Santa Fe*. To their joy, the captives learned that Mexico had won its freedom from Spain. From then on, traders would be welcome in Santa Fe.

Becknell and his friends took their trading goods to Santa Fe and sold out quickly. They returned to Missouri and immediately began to prepare to trade with the people of Santa Fe.

The trail to Santa Fe was long and dangerous. Traders crossed hot, dry plains and could expect Native American attacks at any time. Guides like Kit Carson acted as scouts for many wagon trains of traders bound for Santa Fe.

Once the plains were crossed, the traders had to survive the Cimarron Desert as well as the steep climb to a pass through the Rocky Mountains.

For those who survived the trip, the rewards were great. Traders brought clothing and other trade goods and went home with hides, furs, and gold and silver. A group of traders leaving Missouri with $30,000 worth of goods and 25 wagons could expect to return with close to $200,000 worth of gold, silver, and furs.

For over 20 years traders moved back and forth along the *Santa Fe Trail*. It was the first use of covered wagons on the plains and a time when travelers learned to defend themselves against Native Americans. Not everyone survived, but those who did made great profits.

---

In Texas, a piece of land three miles long and two miles wide cost $30. Over 30,000 settlers came to Texas by 1836!

So many Americans came that they frightened the Mexican government. The Mexicans said no more Americans could come to Texas. This angered the settlers. On March 2, 1836, the settlers decided Texas was a nation all its own.

Mexican General *Santa Anna* led an army to fight the Texans. The first battle took place at the *Alamo*, an old Spanish mission in San Antonio, Texas. The battle began on February 23, 1836, a week before Texas declared its independence. For 11 days the battle went on until at last the 3,000 Mexicans defeated and killed the 187 Americans defending the church. Several days later, a second battle was fought in which the Americans surrendered. Santa Anna had them all killed, anyway.

The Alamo

On April 21, General **Sam Houston** and 800 furious Texans met the larger army of Santa Anna at **San Jacinto**. When the battle was over, the Mexican army was defeated, Santa Anna was a prisoner, and Texas was a free nation. The **Lone Star Republic** chose Sam Houston as its first president.

Even though Texas wanted to join the United States at once, it was not accepted as a state until 1845. Many Northerners had not wanted Texas as a state because slavery was allowed there. However, America realized it was better to have Texas as a state than to have to worry about some other nation attacking the little republic. Therefore, the Lone Star Republic became the Lone Star State, and the United States grew in size again.

The government of Mexico was unhappy about Texas. When it seemed certain the United States would **annex**, or take over, Texas, Mexico threatened war. The United States annexed Texas and war began. In the summer of 1846, General **Zachary Taylor** crossed the Rio Grande to invade Mexico after the Mexicans had attacked some Americans. In March 1847, General **Winfield Scott** crossed the Gulf of Mexico and also landed on Mexican soil.

**Think About It:**

Why was it reasonable for the Mexican government to be angry with the Texans?

Meanwhile, Colonel **Stephen W. Kearny** and a small army captured Santa Fe from Mexico. The Americans already living in California began the **Bear Flag Revolution** and took control of part of California. Soon Colonel Kearny arrived and took over the rest of California for the United States. By 1847, the United States had control over most of the Southwest. The next February, peace was made. The captured land, called the **Mexican Cession**, became property of the United States. Mexico got $15 million in cash, and another $3 million was paid to the Americans for debts owed them by Mexico. The war was over!

Five years later, the United States again paid Mexico $10 million. This time it was for some land in southern Arizona and New Mexico. A railroad was planned to run across this land from the Mississippi River to California. This land was known as the **Gadsden Purchase**.

The **Oregon Country** became part of the United States during this same period. In 1846, the United States and England signed an agreement giving the southern part of the Oregon Territory to the Americans and the northern part to the English. The two nations had both claimed this land since fur traders from both countries had built trading posts in the area. Russia and Spain also claimed the same land, though neither had tried to settle or use the land.

# Territories as They Became States: 1783–1959

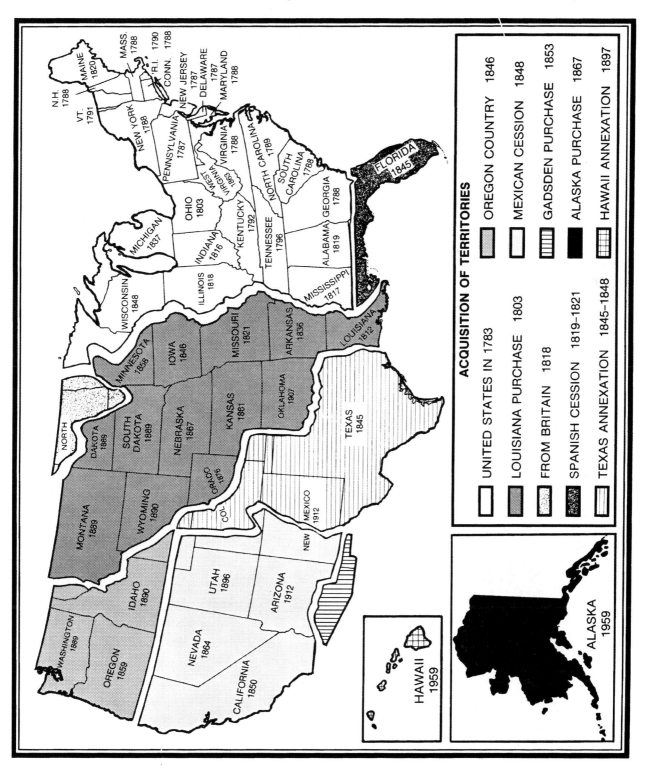

In 1836, ***Dr. Marcus Whitman*** and his wife moved to Oregon and started a mission to help the Native Americans there. Other pioneers began using the Oregon Trail as they traveled west looking for new land. As more Americans arrived, they wanted to be ruled by the United States. For this reason in 1846, the United States and England signed the Oregon Agreement.

The United States had reached the Pacific Ocean. The nation had grown greatly.

## Americans Settle the West

Gold! What a magic word! When ***James Marshall*** found gold near ***John Sutter's*** sawmill in 1848, he was a happy man. By 1849, thousands of people were crossing the prairies, mountains, and deserts to share this happiness. The "Forty-niners" came by land and sea. Sailors deserted their ships in California to hunt for gold. Miners, as well as people who did not know a mine from the moon, came to hunt gold. For a time, it seemed as though *everyone* was coming to California.

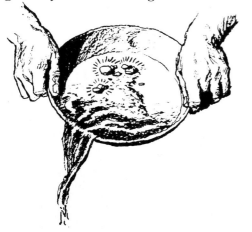

The trouble was, they *all* wanted to hunt for gold. Very few people wanted to grow food or build houses. Prices for food, clothes, housing, and other things went sky-high. For example, eggs—when you could get them— sold for a dollar apiece. The gold hunters found it was cheaper to send their laundry across the ocean to Hawaii than it was to find someone to do it for them in California. Still, California grew. So many people came that California had enough population to become a state in 1850. It entered the Union as a *free* state. No slaves were to be allowed in California. That magic word "gold" brought over a third of a million people to California in ten years.

---

**Think About It:**

Few people became rich hunting for gold. Many became wealthy because of the gold rush. How did people get rich without even trying to find gold?

---

**Supplies Needed to Travel to California in 1849**

Here's what one newspaper said was needed for a family to travel from New York to California in 1849:

One good wagon

Four or five yoke of oxen

Three or four cows and three horses

For every person, 250 pounds of flour, 150 pounds of bacon, 30 pounds of coffee, 50 pounds of sugar, and 20 pounds of rice

Two blankets per person

Cooking pots and pans

A rifle for each male 14 years old or older, 10 pounds of powder, 20 pounds of lead, and 2,000 percussion caps

---

With that many people on the West Coast, there had to be some way to link California with the rest of the nation. A trip by covered wagon took months or even a year. Sailing around South America usually took four months, though once the clipper ship *Flying Cloud* made the trip in 89 days.

Stagecoaches were able to travel from St. Louis, Missouri, to San Francisco in three to three and a half weeks. Such a trip meant day and night travel. The only stops were to change horses every ten miles or so or to pick up mail and passengers. Native Americans and thieves made the trip dangerous.

(In 1860, the **Pony Express** began. A rider carrying only mail rode for about a hundred miles, changing horses every ten miles. Then another rider took the mail pouch and rode for another hundred miles. The Pony Express could carry a letter from Missouri to California in eight days. The cost of a letter was $10 an ounce.

In 1861, a telegraph line to California was finished, and the Pony Express went out of business. It was cheaper and faster to send a telegram than it was to use the Pony Express. Eight years later, the railroad linked California to the rest of the nation, and the stagecoach lines began to lose business. The United States was quickly becoming more and more modern.

The Pony Express

During the 1849 gold rush, people on their way to California usually traveled either north or south of Colorado. Colorado's high mountains were not easy to cross, and most people stayed away from them. However, in 1859, many people who had avoided Colorado rushed to it. Once again the magic word "gold" brought people from all over the world. Now people left California to go to Colorado.

## Westward Ho!

The map on page 77 shows the various ways to get into the western part of the United States. Below is listed a clue for each item you are to identify. Check the map to be sure, and then fill in the blank spaces.

1. This trail starts in Independence and ends in Santa Fe.

   — — — — —   — —   — — — — — —

2. The Willamette Valley can be reached only by this trail.

   — — — — — —   — — — — — —

3. This trail followed part of the Arkansas River until it reached Bent's Fort.

   — — — — —   — —   — — — — — —

4. Just after leaving Fort Hall, this trail branches off to Sacramento.

   — — — — — — — — —   — — — — — —

5. This route connects Sacramento with St. Joseph most directly.

   — — — — —   — — — — — — — —

6. This famous stage route connected St. Louis and Los Angeles.

   — — — — — — — — — —   — — — — — — — — —

   — — — — — — — — —   — — — — —

7. All the trails had to go through these to get from the Mississippi River to the Pacific Ocean.

   — — — — —   — — — — — — — — —

8. This group settled around the Great Salt Lake.

   — — — — — — — —

9. Both the Oregon Trail and the Santa Fe Trail started here.

   — — — — — — — — — — — — —

10. To travel from Santa Fe to Los Angeles, you would take this trail.

    — — —   — — — — — — —   — — — — —

## Westward Ho!: 1800–1850

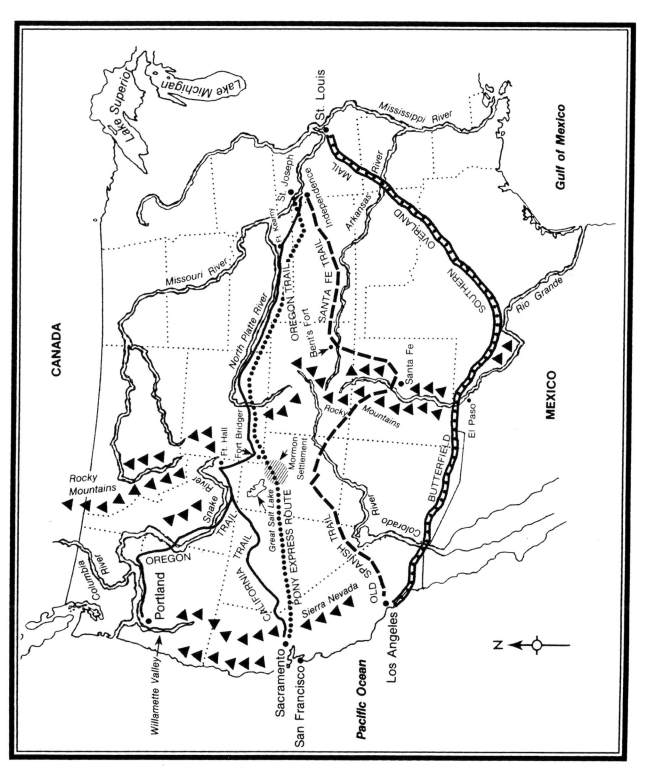

# Western Expansion

**Directions:** Use words from the pages you just read to fill in the blanks above the clues. One letter of each word is filled in to help you check your answers.

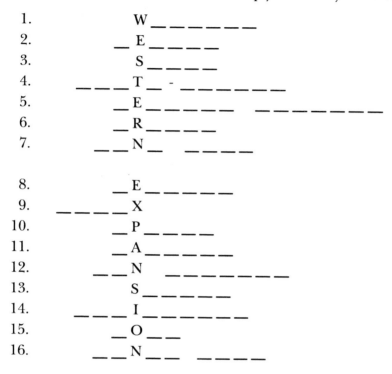

1.    W _ _ _ _ _ _
2.    _ E _ _ _ _ _
3.    S _ _ _ _ _
4.    _ _ _ T _ _ - _ _ _ _ _ _ _
5.    _ E _ _ _ _ _   _ _ _ _ _ _ _ _
6.    _ R _ _ _ _
7.    _ _ N _   _ _ _ _ _

8.    _ E _ _ _ _ _
9.    _ _ _ _ _ X
10.   _ P _ _ _ _
11.   _ A _ _ _ _ _
12.   _ _ N _   _ _ _ _ _ _ _
13.   S _ _ _ _ _ _
14.   _ _ _ I _ _ _ _ _ _
15.   _ O _ _
16.   _ _ N _ _   _ _ _ _

## Clues

1. Early missionary in Oregon
2. General who captured Santa Fe
3. General who invaded Mexico with his soldiers
4. Name for California gold hunters
5. Name for land taken from Mexico
6. Land American and English fur traders shared for many years
7. Texas was once the _____ _____ Republic.
8. When a state withdraws from the rest of the nation, it _____.
9. To take over territory and add it to the nation
10. System when a leader gives government jobs to his friends
11. First western president
12. Battle in which Texans defeated Santa Anna
13. Owner of California sawmill where gold was discovered
14. State that once received important mail by Pony Express
15. Reason so many people went to California
16. Mexican general who captured the Alamo

# BROTHER AGAINST BROTHER (1819–1877)

## Time Line

| Events Elsewhere | Date | Events in America |
|---|---|---|
| | 1820 | Missouri Compromise |
| *Mexico gained freedom from Spain* | 1821 | |
| | 1823 | Monroe Doctrine |
| | 1846 | Mexican War began |
| | 1847 | Mormons settled Utah |
| | 1848 | Mexican Cession; Mexican War ended |
| | 1850 | Compromise of 1850 |
| | 1852 | *Uncle Tom's Cabin* |
| | 1853 | Kansas-Nebraska Act |
| | 1854 | Republican party formed |
| | 1857 | Dred Scott decision |
| | 1858 | Lincoln-Douglas debates |
| *Darwin's Theory of Evolution* | 1859 | Harper's Ferry |
| | 1860 | Lincoln elected President; Pony Express began |
| | 1861 | Confederate States of America formed; Fort Sumter attacked |
| | 1862 | *Monitor* and *Merrimac* fought; Homesteader Act |
| | 1863 | Emancipation Proclamation; Vicksburg fell; Battle of Gettysburg |
| *Red Cross established in Switzerland* | 1864 | Sherman's march to the sea |
| | 1865 | General Lee surrendered; Lincoln assassinated |
| | 1867 | Reconstruction Act |
| *Suez Canal completed* | 1869 | |
| | 1876 | Battle of the Little Bighorn |

## Introduction

During the 1800's, Northerners and Southerners found they disagreed about many things. They lived and thought differently. The two parts of the country seemed to be more like two different countries. Slavery was a big problem. Northerners wanted to stop the spread of slavery; Southerners wanted new states to allow slave-holding.

Slavery was not the only problem. Foreign trade and taxes also caused hard feelings between the two sections of the nation.

Finally, the people of the United States went to war. Rarely in human history has war *really* settled a problem. The Civil War made as many problems as it solved. It divided the nation so completely that some problems left over from the Civil War are still around today.

## What Led to the Civil War

When slave owners moved west, they took their slaves with them. Problems often arose when Northerners and Southerners lived together in new territories. This was shown when Missouri asked to become a state in 1819. Slave owners asked that the new state be *admitted*, or let into the Union, as a *slave* state. Northerners demanded it be a *free* state. An argument followed. The nation had a problem.

Then a solution was seen. Maine asked to join the nation as a free state. Congress agreed to admit Maine as a free state and Missouri as a slave state. In addition, it was agreed that any states made from the Louisiana Purchase would be free states if they were north of the southern edge of Missouri; any states south of the southern edge of Missouri would be slave states. This was called the *Missouri Compromise* or the *Compromise of 1820.*

---

### Abolitionists

Those people who believed slavery was totally wrong were called *abolitionists*, since they wanted to abolish the use of slaves. Thirty years before the Civil War, William Lloyd Garrison printed a newspaper called *The Liberator* that opposed slavery.

Abolitionists went on speaking tours, formed antislavery societies, and published books, pamphlets, and newspapers opposing slavery. They called on Congress to free the slaves and end the practice of allowing one person to own another human being.

Some abolitionists wanted to end slavery gradually. Others, like Garrison, wanted the end brought at once. So strong was the demand of those who agreed with Garrison that in 1850, trading in slaves was no longer allowed in Washington, DC.

Former slaves who had escaped to the North often worked as abolitionists. They knew from their own experience how terrible it was to be a slave.

One of the most famous African American abolitionists was *Frederick Douglass*. It was Garrison who first got Douglass to speak at abolitionist meetings. Douglass always said one thing concerning slavery. He said, "The Negro must be a free man in the United States." His words summed up the feeling of all abolitionists.

## Frederick Douglass (1817–1895)

Douglass was born a slave in Maryland. At the age of seven, he was separated from the grandparents who had raised him. It was time for him to begin his work as a slave. He was one of the few slaves who was taught to read. When he got older, he escaped to New York, pretending to be a sailor. Frederick sent for his wife and moved to Massachusetts to live as a free man. He told people about slavery.

In 1845, Frederick Douglass wrote a book about his life as a slave. After it was published, he had to live in England for two years until he could buy his freedom. Otherwise, he was afraid his old master would make him a slave again.

Douglass worked all his life to end slavery. He helped with the Underground Railroad—a trail slaves used to escape to freedom. When slavery was outlawed and black males got to vote, Douglass became U.S. Minister to Haiti. He also worked for women's rights, including the right to vote.

Then another problem appeared. The new problem was whether or not the national government had the right to manage the affairs of individual states. *John C. Calhoun* of South Carolina became the leader of those people in favor of *states' rights*. This group of Southerners felt the states had more rights than they were often given. *Daniel Webster*, from Massachusetts, led the Northerners, who believed the federal government had to have control of the states or else the Union would fall apart.

The great amount of land acquired from Mexico only stirred up the situation more. Should the new lands be free or slave?

Neither part of the nation wanted the other to have more members of Congress. Each side wanted to be able to control the nation.

Slave being whipped

Then, in 1850, California asked to join the Union as a free state. Congress finally agreed to the *Compromise of 1850*. This compromise let California join the nation as a free state. It also set up the territories of New Mexico and Utah out of land taken from Mexico. When these areas became states, the people living in them could decide whether to be slave or free. A *Fugitive Slave Law* was also passed ordering people in free states to help capture escaped slaves. And, finally, slaves could not be bought or sold in Washington, DC.

Instead of improving, things rapidly got worse. Many Northerners refused to capture escaping slaves. The *Underground Railroad* was set up.

This was not a railroad at all but a group of people who helped slaves reach Canada and freedom. Members of the Underground Railroad guided escaped slaves from house to house at night until they reached Canada. This was against the law and made the Southerners angry.

## Harriet Tubman (1820–1913)

Around 1820, *Harriet Tubman* was born a slave in Maryland. As a young child, she saw the overseer beat many slaves. Harriet herself was beaten more than once.

When Harriet was 14, she tried to help a young boy who was about to be beaten. She shouted at the overseer to stop, and the boy made a dash to escape. The overseer threw a heavy object at the boy and hit Harriet instead. Harriet's head was so badly injured, that it was months before she could work again.

As a result of her head injury, Harriet at times would fall unconscious for a while.

Tubman's master died a few years later. Harriet and her brothers were to be sold. She decided to run away, knowing that if she was to be captured she could be branded with a hot iron or even killed. She and her brothers decided to take the chance and left one night, using the stars to guide them.

At dawn, her brothers were overcome with fear of the slave catchers and decided to return to the plantation and slavery. Harriet moved on. With the North Star as her guide, she traveled toward freedom, over 200 miles away.

After a long and dangerous journey, she reached Pennsylvania and freedom. Soon after Tubman found a job, she decided to attempt to bring her family to freedom.

The Society of Friends, often called Quakers, opposed slavery. These people decided to help Tubman return to free her family. Harriet set out to walk back to Maryland. This time she knew which houses were safe and which friends would help her along the way.

When she reached her family, Tubman convinced them to try to escape. She led them to houses that were part of the Underground Railroad. The homeowners let escaping slaves stay in safety on their way to freedom.

Tubman's family hid during the day and walked at night. Harriet's old injury caused her to become unconscious many times. Each time the family waited until she revived to lead them north.

After reaching safety with her family, Tubman again made the trip to lead other slaves to freedom. In all, she made 19 trips and rescued 300 people from slavery. Eventually, slave owners offered a reward of $40,000 for the capture of Harriet Tubman.

When the Civil War began in 1860, Tubman became a nurse for Union troops. Later she worked as a military scout and intelligence agent. She traveled deep into the South on some of her missions.

In 1913, almost 50 years after the Civil War ended and the slaves were freed, Harriet Tubman died. She is remembered for her courage and desire for freedom.

**Think About It:**

Northerners who helped escaped slaves were breaking the law. Were their feelings about slavery a good excuse or not for breaking the federal law? Why or why not?

In 1852, **Harriet Beecher Stowe** wrote the book *Uncle Tom's Cabin*. This book described all that was wrong with slavery. Northern readers read the book and became furious at the terrible way slaves were treated. Southerners read it and became furious because they felt the book was not all true.

In 1854, the **Kansas-Nebraska Act** was passed. It said that people in the territories of Kansas and Nebraska would decide for themselves about slavery. This act took the place of the Missouri Compromise. Almost at once, Kansas earned the nickname of **"Bleeding Kansas."** People fought and killed each other over the slavery question. The worst tragedy started at **Lawrence**, Kansas. People in favor of slavery attacked the antislave town and killed one person. To get even, **John Brown** and his **abolitionist** friends killed five men. This fighting went on until 1857. When Kansas finally became a state in 1861, it was a free state.

In 1854, a new **political party** was formed. This was called the **Republican party**. One of the new party's main ideas was to stop slavery in the new territories of the United States.

In 1857, a slave named **Dred Scott** came to public attention. He was a slave who had been taken by his owner north of the Missouri Compromise line. Therefore, Scott said, he was free. The Supreme Court, however, decided that slaves were property and could be moved anywhere. The idea of new territories voting for or against slavery was unconstitutional. Slaves could be taken anywhere.

The people of the North were terribly upset. Southerners were delighted.

The next year, the famous **Lincoln-Douglas debates** were held. **Stephen A. Douglas** and **Abraham Lincoln** both wanted to be elected United States senator from Illinois. Douglas, who wrote the Kansas-Nebraska Act, argued that people of an area should decide upon slavery. Lincoln said that slavery was completely wrong and should not be allowed in the territories. He did not, however, say that slave states had to change. The two men discussed this issue in public in several Illinois towns. Douglas won the election, even though Illinois was a free state.

Abraham Lincoln

In 1859, John Brown led an attack on the United States armory at **Harper's Ferry**, Virginia. He and his men captured the armory, where weapons were stored. They were going to give the guns to African American slaves so the slaves could fight and become free. Brown's raid failed, and he was tried and hanged by the United States Army.

Then in 1860, the presidential election was held. The Republican *candidate* was Abraham Lincoln. The Democratic candidate was Stephen A. Douglas. Two other men named Breckinridge and Bell also ran for president, but they were not as important as Lincoln and Douglas. When the votes were counted, Abraham Lincoln became the new president.

**Think About It:**

What reasons might cause people to vote against Lincoln even if they felt slavery was wrong?

## The United States in 1820

The map on page 85 shows how our country looked in 1820. The division between slave and free states was not permanent then. Read the statements below, then look at the map to see if the statements are true or false. If a statement is true, put "true" before it; if it is false, put "false" before it.

_____    1.  There were as many slave states as free states in 1820.

_____    2.  The North had more land that could become free states than the South had for future slave states.

_____    3.  Mexico had become independent from Spain.

_____    4.  Florida had enough people to become a state and had already done so.

_____    5.  The British had sold the Oregon Territory to the United States.

_____    6.  All of the Louisiana Purchase land was closed to slavery.

_____    7.  In the Compromise of 1820, Maine was allowed as a free state and Missouri as a slave state.

_____    8.  There were slave states west of the Mississippi River.

_____    9.  There were free states west of the Mississippi River.

_____   10.  All the free states in 1820 bordered a body of water.

## United States: 1820

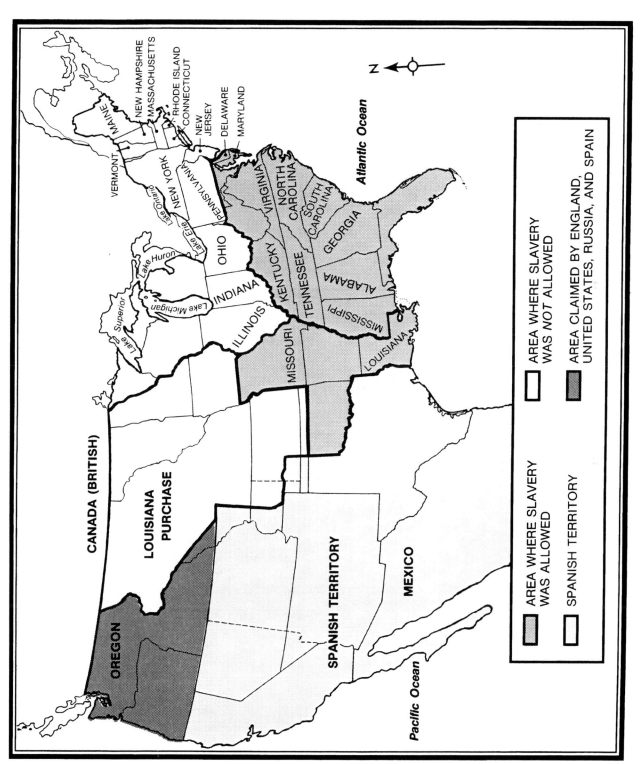

## The United States in 1850

Now look at the map on page 87, the United States in 1850. The division between slave and free states still hadn't become permanent. Answer the questions with "true" or "false." You may need to check the map of 1820 for some answers to see what had happened in 30 years.

_____    1. Some states that were slave states in 1820 were no longer slave states by 1850.

_____    2. Some of the free states in 1820 had changed their minds and were slave states by 1850.

_____    3. Except for the state of California, which entered in 1850, there were still the same number of slave states as there were free states.

_____    4. Mexico had become independent from Spain.

_____    5. The war between Mexico and the United States had occurred by 1850.

_____    6. The United States had made the Gadsden Purchase by 1850.

_____    7. There were still no free states in the Louisiana Purchase area.

_____    8. Oregon still belonged to the British in 1850.

_____    9. The Spanish had lost all of their empire in North America by 1850.

_____   10. The British had no possessions in North America.

_____   11. Starting in 1850, areas were allowed to vote whether they would be a slave or a free state.

_____   12. California was farther south than any other free state.

_____   13. In 1850, more land was closed to slavery than was open to slavery.

# United States: 1850

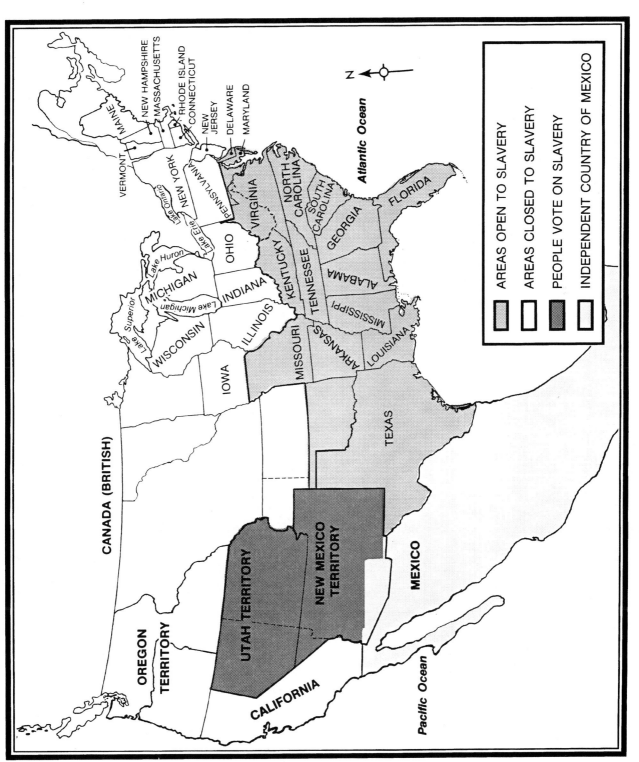

## War!

Several Southern states declared they would secede from the Union if Abraham Lincoln became president. By February 1, 1861, seven states had withdrawn from the United States. They were South Carolina, Mississippi, Florida, Alabama, Georgia, Louisiana, and Texas. These seven states formed the *Confederate States of America.* *Jefferson Davis* was elected president of the Confederacy.

Jefferson Davis

Lincoln became president of the United States on March 4, 1861. He asked the seven states to come back into the United States. He promised to allow them to stay slave states.

Instead, Confederate leaders ordered *Fort Sumter,* in the harbor of Charleston, South Carolina, to surrender. On the morning of April 12, 1861, the Confederates opened fire on Fort Sumter, which had not agreed to give up. The Civil War had started!

When Lincoln asked the states for men to fight for Fort Sumter, four more states quickly joined the Confederacy. They were North Carolina, Tennessee, Arkansas, and Virginia. The mountainous part of Virginia did not like slavery, so it broke away and became West Virginia. West Virginia stayed with the Union and became a separate state in 1863. The slave states of Missouri, Kentucky, Maryland, and Delaware stayed in the Union. Already the South was outnumbered, 23 states to 11.

The North had about 22 million people living in its territory. The South had only about 9 million. Over 3 million of these were slaves who would not be allowed to have a gun or fight. The North had more factories, better transportation, an army, a navy, and the federal government. The North did not have military leaders as fine as the South's leaders, however. Also, since the South was fighting for its life and on its own land most of the time, its armies often did a better job than did Northern soldiers.

Civil War battle scene

Parts of families ended up fighting the rest of their own family. Often one brother lived in the North, another in the South. When a soldier fired at the other army, he never knew for sure whether or not he was firing at a relative or friend.

When the Civil War began, President Lincoln called for 75,000 volunteers to fight the South. Northerners were sure the war would be over in a few months. Soon, the new Northern army marched toward the Confederate capital at Richmond, Virginia. Richmond was only about 100 miles from Washington, D.C. This seemed a good place to begin the war.

# United States: 1861–1865

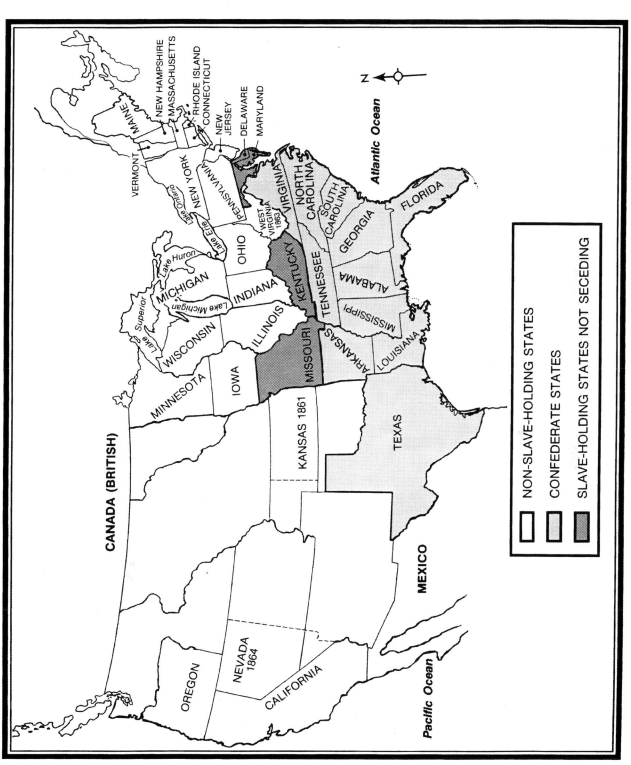

What a surprise the Union army had! The Confederates met them at *Manassas Junction* along a little river called *Bull Run*. People from Washington had packed picnic baskets and followed the Union soldiers to see the fun. They wanted to see the battle that would end the war. The well-trained Confederates defeated the Union soldiers, who turned and ran toward Washington. The sightseers scattered before them, their picnics forgotten in their panic. The North then realized the war might last longer than a few months after all.

The North had two main plans to help win the war. One was to use its navy to *blockade* Southern ports. This would keep supplies from coming in and cotton from going out to be sold. Second, the North planned to cut off one chunk of the Confederacy at a time and conquer it. This tactic is called *divide and conquer*.

The South wanted to hold out until the Union got tired of fighting. Then, Southerners hoped, they would be left alone. Meanwhile, they counted upon getting help from nations in Europe. They were sure England would help them in order to keep getting cotton. Southerners planned to attack the North to win a big victory. One great victory might cause the Northerners to give up the war.

---

**Think About It:**

The North counted on a naval blockade. The South hoped for one big victory. Why was neither idea likely to convince the other side to surrender?

---

Both sides settled down to a war that lasted four terrible years. The war was fought in three areas: the West, the ocean, and the East.

One of the quickest ways to divide the South was to take control of the Mississippi

River. *David Farragut* took a fleet of Union ships to New Orleans in 1862. His fleet defeated the Confederate ships guarding the city, and he captured New Orleans.

Meanwhile, Union General *Ulysses S. Grant* had captured several forts in Tennessee. Then his armies moved south toward Mississippi. Confederate forces met Grant at *Shiloh*, Tennessee. Grant had not expected the attack and, for a time, seemed to be losing. Then more Northern troops arrived, and Grant defeated the Southerners.

Union ships had already captured Memphis, Tennessee, so Grant marched there before going on to Mississippi. After resting, the army marched to *Vicksburg*, Mississippi, where a strong fort overlooked the river. Grant surrounded the fort and began a long *siege* (war of waiting). On July 4, 1863, Vicksburg surrendered. This gave the North control of the Mississippi River and cut Arkansas, Texas, and Louisiana off from the rest of the South.

At the beginning of the war, the North used ships to set up a blockade around the Southern ports. Southern ship captains became *blockade runners*. They sneaked past Union ships and sailed to Europe for supplies. The Southerners also used such powerful warships as the **Alabama** to raid, or attack, Northern *merchant* (supply) ships. The *Alabama* and several other raiders sank 257 Union ships during the war. This was a terrible blow to Northern shipowners.

In March 1862, the Southerners' *ironclad* ship, the **Merrimac**, attacked Union blockade ships at Hampton Roads, Virginia. The *Merrimac* was protected by its armor plate while it sank one wooden ship and captured another. The next day things changed. The *Monitor* appeared from the north and attacked the *Merrimac*. The *Monitor* was also ironclad. It had two guns in an iron turret that turned, so one gun fired while the other loaded. Even though the *Merrimac* had five guns on each side, it could not defeat the *Monitor.* Both ships finally gave up and sailed away, but navy warfare had changed; no longer were wooden ships suitable for war.

The *Merrimac* and the *Monitor*

The Union built more ships like the *Monitor,* but the South built only one *Merrimac.* The *Merrimac* was built around the hull of a ship the South had captured from the North. Later in the war, the Southerners burned the *Merrimac* instead of letting the North capture it. The first *Monitor* sank in a storm and still lies on the bottom of the ocean.

In the East, the Union army tried to capture Richmond and failed. General **Robert E. Lee** of the South was a far better leader than Union General **George B. McClellan.** McClellan was always afraid the South had more men. For this reason, he often held off attacks, waiting for more soldiers. He was so slow going toward Richmond that the Confederates got tired of waiting and attacked him instead.

### Think About It:

If the North had captured Richmond, the South's capital, would the war have ended? Why or why not?

During the summer of 1862, the **Seven Days' Battle** was fought between Lee and McClellan. When the fighting stopped, a total of 16,000 Union soldiers were killed, wounded, or missing. The figures for the South were over 20,000.

The war continued with battles every few days. On September 17, the Battle of **Antietam** was fought in Maryland. This was the bloodiest day of the war. Nearly 5,000 men died and over 18,000 were wounded. The war was not kind to either side.

On January 1, 1863, President Lincoln issued the **Emancipation Proclamation.** This declared that the slaves owned in the states fighting the Union were now free. Of course, it did not free any slaves at the time. This could be done only if the North won the war.

By now both sides were tired of the war. In order to have a large enough army, the North started **drafting** men to fight. From the middle of 1863 until the end of 1864 nearly 1 million men entered the Northern army.

## African American Soldiers and Sailors

After the Emancipation Proclamation of 1863, African American soldiers joined the Union Army. About ten percent of all Union volunteers were free Negroes or former slaves. In all, about 185,000 African American soldiers served in the Union army.

These troops fought in over 450 battles. Twenty African American soldiers received the Congressional Medal of Honor, which was the government's highest award for bravery. Over 65,000 African American volunteers died in the war.

Nearly 30,000 African American volunteers served in the Union Navy, which had accepted African Americans from the beginning of the war. Four of them won the Medal of Honor.

In all, over 300,000 African American volunteers helped the North as soldiers, sailors, hospital workers, laborers, and even as spies.

In the South, African American slaves built most of the Confederate defense lines and did nearly all the heavy work for the Southern armies. At home, slaves kept the plantations going to feed the people and armies of the South.

Near the end of the war, some African American soldiers even served in the Confederate army.

In early May 1863, General Lee fought against General *Joseph Hooker* at *Chancellorsville*. Although outnumbered two to one, Lee won the battle. Both sides lost over 10,000 men each.

Then came the great battle at *Gettysburg*, Pennsylvania. General Lee had marched north into Pennsylvania. General *George G. Meade* met him for a four-day battle. For the first time, General *J.E.B. Stuart* and his Confederate cavalry were late to a battle. General Stuart was the finest horse soldier on either side during the Civil War. On several occasions he and his men had ridden completely around an entire Union army, capturing men and equipment as they went. Once, Stuart had actually gotten into the tent of a commanding Union general and stolen his coat. When Stuart found that the same general had his hat, which Stuart had lost a short time before in a narrow escape, he asked for a *truce*, or cease-fire. Under a white flag, the coat was traded for the hat. Then the fighting went on again!

However, Stuart was late at Gettysburg because he and his men were out capturing a Union supply train. Whether or not his being on time could have saved Lee is just a guess. When the fighting ended, Lee had lost the battle and had to escape with his army into Virginia. There were 50,000 killed or missing in the two armies.

President Lincoln came to Gettysburg the next November and opened a large military cemetery there.

As a result of the battle at Gettysburg, both England and France decided not to deliver ships they were building for the South. This ended any chance the South had of winning the battle on the sea.

In the year following Gettysburg, terrible battles were fought at places like *Chickamauga*, *Chattanooga*, and the *Wilderness*. General Grant was given command of all the Union armies. He began making plans to capture Richmond and defeat Lee.

In May 1864, Union General *William T. Sherman* left Tennessee with 100,000 troops. He marched to Atlanta, Georgia, and again divided the Confederacy. He then marched from Atlanta to the Atlantic Ocean. This last 300-mile march caused terrible destruction. For a width of 60 miles, Sherman's men burned and destroyed everything in sight.

---

**Think About It:**

Sherman's march to the sea caused great suffering. How might his march actually have saved lives?

---

When 1865 arrived, the war was nearing an end. On April 9, General Lee surrendered to General Grant at *Appomattox Courthouse* in Virginia. The Civil War was over at last!

It had been a terrible war. It had also been a war of new ideas. Railroads had been used for the first time to move entire armies quickly from place to place. The telegraph had been used to send messages in seconds. Balloons had been sent high into the air so soldiers in them could see what the enemy was doing. Pinkerton detectives had been used to guard the president and to find out valuable information for Northern generals. The American *Red Cross* had been started by *Clara Barton* to help the wounded on both sides.

By the end of the war, 359,528 Union men and 258,000 Confederates were dead. Nearly 400,000 more had been wounded.

Ulysses S. Grant

Robert E. Lee

## Civil War Sites

The map on page 95 shows you some of the sites mentioned in this chapter. Answer the questions; check the map or the material in the chapter if you are not sure of your answers.

1.  Name the four states that had slaves but did not leave the Union.

    _____         _____

    _____         _____

2.  Sherman marched through the South destroying towns and crops. Most of the destruction occurred in this state. _____

3.  This city in the middle of Georgia was burned by General Sherman. _____

4.  The Chesapeake Bay almost cuts this slave-holding Union state into two parts.

    _____

5.  The capital of the United States, Washington, DC, is nearly surrounded by this state.

    _____

6.  The capital of the Confederacy, Richmond, is in this state. _____

7.  General Lee invaded the North only once. He was stopped at this battle.

    _____

8.  This state, which is located between Kentucky and Maryland, split from Virginia when Virginia left the Union. _____

9.  The first important battle of the Civil War happened in Virginia about halfway between Richmond and Washington, DC. Name this battle.

    _____

10. This important battle in Tennessee took place before General Grant started down the Mississippi River. _____

11. This was a stronghold on the Mississippi River that General Grant captured. It gave the Union forces complete control of the Mississippi. _____

    _____

12. Fort Sumter is located in the first state to leave the Union. Name this state.

    _____

13. Name the Union plan to keep Southern ships from arriving at or leaving their harbors.

14. The Battle of Gettysburg was fought in this state. _____

15. The end of the Civil War came at Appomattox Court House in which state?

    _____

## Civil War Sites: 1860–1865

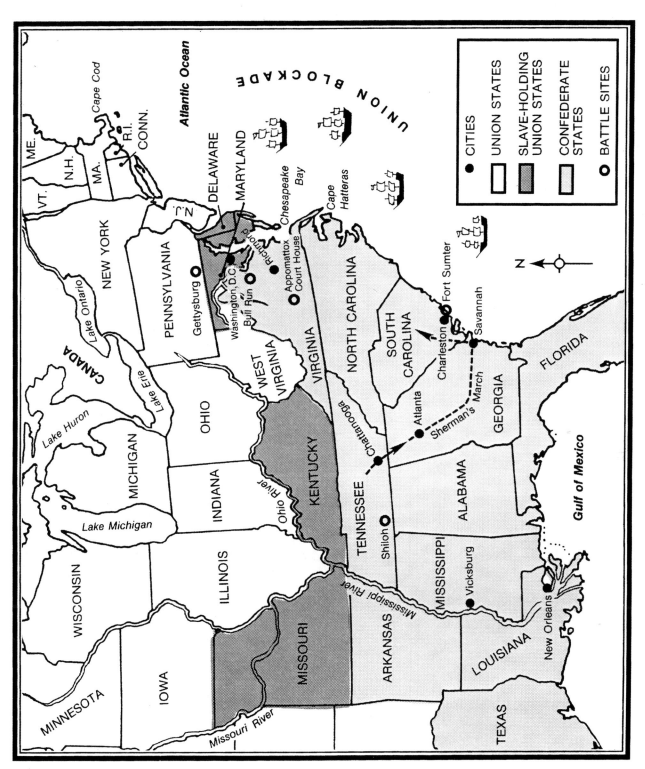

## Civil War

**Directions:**  People at cross-purposes are working against each other. This seems to have happened in America before and during the Civil War. As you can see, each set of answers below, and on the next pages, is at cross-purposes. The answers cross each other. The number beside or above each set of blanks tells which clue matches the answer for those blanks.

       2.     3.     4.     5.     6.     7.     8.

1.

1.  This was the last name of a Southern leader in favor of states' rights.

2.  The Missouri _____ was also called the Compromise of 1820.

3.  The Fugitive _____ Law said Northerners had to help capture escaped slaves.

4.  The Underground _____ helped escaping slaves reach Canada.

5.  _____ Beecher Stowe wrote *Uncle Tom's Cabin.*

6.  John _____ of Kansas led a raid on Harper's Ferry, Virginia.

7.  Stephen A. _____ debated the question of slavery with Abraham Lincoln.

8.  In 1860, Abraham _____ became our first Republican president.

10.   11.   12.   13.   14.     15.   16.   17.

9.

9. The war between the North and South is often called the _____ _____.

10. General Grant won a great victory at _____, Mississippi.

11. This was the South's famous ironclad.

12. Jefferson _____ was president of the Confederacy.

13. This Union ironclad fought the *Merrimac* in 1862.

14. The first big battle of the war was fought at Manassas Junction, or _____ _____.

15. _____ Virginia became a free state in 1863.

16. This ship was a famous Confederate raider.

17. William T. _____ led Union forces in a march that divided the South.

19.   20.   21.   22.   23.   24.   25.   26.   27.   28.

18.

18. This Pennsylvania battle was won by the North.

19. Ulysses S. _____ finally commanded the Union army.

20. Robert E. _____ led the Confederate army.

21. The bloodiest day of the Civil War was during this battle.

22. J.E.B. _____ was the great Confederate cavalry general.

23. In 1862, Lee and McClellan fought the Seven _____ Battle.

24. The Emancipation Proclamation was made to free Confederate _____.

25. Clara _____ helped wounded soldiers on both sides during the Civil War.

26. This is a short halt in fighting, or a cease-fire.

27. The government sometimes uses the _____ to make men enter the army.

28. _____ B. McClellan was a cautious Union general.

## The Nation Needs Rebuilding

The war was over. President Lincoln was already making plans to rebuild the divided nation. He had made plans so the Southern states could quickly get their state governments working again. War-torn farms would have to be rebuilt. Railroads, roads, and bridges needed repair all over the South and in parts of the North. The nation needed to forget the war and live in peace.

Then, on the night of April 14, 1865, President Lincoln was shot while watching a play. He died early the next morning. His killer, *John Wilkes Booth*, was unhappy about the defeat of the South. People in both North and South realized what a terrible thing the death of the president was. Without Lincoln's leadership, rebuilding the nation would be much harder.

The new president, *Andrew Johnson*, was a Southerner who had been chosen to run with Lincoln as vice president. He tried to follow the plans Lincoln had made for the *reconstruction*, or rebuilding, of the South. But Congress would not let him put his plans to work, and Johnson was not strong enough to stop them.

Andrew Johnson

Congress passed three amendments to the Constitution. The Thirteenth Amendment ended slavery in the United States. The Fourteenth Amendment made former slaves citizens, stopped members of the Confederate army from being elected to government office, and said any money owed by the Confederate government was not to be paid by the federal government. The Fifteenth Amendment gave former slaves the right to vote.

Tennessee was the only Southern state that agreed to the Fourteenth Amendment.

Congress then passed the **Reconstruction Act of 1867** for the other 10 states. These states were made into military districts and put under army rule. Almost all Southerners were kept from voting because they had been in the Confederate army. This meant only former slaves could vote and elect officials. Most of these former slaves could neither read nor write.

Northerners stuffed their clothing into cloth suitcases called carpetbags and moved South looking for easy money. The cloth bags gave these men the name **carpetbaggers**. Some Southerners called **scalawags** joined the carpetbaggers. Together, these two groups helped African Americans set up new governments. Of course, many carpetbaggers and scalawags got wealthy because the uneducated African Americans could not see what was wrong. Once in office, the African Americans and scalawags voted for high taxes and greater government spending. The high taxes ruined many Southern landowners, who were already having a hard time rebuilding their land.

Large plantations began to be broken up into small farms. Many big landowners rented parts of their farms to **tenant farmers** or **sharecroppers**. These people paid the landowner their rent in a share of the crop. It seemed a good way to begin farming, but most sharecroppers were always in debt to the landowner. Though cotton and tobacco were still raised, such new crops as peanuts, fruits, and vegetables were grown after the war.

Many Southerners became unhappy. Some former soldiers joined a secret organization called the **Ku Klux Klan**. The Klan members gathered at night disguised in white robes and hoods. They rode through the country frightening African Americans and warning them not to vote for the government of the scalawags and carpetbaggers. When the warnings were not followed, Klan members beat, burned, and killed the African Americans. Soon the Klan was feared throughout the South.

By 1872, most former Confederates were again allowed to vote. All Northern soldiers left the South by 1877. The government of the Southern states was once more in the hands of Southerners. When whites got control of the government, they remembered what poor governments they had during African American leadership. They tried to keep African Americans from ever leading the government again. Many laws were passed that made it impossible for African Americans to vote.

Slowly the South changed. Industries were started and transportation was improved. Once again, the South was part of the United States.

## Booker T. Washington

Washington was born a slave but became one of America's greatest educators. He loved to learn and became a teacher to share that love. When young, he worked for five hours each day before school. When just a little older, he walked most of the 500 miles to go to the Hampton Institute for blacks.

Washington felt black people had to be educated to advance and have a better life. He founded the Tuskegee Institute in 1881. It was a school where blacks could learn a trade or profession. He later became the adviser on racial issues to three presidents—Cleveland, Roosevelt, and Taft.

Washington worked his whole life to help other black people improve their lives economically. But, because he accepted segregation, some more militant black people criticized him.

## The Western Frontier Is Settled

In 1862, the *Homestead Act* was passed. This act made it possible for a family to move onto 160 acres of government land and live there for five years. At the end of that time, the homesteaders could keep the land if they had met certain requirements. Even before the close of the war, thousands of families were "homesteading." When the Civil War finally ended, huge numbers of people decided to begin a new life in the West. The Homestead Act made that new life possible.

Wagon train heading west

A great help in settling the West was the opening of the transcontinental railroad. Towns started to grow along the rail lines. Ranchers could raise cattle hundreds of miles from cities that needed the meat. They would drive the cattle 50 miles or more to the railroad, where they were then shipped the rest of the way to market.

### Think About It:

How did the destruction of the South's economy help cause expansion into Western lands?

For many years cattle grazed on the *open range*, or unfenced land, in the West. With the coming of farmers, the range land was slowly fenced until, today, little open range is left. Terrible fights occurred at times between cattle raisers and farmers, or between cattle raisers and sheep raisers. Gradually, ranchers and farmers reached the point where they could live together in peace.

### Black Cowboys

After the Civil War, freed blacks moved west to find a better life. Many became cowboys and played a huge part in building the American West. They drove cattle to market. They rode horses and even hunted wild horses.

One of the most famous was Nat Love. He was born a slave, was freed, and learned to break horses. Then Nat went west to earn a living. By the time he was 20, he had led cattle drives, explored the West, and learned to speak Spanish. He described his life in a popular autobiography.

Gold and silver brought *prospectors,* or gold hunters, to the Rocky Mountain states of Colorado, Idaho, Nevada, and Montana. Where gold and silver were discovered, towns sprang up overnight. Just as California became a state because of miners, so did Nevada, Colorado, Idaho, and several other mountain states.

Pioneers crossed the Indian Territory on their way to Oregon or California. In 1847, the Mormons passed through Native American lands on their way to Utah, where they settled. Native Americans' hunting grounds were taken and the huge buffalo herds ruthlessly killed.

Time after time the Native Americans fought back. Bloody massacres were carried out by both Native Americans and settlers. A Colorado army group killed hundreds of Native American women and children at the **Sand Creek Massacre**. At the **Little Bighorn** in Montana, the Sioux wiped out General **George A. Custer** and his small army. No matter how hard they fought, the Native Americans always lost in the end.

Beginning in the early 1800's lands were set aside for Native Americans. These lands were called **reservations**. Such lands were almost always poor. This made it hard for Native Americans to live.

Native American warriors

## Matching

**Directions:** Match each word or phrase in the first column with a word or phrase in the second column. Use each item only once. Write the correct letter after each phrase in the first column.

1. Reconstruction _____    a. Greedy Northerners

2. John Wilkes Booth _____    b. Source of free land

3. Carpetbaggers _____    c. Gold and silver hunters

4. Scalawags _____    d. Southern friends of carpetbaggers

5. Ku Klux Klan _____    e. Battle won by Sioux tribe

6. Homestead Act _____    f. Killing of innocent Native Americans

7. Open range _____    g. Rebuilding

8. Prospectors _____    h. Southern terror group

9. Sand Creek Massacre _____    i. Unfenced cattle land

10. The Little Bighorn _____    j. Killer of President Lincoln

# YEARS OF GROWTH AND CHANGE (1831–1936)

## Time Line

| EVENTS ELSEWHERE | DATE | EVENTS IN AMERICA |
|---|---|---|
| | 1859 | First oil well drilled |
| | 1860 | Lincoln elected President |
| | 1861 | Civil War began |
| | 1865 | Civil War ended |
| | 1866 | First Atlantic cable laid |
| | 1867 | The Grange organized |
| | 1869 | Knights of Labor formed; women's suffrage in Wyoming Territory |
| *France gave Statue of Liberty to U.S.* | 1876 | First telephone |
| | 1879 | Edison's light bulb |
| *All men in Britain could vote* | 1884 | |
| *Gold found in South Africa* | 1886 | American Federation of Labor formed |
| | 1889 | Hull House opened in Chicago |
| | 1890 | Horseless carriage appeared; Sherman Anti-Trust Law |
| *Spanish-American War* | 1898 | |
| | 1901 | Wireless invented |
| | 1903 | Wright Brothers' flight |
| | 1908 | Model T sold |
| | 1914 | Clayton Anti-Trust Act |
| *World War I began* | 1914 | |
| *World War I ended* | 1918 | |
| | 1920 | First radio station; Nineteenth Amendment passed |
| | 1936 | Congress of Industrial Organizations formed |

## Introduction

Many changes began to take place in the United States. The country's population was growing. People from other nations came to America in large numbers. Cities increased in size, and life on the farm changed. Changes were made in manufacturing, transportation, and communication. Working people demanded better wages and fairer treatment. Business changed. A few people became very rich and powerful. The nation was changing so fast it was hard to keep up with the new ideas.

## The Farmer's Life Changes

Now that the nation was settled, farmers had more land than ever on which to raise food for the growing nation.

Wooden plows had long since been replaced by those with iron tips. *Cyrus McCormick* had invented the *reaper*, which, when pulled through a field, cut the grain and tied it into bundles. This was much faster than cutting the grain by hand with a scythe. A *threshing machine* had also been invented to separate the grain from the stalks.

---

### *George Washington Carver (1864–1943)*

Carver knew where he was born, but he had to guess his birthday! He was born a slave. He taught himself to read, and at 13 he went to find more education. Carver worked and went to school. He was brilliant and studied all he could about agriculture. He got his M.S. degree in agriculture in 1896.

Booker T. Washington asked Dr. Carver to come to Tuskegee Institute and start a department of agriculture. Carver accepted and began studies that would help to save the economy of the South.

Cotton was still the major crop, but when prices fell, the South suffered. Dr. Carver told farmers to plant peanuts! He found 145 useful products that could be made from peanuts. His birthplace became a national monument 10 years after his death.

---

Following the Civil War, an all-steel plow was invented. Seed-planting machines followed. Then came a *combine*, which cut and threshed the grain all at once. Horses were replaced by *tractors*, and American

farmers found their whole way of life had changed. One farmer could farm more land and produce more food than ever before. Farms grew larger, especially in the West.

Just as the *windmill* had helped cattle raisers by pumping water for thirsty cattle, so *irrigation* helped the western farmer. Irrigation canals were dug to bring water from the mountains to the dry prairies. Dams stored water for use during dry times. Wells were dug, and water was pumped from under the ground. Today, huge *sprinkling systems* are spread across the dry lands of the West.

However, problems came with these improvements. The number of farm jobs decreased. People who had no work other than farming found themselves moving to the city to take any work they could get.

As more and more food was raised, the price for farm crops often went down. This is called the law of *supply and demand*. When a lot of something is produced, it is likely to sell for a lower price. When little is produced, the price goes up.

What were farmers to do when the price fell on the crops they raised? The first thing they tried to do was raise more crops. Often the farmers wore out their land trying to raise more. Lands that were not cared for and *fertilized* soon wore out. Then the farmers were worse off than ever.

It often cost nearly as much to ship a crop to market as it did to buy the crop itself. In 1867, the *Grange* was organized. Farmers joined the Grange to learn about better farming. They also learned that a group of farmers had more strength than one farmer alone. Grange farmers marketed or sold their crops as a group. They protested high *freight* charges set by railroads.

Then farmers discovered another way to help themselves. They asked the government for laws to protect farmers from unfair transportation costs and from loss of their land when they had a bad year and could not pay their debts. When a congressman did not listen to the farmers, they voted against him in the next election. Soon, the farmers had a greater *voice* in government. They had discovered the truth to the saying: "There is strength in numbers."

The government tried hard to help the farmers. Colleges to teach about farming were started. Today, the United States Department of Agriculture gives advice and tries to help solve farm problems. Many farm crops are given government *support*. This means farmers are guaranteed at least a certain price. They may get more, but they won't get less.

> **Think About It:**
> The government has spent billions of dollars in various forms of aid to farmers. Why have farmers received so much help?

## Communication and Transportation Continue to Improve

One area that changed greatly after the Civil War was communication. The telegraph had served well, but it served only the United States. *Cyrus Field* wondered why the telegraph could not connect us to Europe. Since the wire could not go above the ocean, why not under the sea? Huge cables were made to carry many telegraph messages at once. Ships began laying the *Atlantic cable* under the ocean. Cables broke time after time, but Field kept trying. Finally, in 1866, the first cable was completed. Now people in the United States could send a message to Europe in a few seconds!

At the time Field was laying his cable, *Alexander Graham Bell* was trying to send the human voice over a wire. By 1876, the *telephone* worked. Two years later, New Haven, Connecticut, had a telephone system in use.

Alexander Graham Bell

By 1901, an Italian named *Guglielmo Marconi* was sending *wireless* signals across the Atlantic Ocean. By 1920, the United States had its first radio station. The people of the nation seemed closer to each other when the entire nation could listen to the same radio program at the same time.

Television followed radio and made communication that much easier.

Robert Fulton would not have recognized the steamships that now began to travel the oceans. They were many times larger than his little *Clermont,* and they traveled much faster.

Railroads were being built faster and faster. Short rail lines appeared to cover the nation like spiderwebs. Soon, these short lines began to join together to make huge railroad *systems.* Railroad men like ***Cornelius Vanderbilt*** often combined dozens of small railroads into one system and became wealthy from the profits. Today, the railroads still carry huge amounts of freight.

---

**The Electric Railway**

Inventions by Thomas Edison and others helped develop the ***electric railway.*** It did a lot to make cities grow because workers could ride to work quickly and cheaply. This allowed many workers to live in one huge city.

When the electric railway ran on tracks through a city, it was called a streetcar or a trolley. In some cities like New York, if often ran on tracks above the city and was known as an elevated. When it ran underground, people called it the subway.

Lines joined cities and towns and enabled people to live in a small town and work or shop in a city. Millions of people came to depend on the electric railway for transportation.

---

In the 1890's, strange little ***horseless carriages*** began to amuse the citizens and frighten the horses of America. In the time since then, thousands of different makes of cars have been produced in America.

Though ***Henry Ford*** did not make the first automobile, he did more for the auto industry than any other car maker. Ford used the idea of another inventor to make car manufacturing a big business. Do you remember Eli Whitney and his cotton gin? Well, we often forget that Whitney had another idea. He made rifles for the army using ***interchangeable,*** or ***standard***, ***parts.*** This meant the trigger from one rifle was the same as the trigger for any other rifle of the same model.

Ford used this same idea in building his cars. He started an ***assembly line.*** The workers stayed in one place and the work came to them. Each worker did one job in the making of a car. Use of interchangeable parts and the assembly line increased car manufacturing. This ***mass production*** allowed Ford to sell his cars cheaply, since they were made so quickly.

**Think About It:**

Henry Ford made the United States the world's leading automobile maker. Today, people drive vehicles made in many nations. What are some of the reasons for this change?

Model T

When ***Orville*** and ***Wilbur Wright*** made the first successful airplane flight in 1903, the plane flew less distance than that between the tips of the wings of a Boeing 747. People looked on the airplane as just an interesting toy at first. That idea soon changed. The airplane proved itself to be a great aid to rapid transportation.

In the last 100 years, improved communication and transportation have brought the people of our nation and the entire world closer together.

---

### Free Public Education

Originally, girls seldom went past elementary school. Academies and high schools were mostly for boys. By the 1830's and 1840's, a few places did have schools for girls. One of these later became Mount Holyoke College in Massachusetts. In Ohio, one of the first colleges in America to accept both male and female students was Oberlin College.

Though people saw the need for education, very few schools were paid for by public taxes. Only in New England were there very many public schools.

During the time of Andrew Jackson, more people began to favor the idea of tax-supported schools. Labor groups helped push for *free public education*. Workers wanted their children to be educated so they could lead easier lives than their parents had.

Gradually, citizens realized that if people are to have a democracy, they must be educated in order to make responsible choices. Big cities led the way in tax-supported public schools. By the middle of the 1800's, most of the states in the North had free public elementary schools.

Colleges were set up to train teachers. A movement began that resulted in free public high schools for all students.

Gradually public education as we now know it became available for all.

---

## The United States Becomes an Industrial Giant

After the Civil War, industry grew at a great rate. The Industrial Revolution made itself felt all over the country.

The United States had enough iron ore and coal to provide *raw materials* for manufacturing. Swift rivers provided water power to run factories before steam engines and then electricity were used for power. Timber was another plentiful *natural resource*. In 1859, America's first oil well was drilled in Pennsylvania. Kerosene was then used for lighting instead of whale oil. The demand for oil products started a new industry—the *petroleum* industry.

## Drake's Oil Well and the Use of Kerosene

When **Edwin Drake** drilled for oil in Titusville, Pennsylvania, in 1859, people laughed at him. **Petroleum** had been sold for years as a cure for disease. A chemistry professor discovered that purified petroleum could be used for lighting and heating.

Drake's well paid off. After three months of drilling, Drake hit oil. His well produced 30 barrels of oil daily. Each barrel sold for about $20.

Once the oil was purified, **kerosene** was produced. Kerosene burned easily and gave off lots of light and heat. It was better than candles or whale oil for lighting homes and businesses. A new era began as people used kerosene more and more.

Gasoline is also produced when kerosene is made. For many years gasoline was considered worthless and burned off at the oil refinery.

**Thomas Edison** began to put electricity to use when he invented the **light bulb** in 1879. A short time later, electricity was serving Americans in both home and factory.

Thousands of other inventions and discoveries came one after another. American industry was producing more goods every day. **Montgomery Ward** started the idea of buying things from a **mail-order** catalog. Companies such as **F. W. Woolworth** built **chain stores** all over the nation. Huge **department stores** such as **Marshall Field** in Chicago sold thousands of different items in one store.

Huge companies called **corporations** were formed. Many people owned **stock** in a corporation. This meant that each stockholder owned a part of the business. By selling stock, a company could raise millions of dollars for new buildings and equipment so the corporation or company could grow even larger.

This was the time when a few individuals became famous for their huge enterprises. We have already mentioned Ford's mass-produced cars and Vanderbilt's railroad

system. John D. Rockefeller came to control almost all of the American oil industry.

When the first oil well was drilled in 1859, it began one of the greatest money-making industries in the world. Huge oil discoveries were made in other states. People came to the oil **boom towns** just as they had gone to gold strikes.

John D. Rockefeller was a vegetable seller when he bought one oil refinery where **crude oil** was changed to kerosene. Then he bought more refineries, pipelines to carry oil, and all the other things needed to carry on the oil business. Soon his **Standard Oil Company** controlled nearly all the nation's oil business. Rockefeller had a **monopoly** on oil. Later, he was forced to break up his giant company.

In 1848, a 13-year-old boy named **Andrew Carnegie** came to America to work in a cotton mill. He earned a little over a dollar a week. He moved on to different jobs, working hard and saving his money. Eventually, he got into bridge building. He needed **steel** for his bridges. Even though America had long had an iron and steel industry, most bridge steel came from England. There, a new process made it easier to make steel from iron. Carnegie took a chance and set up his own steel mill in America, using the English method.

As Carnegie's steel mill grew, he bought iron ore deposits along the Great Lakes. Then he bought a fleet of Great Lake ships and a railroad to carry the iron ore to his plant. His business became known as the *United States Steel Corporation*. It was the largest producer of steel in America.

Carnegie was a man who felt he should do good for America. He began giving money to towns and cities to build public libraries. Even though he gave away more than $300 million, he was still a rich man.

---

## Mary McLeod Bethune (1875–1955)

Ten miles was not too far to walk to school if you loved to learn. Mary McLeod would not have had to walk so far if she had been white. She passed that school on the way to her school every day.

When Mary McLeod finished college, she became a teacher. She married and moved to Florida, where she started her own school. For many years most of her students were girls. But in 1923, her school merged with a nearby men's college. When the school needed money, she asked John D. Rockefeller for help. He and others gave money when Mrs. Bethune needed it. She did so well with her school that she became an adviser to Franklin D. Roosevelt! Her desire to provide education made a difference to many black children.

---

By 1893, *James J. Hill* controlled the huge *Great Northern* railway system. His 20,000-mile-long system covered most of the Northwest from the Great Lakes westward. Hill realized that ranchers and farmers needed a way to get their crops to market. Hill gave them that way. Good rail transportation encouraged more ranchers and farmers to settle in the West. The more settlers, the more business for Hill's railroad.

Dozens of men made fortunes in railroads, coal, oil, timber, iron, and steel. Many of these men made their money by overworking those who worked for them, by destroying the countryside, and by crushing anyone who got in their way. Such men came to be known as robber barons because of their ruthless ways. In spite of their selfishness, however, they did much to develop American industry.

---

### Think About It:

The robber barons were responsible for much of America's industrial and transportation growth. How would American industry and transportation be different today if these men had not done what they did?

# Building America

**Directions:** Answer the following questions or statements using words from the unit so far. When you have answered the questions, find all of your answers in the letter maze below. These answers are written across and up and down. A few are written backwards. Some answers cross each other. Circle each answer as you find it.

| | | | | | | | | | | | |
|---|---|---|---|---|---|---|---|---|---|---|---|
| R | I | R | R | I | G | A | T | I | O | N | O |
| E | D | L | E | I | F | O | R | D | E | L | I |
| A | E | N | O | H | P | E | L | E | T | I | L |
| P | M | S | Y | S | T | E | M | I | C | N | L |
| E | A | I | R | P | L | A | N | E | F | E | E |
| R | N | P | E | T | R | O | L | E | U | M | E |
| A | D | R | A | W | K | H | I | L | L | H | T |
| C | O | R | P | O | R | A | T | I | O | N | S |
| Y | L | O | P | O | N | O | M | B | J | D | G |

1. What farm machine did Cyrus McCormick invent?
2. What word means watering farm crops?
3. Prices go up and down according to supply and _____.
4. Cyrus _____ laid the Atlantic cable.
5. What did Alexander Graham Bell invent?
6. What word describes a number of railroads that are joined into one group?
7. Henry _____ was a famous automaker.
8. When a car moves from worker to worker as it is being built, the car is on an assembly _____.
9. Orville and Wilbur Wright made the first _____.
10. What is another word for oil?
11. Montgomery _____ began using mail-order catalogs.
12. What are companies owned by stockholders called?
13. When one person or company controls all of one industry, we call it a _____.
14. John D. Rockefeller controlled the Standard _____ Company.
15. Andrew Carnegie made a fortune making what?
16. James J. _____ once controlled the Great Northern railway.

## American Workers Demand Better Treatment

Before the Industrial Revolution, people worked at home or in small shops. With the coming of machines, hundreds or even thousands of workers labored together in factories. Here an employee did one kind of work or made one part of a product. Long hours and low pay made the life of working people hard. Something needed to be done to help them.

Just as farmers joined together, so did working people. *Labor unions* were formed in which workers joined together to try to get better wages and improved working conditions.

In 1869, the ***Knights of Labor*** was formed. This labor organization took members from various jobs in different industries. Since its members faced so many different problems, the Knights of Labor lost power because it tried to help everyone. Even though it did much good for many workers, it was no longer popular by 1890.

A new kind of union was formed in 1881 and reorganized in 1886. ***Samuel Gompers*** thought the members of each kind of work should have their own union. He organized the ***American Federation of Labor***. The A.F. of L. (as it was called) included many unions. For instance, carpenters had a union, cigarmakers had a union, and so on. All the unions in the A.F. of L. tried to help each other whenever possible.

Union symbol

In 1935, the ***Congress of Industrial Organizations*** was formed. This labor organization was made up of unskilled laborers such as autoworkers and steelworkers. The CIO and the A.F. of L. finally joined in 1955 and became the ***AFL-CIO***.

How did unions help their members? If one worker asked for better pay and shorter working hours, that worker might be ignored. If every worker demanded the same thing as a group, the *employer* or business owner was more likely to listen. Often the union would make a bargain with the employer. Union members would work in an agreed-upon way. In return, the employer would promise to provide certain pay and benefits. This is called ***collective bargaining***.

If the union and the employer could not agree, a group might be called in to listen to both sides. This neutral party would then make suggestions to both the union and the employer. This ***arbitration*** often helped solve labor problems.

## Samuel Gompers (1850–1924)

In 1863, a 13-year-old boy immigrated to the United States from London. That boy was *Samuel Gompers*. Because his father was a cigar-maker, Samuel was apprenticed to that trade when he was 10. When the family moved to America, Samuel helped his father make cigars in their tenement home in New York.

In 1864, Samuel got a job of his own and joined a union. Later, he helped organize the first cigar-makers union of New York. Eventually, he was secretary and finally president of that union.

A cigar-makers' strike against poor working conditions failed. The members learned from failure. They raised money through high union dues and initiation fees so in future strikes they would have enough money to survive. They also added sickness and death benefits for their members.

Other unions copied the Cigar-Makers Union. In 1886, the *American Federation of Labor* was formed, with Gompers as its first president. Gompers was the driving force behind the A.F. of L. He was president every year except one from 1886 to 1924.

Gompers insisted that unions would bargain with employers and avoid getting involved with government. He supported labor laws to protect working women and children.

When World War I began, Gompers worked to have labor and government cooperate for the good of the nation. He worked to create a Department of Labor to deal with labor problems in wartime production.

Gompers also worked for passage of the *Clayton Anti-Trust Act* of 1914. The Act affected the rights of labor. It said unions were legal and that employers could not get injunctions in all strikes. An *injunction* was a court order making a strike illegal. The Clayton Anti-Trust Act also legalized peaceful strikes, picketing, and boycotts.

Gompers often gave more money to the unions than he could afford. He did not become rich as a union president. To him the needs of working people were more important than eating.

When he was 74, Gompers was in Mexico City on a labor visit. He became ill and was rushed back to the United States. He died in San Antonio, Texas, on December 13, 1924.

Sometimes no agreement was reached. Then the union members might refuse to work until an agreement was reached. This was called a *strike*. During a strike, the employer made no money and the strikers got no pay, or *wages*. The workers hoped to get more pay after the strike than before. Once in a while, a strike would be *broken*, and the workers would go back to work no better off than before the strike.

### Think About It:

Strikes are a major weapon of labor unions. How can a strike in one plant cause workers in other locations to be laid off?

Sometimes a business owner would shut down a factory when labor troubles began. This was called a *lockout*, and it meant that workers were not allowed to work. Some union members were *blacklisted* by business owners when they tried to get better treatment for the workers. A list of their names was sent to other employers saying they were troublemakers. It was often hard for a worker on the blacklist to get a job.

Some labor troubles ended in riots and killings. Strikers often came to blows with fellow workers who, rather than strike, continued to work. Union officials were sometimes killed. At times, employers died violent deaths. Even so, business owners have kept on making money and workers have been better treated since the unions began.

The government tries to see that both business and labor play fair with each other and with the American people. If a threatened strike might harm too many people, the government may require the workers to have a *cooling-off period*. This means that for perhaps two months the strike cannot be called. During this time, both labor and employer are asked to try to solve the problem.

### The First Major Railway Strike

Unions used the *strike* as a weapon to force employers to listen to their demands for better pay and improved working conditions. In 1877, four major railway lines in the East cut the pay for their workers.

The workers went on strike to protest. Railway workers in other states joined, and soon the trains stopped running. It looked as though the strike was a success.

Fights between strikers and company officials broke out. People were injured, some were killed, and property was destroyed. The governors in four states called for military troops to stop the fighting.

The army came in and broke the strike. The beaten strikers went back to work for less pay. The first major railway strike had failed.

But government goes much further in control of American business and labor. Remember the oil monopoly that Standard Oil had? In 1890, the *Sherman Anti-Trust Law* was passed. This made it illegal for any one company to control all of most businesses or industries.

The amount that such businesses as the railroads and utility companies can charge is regulated by the government. In this case, a company may have a limited monopoly on providing something like water to a particular area. The government tries to make sure that companies with limited monopolies do not charge too much and that they give good service.

The government also sets the bottom or *minimum wages* paid to certain workers. It sets certain health and safety requirements for some businesses, such as mining. Children are protected by other laws. No longer can a 10-year-old child work 12 hours a day, 6 days a week. Workers injured at work receive certain help and pay under *workmen's compensation laws*.

---

## Muckrakers

By the early years of this century, big business had become extremely powerful in the United States. Politicians passed laws that favored business and often ignored the problems of workers and farmers.

A group of writers set out to call attention to these problems. They were nicknamed *muckrakers*. Millions of readers learned from these people just how bad things were for labor and farmers.

Ida Tarbell wrote about how laws helped make Standard Oil so powerful that new companies could not compete. Lincoln Steffens told how politicians in cities got rich by taking bribes from big business. Author Frank Norris told how the railroad and grain trusts cheated farmers.

The most famous of all muckraking books was *The Jungle* by Upton Sinclair. This book told about the cruelties of the stockyards and the meat packing industry. Because of that book, laws were passed to make meat products cleaner and to protect consumers and workers alike.

---

Today, many businesses provide their workers with more than the government requires. Workers in many industries are given paid vacations and time off with pay during sickness. Some workers have health insurance and life insurance paid by the company for which they work. Others get a bonus or extra pay at the end of the year from the *profits*, or money, the company made that year.

---

### Think About It:

The government passes laws to protect workers and consumers. How might government rules and regulations help a new business to succeed or fail?

---

## "Give Me Your Tired, Your Poor"

In 1876, the people of France gave the people of America the Statue of Liberty, which stands in New York Harbor. For many people coming to the United States to make new homes, this famous statue was the first thing they saw. At the base of the statue are these words:

> *Give me your tired, your poor,*
> *Your huddled masses yearning to breathe free,*
> *The wretched refuse of your teeming shore,*
> *Send these, the homeless, tempest-tossed, to me:*
> *I lift my lamp beside the golden door.*

Statue of Liberty

From the beginning of its history, the United States has been a magnet for people of other lands. In the last 150 years, about 48 million people from other nations have *immigrated* to the United States. People came for religious freedom, for a place to begin a new life, or just to see the new land. Usually these people were poor or were hunting for a better life than they had in their native lands.

When Ireland had great crop failures in the mid-1800's, many people left that nation to keep from starving. When these people arrived in the United States, they had no money and no one to help them. The Irish took any job they could find. Many of these people lived in crowded cities in the East.

In western America, Chinese laborers built many of the early railroads in the 1800's. Their *descendants* now live in western cities like San Francisco.

Many midwestern farmers have relatives who came from Germany during this period. Great cities such as St. Louis and Milwaukee were settled by early immigrants from Germany.

Much of the land west of the Great Lakes was settled by people from Sweden, Norway, and Denmark. Louisiana and northern New England have many people whose *ancestors* were French. The southwestern states show the influence of Spanish immigrants.

Life was not easy for these newcomers. Usually they did not speak English, and they had no friends to help them get a start. They had to find jobs where language was not important. This usually meant that the poorest paid and the hardest jobs went to immigrants.

In spite of these hardships, most immigrants learned to speak English and became *citizens* of the United States. Many became well-to-do and respected Americans.

By about 1900, some Americans began to fear the country would be taken over by these newcomers. Congress passed laws to limit the number of immigrants who could come to the United States. *Quotas*, or limits, were set on the number of people who could come from each foreign nation in a year. Immigrants from some nations, such as China, were no longer allowed. People who could not read were told to stay home. So were those with certain diseases. Canada was one of the few nations from which an unlimited number of people could come to the United States.

Quotas and limits on immigration changed as the years passed. Events such as the war in Vietnam or the communist take-over of Cuba caused the United States to allow large numbers of refugees from such nations. People in Mexico and Latin American nations wanted a better life for themselves and their families. They came to the United States in large numbers. Many of these new immigrants came illegally and are not included in immigration figures.

Europe, once the source of most of the nation's immigrants, supplied fewer of the newcomers to the United States. Many new arrivals now come from Asia and Latin America. As a result, the nation is finding it necessary to help those from many cultures adjust to life in the United States.

---

**Think About It:**

At any time, several million immigrants are in the United States illegally. What services should be provided for these people, and why should this help be given?

---

## Problems of Our Nation

Changes bring problems. The Industrial Revolution brought more and more people to the cities. Farmers came to town looking for jobs. Immigrants without money settled in the cities. Too many poor people were crowded into too little space in the cities. *Slums* were the result. Overcrowding and low income forced people to live in crowded, dirty conditions.

Many people knew the problem of slums. The people who lived there often could not help themselves. Other people seemed not to care. Some people did care, however. One of these was *Jacob Riis*, an immigrant from Denmark who had become a writer and newspaper reporter. He wrote and published articles about the terrible conditions so everyone could see how bad slum living was. Another slum fighter was *Jane Addams*. She built **Hull House** in Chicago in 1889. Hull House worked especially to help the women and children of Chicago's slums. Gradually, the work of people like Riis and Addams did improve the lives of many poor people in the big cities.

Other problems bothered Americans. women were not given equal rights with men. Many colleges would not accept women. Many jobs were open to men only. Women were not allowed to vote. They had no say in choosing the men who governed them. In 1869, Wyoming Territory allowed women to vote. A few other western states followed Wyoming's example and granted *woman suffrage*, or voting. It was not until 1920 that the nation finally passed the *Nineteenth Amendment*, which gave all women the right to vote.

The question of the use of alcohol had bothered some Americans for years. In 1919, *Prohibition* began in the United States. The *Eighteenth Amendment* said no liquor was to be made or sold in the nation. People who were usually honest broke the law and laughed about it. Finally, in 1933, Prohibition was *repealed*, or stopped, by the *Twenty-first Amendment*. Once more, most states allowed the sale of liquor.

## Problems

**Directions:** Each numbered item below has several related items at the right. The number following the term at the left tells how many related items match it. Use each right-hand item for only one left-hand term. After each right-hand item, write the number of its corresponding left-hand term.

1. Labor organizations (4)

2. Labor union words (5)

3. Americans from other nations (3)

4. Jane Addams (2)

5. Women's rights (3)

6. Use of alcohol (4)

strike _____

American Federation of Labor _____

immigrate _____

Wyoming _____

Prohibition _____

Hull House _____

Knights of Labor _____

collective bargaining _____

suffrage _____

quota _____

arbitration _____

repeal _____

Chicago slums _____

Congress of Industrial Organizations _____

citizens _____

cooling-off period _____

Nineteenth Amendment _____

Eighteenth Amendment _____

AFL-CIO _____

wages _____

Twenty-first Amendment _____

## Jane Addams (1860–1935)

*Jane Addams* was one of the few rich people willing to spend her life helping the poor. When she was born September 6, 1860, her father was a banker, a mill owner, a lawmaker, and a friend of President Lincoln. After Jane's mother died when Jane was two, her father raised her.

Her father used to take Jane for drives. When she was only six, they drove through poor neighborhoods, which depressed Jane. She told her father she was going to live next to poor people so they could play in her nice yard.

Jane graduated from college. She attended medical school but quit when back trouble kept her in bed for a year. Her father died soon after, and Jane's doctor sent her to travel in Europe to regain her health.

In London Addams saw terrible poverty. There, she learned of Toynbee Hall, where college students helped the poor. Jane observed this social work and thought it was wonderful.

In 1887, Addams decided what she wanted to do with her life. With her friend Ellen Starr, Addams decided to help the poor of Chicago. The two women located Hull House, a huge old home, to use as headquarters. The women moved in in 1889.

The two women were ready to help people living in the slums around them. Nobody came for help. Most of the residents were from foreign countries and did not understand the offer of help.

It was children who first came to play. They were followed by factory girls who stopped for tea. As Addams and Starr learned to speak a number of languages, their efforts to help were better received. They helped mothers with housework and taught them how to cook food properly. They showed children how to keep clean. Addams read aloud to any who wished to listen.

After Addams complained to the city that the streets were not being kept clean, she got a city job. She became "Inspector of Streets and Alley Ways in the Neighborhood of Hull House."

Her settlement house kept on working. English was taught. Food and medicine were given to the needy. When Addams ran out of money, she asked wealthy Chicago women to donate funds.

Concerts were given on Sunday afternoons. Art classes began. A branch library opened at Hull House. Addams started a public bath house for the poor. A boarding house was begun for working girls. More buildings were added. Addams was elected to the school board and demanded better and safer schools for slum children.

Addams bought coal cheaply by the load for a cooperative so poor people could buy if from the cooperative by the bag. She asked lawyers to give legal aid to the poor. She fought against child labor and worked for insurance and old-age pensions for workers.

Kings and rulers visited Hull House as Jane Addams's social work became known. Addams opposed war and felt people of all races could live in peace. In 1931, she received the Nobel Peace Prize. Cities across the nation copied her ideas.

Addams's good works lived on after her death in 1935. She was a good neighbor to Chicago's poor when many had no real neighbors.

# THE UNITED STATES BECOMES A WORLD POWER (1867–1959)

8

## Time Line

| EVENTS ELSEWHERE | DATE | EVENTS IN AMERICA |
|---|---|---|
| | 1867 | U.S. purchased Alaska |
| | 1889 | Pan American Union formed |
| | 1898 | Hawaii annexed by U.S.; Battleship *Maine* sunk; Spanish-American War |
| | 1899 | U.S. controlled Samoan Islands |
| *Panama broke from Colombia* | 1903 | |
| *Archduke Francis Ferdinand assassinated; World War I began* | 1914 | Panama Canal opened |
| | 1915 | *Lusitania* sunk by Germany |
| | 1916 | General Pershing sent to Mexico to capture Pancho Villa |
| | 1917 | U.S. bought Virgin Islands; people in Puerto Rico became U.S. citizens; U.S. entered World War I |
| | 1918 | Armistice in World War I; Wilson's Fourteen Points |
| | 1919 | Treaty of Versailles |
| | 1920 | Vote given to women |
| | 1921 | U.S. signed treaty with Germany |
| *Mussolini gained power in Italy* | 1922 | |
| | 1929 | Stock Market collapsed; Depression began |
| | 1932 | Roosevelt elected President |
| *Hitler appointed chancellor of Germany* | 1933 | Worst part of Great Depression |

## Introduction

In the years following the Civil War, the United States began to pay more and more attention to what was going on in the rest of the world. It emerged as a major world power.

And the United States continued to expand. It got land by buying it, by going to war, and by giving smaller countries help. Just like any landlord, America had problems with some of these new holdings.

Then the United States used the Monroe Doctrine as a reason for getting involved with *Latin America*.

All too soon, America had been drawn into a great war in Europe. Following that war, when things were looking just fine, the nation was suddenly in the worst shape it had been in since the Civil War.

## Alaska

In 1867, *William Seward* was secretary of state. He was a man who believed in *expanding*, or making the United States bigger. One day a Russian official offered Seward a real bargain. Russia would sell *Alaska* to the United States for about two cents an acre. Seward hurried to get Congress to approve the deal. Later that year the United States bought Alaska for $7.2 million. Many people called Alaska "Seward's Icebox" and "Seward's Folly."

When gold was discovered in Alaska, people no longer asked why the United States needed the territory. Salmon, timber, furs, and oil added to Alaska's products. In 1959, Alaska became our forty-ninth state.

Usually Americans do not think of Russia as being too near the United States. However, if you look closely at the Diomede Islands in the Bering Sea, you can see an interesting fact. Russia owns Big Diomede and the United States owns Little Diomede. Three miles separate the United States from Russia!

## The Hawaiian Islands

In 1898 *Hawaii* was annexed by the United States. Even though American missionaries and traders had lived in Hawaii for years, the United States seemed unwilling to take over the islands. The Hawaiians had promised not to sell any of the islands to any other nation. Also, American ships could use *Pearl Harbor*. Other than that, the government left Hawaii pretty much alone.

However, a revolution took place in 1893, and Hawaii began to have troubles. It had been a free country for several years but finally asked the United States to take over its government. In 1898, Hawaii became a territory of the United States. Then, in 1959, it became the fiftieth state.

The Hawaiian Islands are a series of volcanic islands in the Pacific Ocean. The people of the Hawaiian Islands have come from various places—from the Polynesian islands many miles to the south, and from China, Japan, America, and Korea.

Hawaii is the largest of the islands. Mauna Kea and Mauna Loa are two volcanoes on Hawaii. The island of Lanai is known for pineapples. Honolulu is the capital city of the Hawaiian Islands. It is located on the island of Oahu. Also on Oahu is Pearl Harbor, where much of the United States Navy was stationed before the start of World War II. Oahu has half the population of all the Hawaiian Islands. Niihau has been reserved for only pure Hawaiians. Tourists cannot even visit the island.

# The Hawaiian Islands: 1959

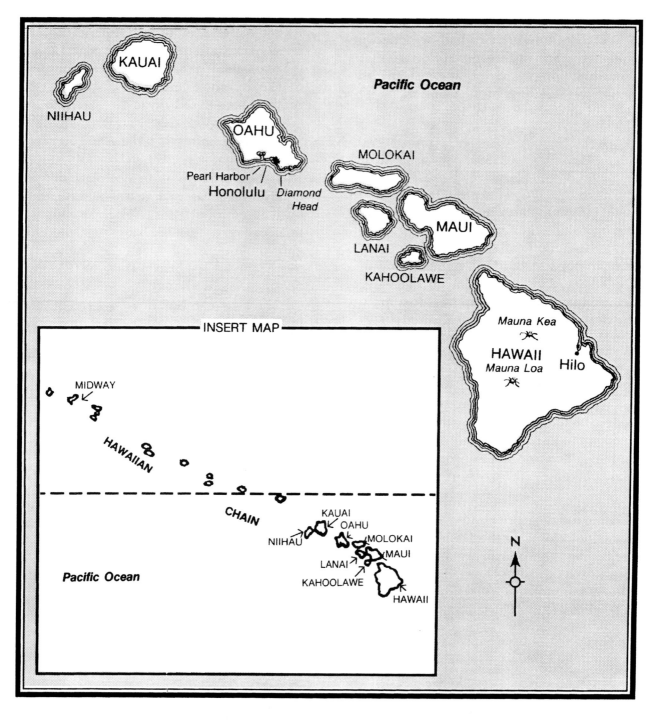

## Alaska: 1959

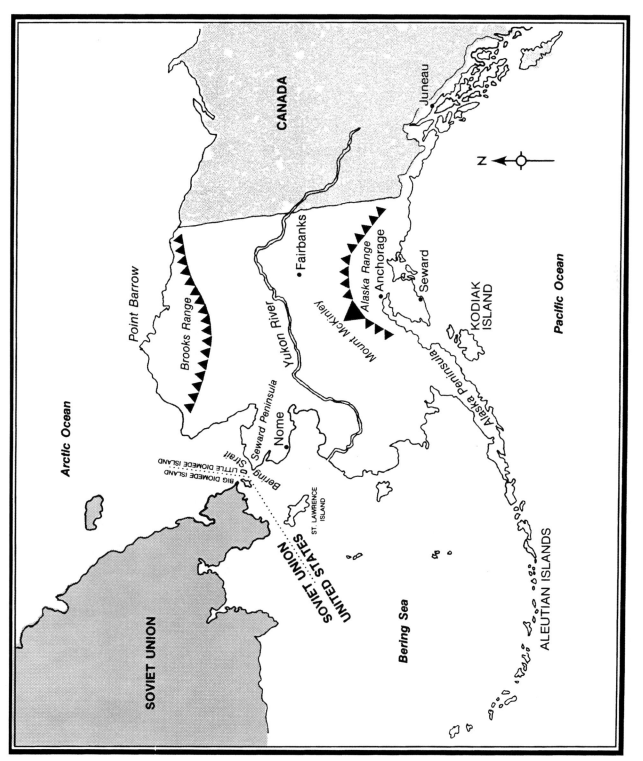

## Alaska and Hawaii

**Directions:** Use the information and maps on Alaska and the Hawaiian Islands to complete this puzzle.

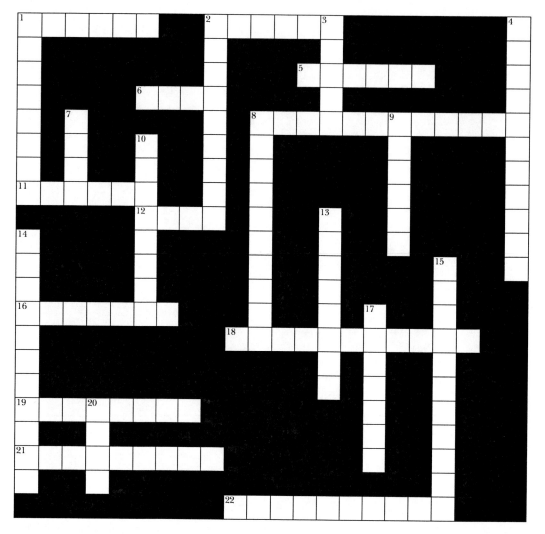

## Across

1. This became our forty-ninth state.
2. A large island south of Seward, Alaska
5. Capital city of Alaska
6. Largest city on the island of Hawaii
8. This body of water separates Alaska from Russia.
11. This Hawaiian island may not be visited by tourists.
12. Alaskan city on the Seward Peninsula
16. Hawaiian island north of Lanai

*(continued)*

18. Famous naval base west of Honolulu
19. Capital city of the state of Hawaii
21. This city, which is north of Seward, has more people than the capital of Alaska.
22. This large island is south of the Bering Strait.

## Down

1. Chain of islands off Alaska's southwestern coast
2. A small Hawaiian island south of Maui
3. Island northwest of Oahu
4. This piece of land reaches farther north than any other part of the state of Alaska (two words).
7. The island of Hawaii seems to be pointing a finger at this island.
8. This small island in the Bering Strait is only three miles from Little Diomede Island (two words).
9. This man was responsible for the United States purchase of Alaska. A city and a peninsula are named after him.
10. The northern volcanic mountain on the island of Hawaii is the highest in the state (two words).
13. Southwest of Hilo is this volcanic mountain on the island of Hawaii (two words).
14. When people fly into Honolulu, they often see this mountain (two words).
15. These mountains are in northern Alaska (two words).
17. Both Hawaii and Alaska are in this ocean.
20. One half of the total population of the state of Hawaii lives on this island.

## The United States as Landlord

Shortly after Hawaii had its revolution in 1893, the people of **Cuba** revolted against Spain, the country that owned their island. The fight between Spanish soldiers and the Cuban people went on for some time. Since many Americans lived in Cuba, the United States was very interested in what was going on. In 1898, the battleship *Maine* sailed to Cuba to protect Americans living there. About a month after the *Maine* reached **Havana** harbor, it blew up one night. The terrible explosion caused the ship to sink at once. Nearly 300 American sailors died that night. All over America, the cry of "Remember the *Maine*!" was heard. On April 25, the United States declared war on Spain.

REMEMBER
THE MAINE

## Yellow Press

Sometimes called "yellow journalism," the **yellow press** got its name from a newspaper circulation war. In the late 1800's, several New York newspapers each tried to outsell the others. The *Journal* and the *World* tried to give readers more news and sent reporters all over the world. The use of big headlines helped attract readers.

Joseph Pulitzer published the *World*. He used lots of drawings, as well as huge headlines, to attract readers. His paper began to print comics and carried many stories about crime and the problems of famous people. The *World* added color to its pages in 1893.

William Randolph Hearst published the *Journal*. He wanted his paper to be even more widely read than the *World*. He also used color in his newspaper and began printing colored comic strips. Of course he, too, printed many stories about crime and what people did wrong.

Both papers had a comic strip with a young boy who wore a shapeless yellow sack. The comic-strip character was called the "yellow kid." This all led to the term "yellow journalism" or the "yellow press."

The yellow press became famous when the United States was having troubles with Cuba in 1898. When the battleship *Maine* blew up and sank in Havana Harbor, the newspapers went wild.

Stories began to appear about the terrible treatment of rebels in Cuba, which was governed by Spain. Some papers called for war. Though the stories these papers printed were not always totally true, people believed what they read.

Historians have suggested the Spanish-American War was as much the fault of newspapers as any other cause.

The United States planned to blockade Cuba and destroy the Spanish fleet. On May 1, Commodore *George Dewey* and a fleet of American ships attacked the Spanish fleet in *Manila Bay* in the *Philippine Islands*. At the end of the battle, eight Americans were wounded and no ships damaged. The entire Spanish fleet was either sunk or captured, and 381 Spaniards were killed. In one battle, much of Spain's sea power was gone.

On land, things went a little more slowly. U.S. forces invaded the Philippine Islands and, after hard fighting, took control of them. In Cuba, the army had a terrible time. American soldiers died from diseases and improper food. Even though it was summer, they were dressed in winter uniforms. A group of volunteers called the *Rough Riders*, commanded by Colonel Leonard Wood and Lieutenant *Theodore Roosevelt*, won a great victory at *San Juan Hill*.

Soon after this, the few Spanish ships in Cuban harbors tried to escape to Spain. They were all destroyed by the waiting American fleet.

Shortly afterward, Americans captured the island of *Puerto Rico*. On August 12, the three-and-a-half-month war ended. The United States now owned Puerto Rico, the Philippines, and Guam. Cuba was given its freedom, but American soldiers stayed on the island for the time being.

### Think About It:

Secretary of state John Hay called the war with Spain a "splendid little war." What could he have meant by that?

America's next land additions were small islands. The United States had taken over *Midway Island* in the Pacific Ocean in 1867. In 1899, *Wake Island* in the Pacific was taken over by the navy. Wake is about 2,000 miles west of Hawaii and about three square miles in size. Nobody lived there. Why did the United States want it, then? Its location is the answer. The navy wanted it as a stopping place for ships. Later, it became an air base for planes flying across the Pacific.

*Guam* also became a naval base and later a stopping place for flights.

In 1899, America also took control of the *Samoan Islands* as a stopping place between the United States and Australia.

The map on page 126 shows the great area over which United States power is felt in the Pacific. In addition to the possessions shown on the map, the United States "looks after" many small islands in the Pacific.

---

### Melodramas

In the late 1800's, a form of entertainment called a *melodrama* became popular. Melodramas were funny little plays that all had pretty much the same theme.

Every melodrama had a villain, a heroine, and a hero.

The villain was truly bad and always dressed in black. He was always male and spent lots of time twirling his mustache.

The heroine was a helpless young woman who had some terrible problem. She could not pay the rent, or she needed money to care for her sick mother.

Just as the villain was about to take advantage of the heroine, the brave hero appeared. He was always perfect, handsome, and wonderful. Best of all, he saved the heroine from the villain's clutches.

When movies first came into being, many of them were actually melodramas on film.

---

The United states decided to dig a canal across Central America so ships could move from ocean to ocean without having to sail around the tip of South America. The question was: Should the canal cross *Panama* or *Nicaragua*? Crossing Nicaragua was longer but easier. Congress had to decide. Someone gave each member of Congress a postage stamp from Nicaragua. Each stamp showed that country's volcanoes. The question was decided. Panama was to have the canal.

The government of Panama was controlled by *Colombia*. Colombia did not want the canal; Panama did. In 1903, Panama revolted. President Theodore Roosevelt sent a fleet of American ships to keep Colombia from sending in troops. When the revolt was a success, the United States paid Panama $10 million for a piece of land across Panama about 10 miles wide. The story of how a canal was built there is told on pages 127 and 128.

Later, in 1917, the United States paid Denmark $25 million for the *Virgin Islands* in the Caribbean Sea. There a military base was built to help protect the new canal across Panama.

## United States Expands: 1867–1917

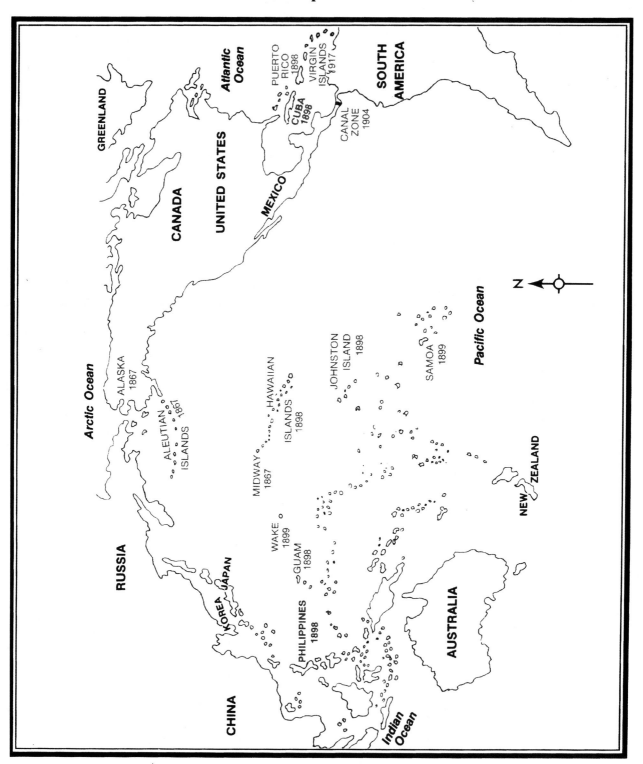

**Iced Tea and Ice Cream Cones Arrive**

The Louisiana Purchase Exposition was held in St. Louis during the summer of 1904. The weather was hot and sticky as thousands upon thousands of people came to the World's Fair.

Visitors found the heat easier to stand because of two treats offered there for the first time.

Americans were used to drinking hot tea. But here, for the first time, they bought cold tea with ice in it. The love of *iced tea* was born that hot summer in St. Louis.

*Ice cream* had long been popular in the nation. It was eaten out of a dish or bowl. At the Fair, customers were served a scoop of ice cream held by a sugar-wafer holder. It was not called a cone, however. What we now call a cone was sold then as a cornucopia.

## Landlord Problems

The United States found many problems resulted from owning property. When American soldiers were in *Cuba* fighting Spanish troops, more Americans died of disease than were killed by the enemy. Something had to be done about *yellow fever* and *malaria*. *Dr. Walter Reed*, an army doctor, and *Dr. Carlos Finlay*, a Cuban doctor, worked on the problem. Finlay thought mosquitoes carried the disease. Soldiers volunteered to be bitten by mosquitoes that had bitten men with yellow fever. The volunteers got yellow fever. Mosquitoes did carry the disease!

The answer was to kill the mosquitoes. Oil was spread over mosquito breeding grounds; swamps were drained. In a few months, Cuba was a safer place to live.

By 1902, Cuba had set up its own government. The United States kept a naval base there in case trouble developed. In 1934, Americans gave up any claim to Cuba except for the naval base.

In addition to Cuba, the United States was also involved with *Puerto Rico*. Americans built roads, worked for better education, and improved health conditions for the people of that little island. Their sugar and bananas were shipped to the United States. In 1917, the people of Puerto Rico became United States citizens. They make their own laws but are protected by the United States. Some people say Puerto Rico will one day be the fifty-first state.

**Think About It:**

Many of its citizens wish Puerto Rico to remain a territory. Why might they rather live in a territory than a state?

The next question was what to do with the *Philippines*. A revolt against the Americans took place soon after the Spanish troops left. With that bad beginning, work was begun to improve health, education, and farming. Here, too, Americans bought products from the people, built schools, and improved living conditions.

For years the people of the Philippines made their own laws and elected their own lawmakers. In 1934, they became completely self-governing with American protection. In 1946, they became an independent nation.

But what about the *Big Ditch* across Panama? A huge French company had already tried to dig a canal across the narrow *isthmus* of *Panama*. That company spent over $250 million and lost 40,000 men before it gave up. After helping Panama revolt, the United States bought the French claims in 1904. Now the U.S. was ready for business.

Colonel *William Gorgas* was sent to Panama to control yellow fever. He had done the same thing earlier in Cuba. In two years, the mosquitoes were under control and the water supply was safe. Work could begin!

The Army Engineers under Colonel *George Goethals* did the work. They blasted through mountains of solid rock.

The canal has large sections called *locks*. The locks have gates at each end. They can raise water and ships in the canal above sea level in some places. In 1914, the Panama Canal was open for use.

## Matching and Ordering

*Directions:* This is a matching exercise. The items to be matched are written in groups of three. Do each group by itself. Each item in the first column has a strong association with one item in the second column. Write the best answer from the second column after each item in the first column

I.
1. Alaska _____
2. Hawaii _____
3. Virgin Islands _____

1917
1867
1898

II.
1. Alaska _____
2. George Dewey _____
3. Theodore Roosevelt _____

Manila Bay
Rough Riders
Seward's Folly

III.
1. San Juan Hill _____
2. Manila Bay _____
3. *Maine* _____

Havana Harbor
Cuba
Philippines

IV.
1. Alaska _____
2. Virgin Islands _____
3. Panama _____

$10 million
$25 million
$7.2 million

V.
1. Walter Reed _____
2. George Goethals _____
3. Panama Canal _____

The Big Ditch
Yellow fever
Panama Canal builder

## Troubles South of the Border

The people of South and Central America had formed independent nations in the years following the American Revolution. These countries south of the United States are known as *Latin America*. President Monroe had included Latin America in his Monroe Doctrine in 1823.

During the Civil War in the United States, the leader of France had sent troops to take over Mexico. For several years France controlled Mexico. When the Civil War ended, the American president warned France to withdraw the troops. The Mexican people revolted against the government France had forced upon them. Once again, Mexico was ruled by its own people.

## The Pan American Union

In 1889, a conference was held to develop friendship and cooperation among the nations of North and South America.

Dating back to the Monroe Doctrine in 1823, the United States had warned Europe to stay out of American politics. Now it was hoped the 21 nations that joined the **Pan American Union** could work together to make sure the member nations were safe from European interference.

Headquarters were set up in Washington, DC. Every few years meetings were held in various member nations. Even though the members thought the Union was a good idea, many did not trust the powerful United States.

Though the nations of North and South America continued to work together, the term "Pan American" was eventually dropped. To many, it meant control by the United States, which was something none of the smaller nations wanted. In 1948, a new inter-American organization was started. It is called the **Organization of American States (OAS)**.

Then, in 1895, Great Britain and the United States came close to war over **Venezuela** in South America. The border between Venezuela and British Guiana was the cause of the trouble. Great Britain agreed to discuss the problem rather than risk war with the United States.

In the next few years, the United States became more and more involved in Latin America. In 1905, United States officials took over the money affairs of the **Dominican Republic**. Then the United States did the same in **Haiti**. U.S. Marines went to the island of Haiti in 1915 and stayed for 19 years. In 1912, U.S. Marines had gone to Nicaragua to protect United States property there. The marines stayed in Nicaragua for 21 years.

Between 1910 and 1920, **Mexico** had one revolution after another. Changes in Mexico gave poor people land to farm and gave the oil and minerals to the government. The United States tried to calm things down in Mexico and protect Americans living there.

In 1916, **Pancho Villa**, a revolutionary leader, took 18 Americans from a train and killed them. Then he came into a small town in New Mexico and killed 17 more Americans. General **John J. Pershing** was sent into Mexico to punish Villa. After several battles with Villa's troops, the Americans came home the next year. Pershing had chased Villa all over northern Mexico without capturing him.

By now the nations of Latin America were sick and tired of the United States acting as a watchdog for them. They were afraid of the big nation north of them and thought it was likely to take them over.

In the years that followed, the United States tried to keep its military hands off the Latin American nations. Marines came home. Even when Mexico **nationalized**, or took away, land belonging to American oil companies in 1938, the U.S. government did not fight back. The oil companies were paid a low price for their land but took it rather than cause trouble.

In the 1930's, important meetings were held among members of the **Pan American Union**. Latin America and the United States tried to work together. When World War II came, most of the Latin American countries helped the United States.

Today, Latin America is an important American trading partner.

---

**Think About It:**

Mexico nationalized land belonging to American oil companies. What may be some reasons the United States government did not use force to prevent this?

---

## Protectorates and Territories

Check the map on page 131 for the answers to these three questions.

1. Five countries on the map were protectorates of the United States at one time. All of them are now independent. Names these five countries.

   _____  _____  _____  _____  _____

2. Other than the mainland of the United States, what two areas on the map are still territories of the United States?

   _____  _____

3. What direction would you be going in if you went from the Caribbean Sea through the Panama Canal to the Pacific Ocean? Be very sure of your answer.

   _____

# United States Influence in the Caribbean and Central America: 1867 to Present

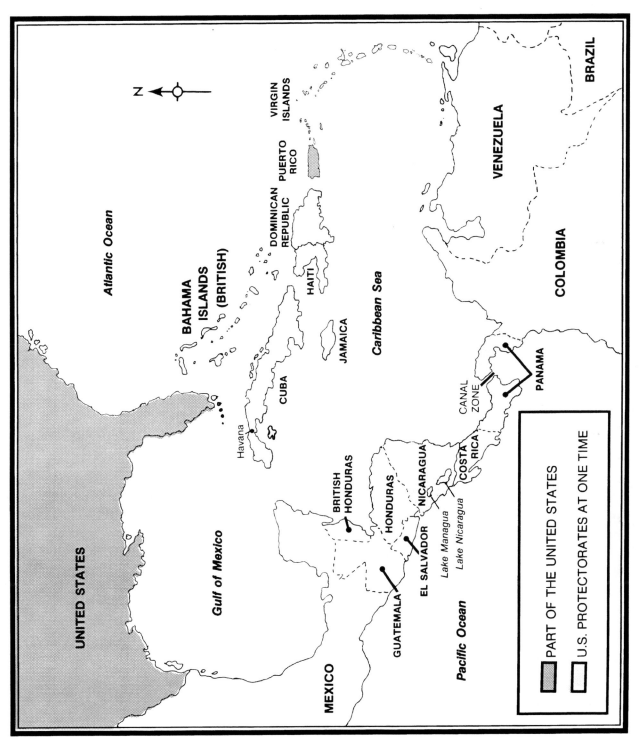

## The United States in World War I

While the United States was having its troubles in Latin America, Europe was working its way toward a great war.

*Germany* was unhappy because other European nations had numerous *colonies* on the continents of Africa and Asia. For years the nations of Europe had been taking part in an *arms race*. Each nation was trying to have a bigger and better army and navy than its rivals. When some of the smaller nations argued, the larger nations took sides.

Soon this choosing of sides caused two *alliances* to form. The idea of an alliance was that if one member was attacked, the other members would come to its aid. Three nations formed the *Triple Alliance*. They were Germany, Austria-Hungary, and Italy. Great Britain, France, and Russia were members of the *Triple Entente*, the other alliance.

On June 28, 1914, the archduke of Austria-Hungary, *Francis Ferdinand*, was shot. This was the spark that set off *World War I*.

War was declared. Armies began to march, and fighting began. The members of the Triple Alliance eventually were called the *Central Powers*, with the exception of Italy. Italy joined the Triple Entente nations, which were called the *Allies*.

I WANT YOU FOR U.S. ARMY
NEAREST RECRUITING STATION

German armies invaded France after defeating Belgium. Great Britain rushed in to help France. *Trenches*, or ditches, were dug across France, and Europe was at war.

What should the United States do? President *Woodrow Wilson* and many other Americans said it should not take sides, that it should stay *neutral*. From 1914 through 1916, the United States did stay neutral. It traded with both the Central Powers and the Allies. Slowly the United States did more and more trading with the Allies.

Americans were friendlier toward the Allies than the Central Powers. It was also easier to trade with the Allies. The Allies had set up a great naval blockade around the ports used by Germany and its friends.

In order to hurt the Allies, the Germans started using *submarine* warfare. German submarines, or *U-boats*, went looking for Allied ships to sink. Soon the Germans used *unrestricted* submarine warfare. Ships of any nation were sunk, whether they were supply ships or passenger ships.

Then, on May 7, 1915, the British passenger ship **Lusitania** was sailing from New York toward England. The German sub **U-20** torpedoed the great ship off the Irish coast. In a few minutes the *Lusitania* was sunk. Out of more than 1,000 who drowned, 114 were Americans. Angry Americans were ready to fight!

In spite of this, President Wilson felt the United States should still stay out of the war. But, in early 1917, German submarines sank several American ships without warning. At about this time the British got hold of a top-secret note from the Germans to Mexico. A top German official named *Alfred Zimmermann* had sent the message to another German official in Mexico. The note said that if the United States went to war, Mexico should help Germany by invading the American Southwest. In return, Mexico could get back Texas and the Southwest. The British gave the note to the Americans. The Americans were angry. Other American ships were sunk, so finally, on April 6, 1917, the United States declared war.

**Think About It:**

It was to Germany's advantage for the United States to stay out of the war. Why did German submarines sink American ships, which they knew would anger Americans?

American soldiers arrived in France just when the Allies were in the most trouble. Russia had a great revolution, which changed its government. The Russians had signed a peace treaty with Germany and stopped fighting. This had taken them out of the war on the side of the Allies. German troops left Russia and were moving toward the *western front* in France. Only the fresh American troops kept the Allies from being overrun and pushed back. The German drive slowed, then stopped. By July 1918, the Germans were falling back in *retreat*.

On November 11, 1918, an *armistice*, or cease-fire, was signed. The war was over. Today, this date is celebrated every year in the United States as Veterans Day.

## World War I

**Directions:** The answer to each question is written in mixed-up order after the question. Unscramble the letters to spell each answer correctly.

1. To what Latin American nation were United States Marines sent in 1912?
   c a r a n i a u g _____

2. What Mexican revolutionary leader did General Pershing hunt in 1916 and 1917?
   c a n h o p   a l l i v _____ _____

3. What was the Triple Entente called after World War I began?
   i a l e l s _____

4. What was the name of the Central Powers before World War I started?
   p i t l e r   l a n c e i a l _____ _____

5. Whose death started the First World War?
   f a r i c n s   f a n d d e r n i _____

6. What word means "not taking sides"?
   l e n t r a u _____

7. What great passenger ship did the German *U-20* sink?
   t a n i l u s a i _____

8. Who was the German who tried to get Mexico to go to war against the United States?
   f a l d e r   m m m a z i e r n n _____ _____

9. What was a U-boat?
   m u s a b e i r n _____

10. What agreement was signed on November 11, 1918?
    i c e m a r t i s _____

# Europe: 1914

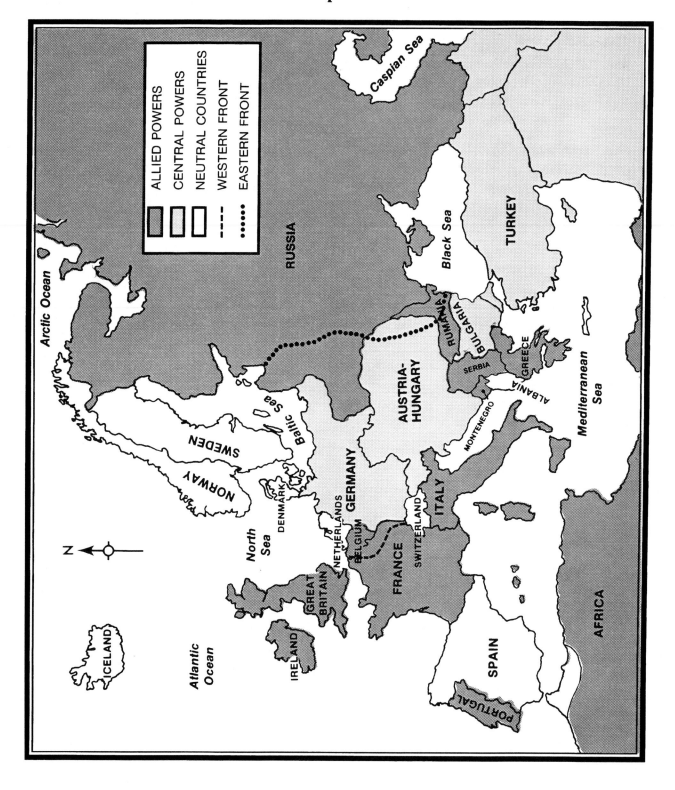

## Europe in 1914

Refer to the map on page 134 to answer the questions and fill in the blanks. Below some blanks are numbers. Collect the numbered letters, put them in order at the bottom of the exercise, and spell out our topic.

1. The eastern front lay mainly within the boundaries of this large Allied country.

   __ __ __ __ __ __
   3

2. The western front lay mainly within the boundaries of this country.

   __ __ __ __ __ __
      7

3. What was the name given to Germany, Austria-Hungary, Bulgaria, and Turkey in World War I?  __ __ __ __ __ __   __ __ __ __ __ __
                                                                      9

4. Those nations that didn't join either the Central Powers of the Allied Powers were called this.  __ __ __ __ __ __ __
                                                                      8

5. This large island off the coast of France became an Allied nation.

   __ __ __ __ __   __ __ __ __ __ __ __
                                      10

6. If Germany had used either the Baltic Sea or the North Sea for its navy, the ships would have had to go past this Allied country.

   __ __ __ __ __ __   __ __ __ __ __ __ __
      11

7. The smallest of the Central Power countries.   __ __ __ __ __ __ __ __
                                                              4

8. These two neutral nations shared a large peninsula north of Germany and Denmark.

   __ __ __ __ __ y  and  __ __ __ __ __ n
      2   1                     6   5

   __ __ __ __ __   __ __ __   __ __ __
   1  2  3  4  5    6  7  8    9 10 11

## President Wilson's Plan for Peace

President Wilson had a plan for peace. He called it the *Fourteen Points*. His ideas were good ideas. Such things as freedom of the seas and smaller armies and navies were mentioned. People living in colonies were to be helped to govern themselves. Trade among nations was to be made easier. A *League of Nations* was to be set up so nations could settle their differences by talk rather than by war.

President Woodrow Wilson

Many nations did not agree with all of Wilson's ideas. When the peace treaty, or *Treaty of Versailles*, was finally signed, it had some of Wilson's ideas and some things he did not want. The League of Nations was formed. Germany, as punishment for the war, had to pay *reparations*, or money, to the countries it had hurt. Some new nations were formed in Europe, such as Austria, Hungary, Czechoslovakia, and Yugoslavia. Land for these nations was taken from Germany, Austria-Hungary, and Russia (which had become the Soviet Union, or U.S.S.R.). Germany was forbidden to have an army and navy. Germany's foreign colonies were taken away.

The United States neither joined the League of Nations nor signed the Treaty of Versailles. Rather, in 1921, it signed a separate peace agreement with Germany.

President Wilson was brokenhearted that his own nation would not join the League. He made a long, hard trip across the United States trying to gain support for his ideas. During the trip he became very ill and had to return to Washington. Never again was

Wilson well. He had destroyed his health trying to make a better world.

In the years that followed, the United States worked for world peace. The United States joined in many things done by the League of Nations. The U.S. took part in the *World Court*, which worked to settle problems of law between nations.

The United States led the world in cutting down the size of its army and navy. President *Warren G. Harding* got the nations of France, Great Britain, Japan, and Italy to join the United States in limiting the number of warships built.

At one time the U.S. even tried to get the nations of the world to outlaw war. The United States wanted world peace.

## Boom to Bust

After World War I, the people of the United States wanted to forget the fighting. They were anxious to pick up their lives again and have fun. For this reason, the time after the war is called the *Roaring Twenties*.

A "flapper" of the Roaring Twenties

The automobile had become popular. People were able to move about the nation quickly and easily. Pay was good and jobs were easy to find. Everyone seemed to be doing well. The nation seemed well off, too.

Prohibition was then law, but the law was not followed very well. Even though it was against the law, many people made wine and whiskey at home. *Speakeasies* sold illegal whiskey to anyone who had the money, and most people had the money. New dances became popular, women's dresses got shorter. All in all, the nation was having a pretty fine time.

---

## Louis Armstrong (1901–1971)

*Louis Armstrong* was a musical talent even at a young age. He sang for money, but he also got in trouble. He ended up getting a year's discipline in a home for black children. It was here that Louis was taught to play a cornet. He learned the trumpet and the beginnings of jazz after he left the home.

Soon he was making people happy with his music. He played in big bands in both Chicago and New York. In 1925, he formed his own jazz band. A story says he introduced scat singing (singing nonsense syllables in interesting rhythms) because he dropped his sheet music. He also made playing jazz solos popular. He had a rasping, gravelly voice that people recognized and loved to hear. Armstrong travelled to Europe and Africa and became known as America's Ambassador of Goodwill.

---

Sure, there were problems. The American gangster was becoming bolder all the time. *Bootleggers*, or sellers of illegal whiskey, shot it out with the police every so often. Once in a while, an innocent person got killed.

Then many people discovered a new game to play. It was called the *stock market*. The rules were easy. You picked a stock you thought looked good. You bought the stock. If its price went up, you won. If it went down, you lost. More and more people began to play the market. The prices seemed always to go up. To make it easier to play, people were allowed to buy stock on *margin*. This meant they had to pay for only part of what they bought. For instance, a person could buy $1,000 worth of shares in General Motors for $100 down. It sounded easy and fun. So long as your stock went up, you were winning.

Then something went wrong. In the fall of 1929, prices began to drop. *Stockbrokers*, or sellers of stock, called people who had bought stocks on margin. These people were asked to pay what they owed on the stocks they had bought. When they could not pay, their stocks were sold. Suddenly everyone was selling, and the prices dropped even more. Panic set in.

Things got steadily worse. The United States was in the *Great Depression*. Almost overnight, nothing seemed to go right. Prices on farm goods dropped. Cows that had been bought for $150 sold for $10. Butter brought only a few cents a pound. Thousands of farmers could not pay loans due on their farms and lost their homes and farms.

Factory workers suddenly were out of jobs. The factories could not run when people did not have money to buy their products. Lines of jobless people formed in nearly every city.

---

**Think About It:**

Not all people suffered during the Depression. Some became much better off than before. Which people would you expect to have profited during the Depression, and why?

The land east of the Rocky Mountains became the center of the ***Dust Bowl. Drought***, or lack of rain, and strong winds caused black dust clouds to cover entire states. People from states like Oklahoma headed toward California looking for work. Usually they were no better off after they arrived.

No one knew when the Depression would end. The people of the nation were frightened. In 1932, ***Franklin D. Roosevelt*** was elected president. He had some ideas he thought might help the nation.

## Review Exercise

**Directions:** Each sentence below has one incorrect word in it. Find the wrong word, cross it out, and write the correct one over it.

1. Woodrow Wilson's plan for peace was called his Fifteen Points.

2. The League of Countries was Wilson's idea.

3. The Agreement of Versailles was not signed by the United States.

4. The World Trial was set up by the League of Nations.

5. The years after World War I were called the Booming Twenties.

6. Talkies were places to buy illegal whiskey.

7. Legbooters sold illegal whiskey during Prohibition.

8. In the 1920's, many people played the black market.

9. In 1929, the Great Regression began.

10. Drought and wind helped cause the Dust Bin on the Great Plains states.

# AN UNEASY WORLD (1922–1970)

9

## Time Line

| EVENTS ELSEWHERE | DATE | EVENTS IN AMERICA |
| --- | --- | --- |
| *Mussolini gained power in Italy* | 1922 | |
| | 1929 | Stock market crashed |
| *Hitler appointed chancellor of Germany* | 1933 | New Deal began |
| *Italy invaded Ethiopia* | 1935 | |
| *Japan invaded China* | 1937 | |
| *Munich Agreement signed* | 1938 | |
| *Hitler invaded Poland; World War II began* | 1939 | |
| *Germany invaded Russia* | 1941 | Japan attacked Pearl Harbor, Hawaii; U.S. entered war; Atlantic Charter; Lend-Lease Act |
| | 1944 | D-Day invasion of France |
| *Yalta conference; United Nations began* | 1945 | A-bomb dropped on Hiroshima and Nagasaki; end of World War II |
| | 1947 | Marshall Plan; Jackie Robinson became first black professional athlete |
| | 1948 | Berlin Airlift |
| *China became Communist* | 1949 | North Atlantic Treaty Organization established |
| | 1950 | Korean War began |
| *Death of Stalin* | 1953 | Korean War ended |
| *Fidel Castro took control of Cuba* | 1959 | Computer chip patented by American scientists |
| *Berlin Wall built* | 1961 | |
| | 1962 | Cuban missile crisis |
| | 1963 | U.S. troops in Vietnam; President Kennedy assassinated |
| | 1964 | Gulf of Tonkin |

## Introduction

Not only the United States but also much of the world was in a great depression. President Roosevelt and the United States chose one way to improve things. Nations such as Germany chose a completely different way.

All over the world, small troubles were growing bigger. Heads of several nations were leading their nations into war against weaker neighbors.

Twenty years after the end of World War I, World War II was already beginning. Once again the United States tried to stay out of it, waiting almost too long before deciding to enter.

## President Roosevelt's "New Deal"

When President Franklin D. Roosevelt took office, the nation was in trouble. Something had to be done and soon! People were out of work. Many had lost their homes as well as their jobs. Farmers were not making enough money to stay in business. In order to try to bring the nation out of the depression, Roosevelt offered his *New Deal.*

Franklin D. Roosevelt

Laws were passed to let the government loan money to farmers to improve their farms or to pay off old loans. Farmers were told to grow fewer crops in order to raise farm prices.

Jobs were found for unemployed people. The *Public Works Administration (PWA)* and *Works Progress Administration (WPA)* were government organizations that created jobs. Roads, public parks, public buildings, and so on, were built by WPA and PWA workers. Great amounts of government money were spent on these projects to give work to people needing it. Young people often found jobs

with the *Civilian Conservations Corps (CCC)* working in mountains and forests.

As people began to make money from these government programs, they had money to spend. The money they spent gave people jobs in stores and factories. This was a great help in getting the nation back on its feet.

---

### Early Television

In the 1930's, TV sets were shown in science fiction movies. The funny thing was that had it not been for wars and distrust among nations, *television* might have been developed during the time of World War I.

Inventors knew the basics for TV. They needed time, money, and cooperation to develop TV. For example, a picture was transmitted from London to New York as early as 1928. The next year, Bell Telephone tested its first color television system. In 1930, RCA had its first telecast, which featured Felix the Cat out of the comics.

The depression of the 1930's slowed down development of television. Even so, by 1937 BBC had TV broadcasts in England. Two years later, the Easter Parade was televised in New York City. The opening of the World's Fair was also telecast in March 1939, and TV was on its way. That month, sets were advertised for sale at prices ranging from $200 to $2,000 depending on size and capabilities. Television as we know it had become part of American life.

---

Laws were passed to help workers, too. The *National Labor Relations Act* protected the rights of the American laborer. Then the *Wages and Hours Act* was passed setting *minimum wages* for certain workers and the 40-hour week as the standard workweek. The act started the idea of *time and a half* for *overtime* (work over 40 hours a week). It also required that workers be at least 16 years old.

## *Amelia Earhart (1898–1937)*

On July 24, 1898, *Amelia Earhart* was born in Kansas, just a few years before the Wright brothers flew for the first time. Even as a young girl, Amelia knew she wanted to fly. When she was eight, she and her sister built a roller coaster that began at the top of a shed. The flying was fine, but the crash landing wasn't all that great.

During World War I, Earhart visited her sister, who lived in Canada. Amelia decided to be a nurse's aide. She spent her time off at the airfield near the hospital. After the war she studied medicine for a time but quit to go to California when her parents moved.

In California Earhart got to fly. She paid for an airplane ride at an airshow. She loved it. She got a job to pay for flying lessons. Her teacher was Neta Snook, who was one of the first women in the world to be a pilot.

Eventually, Earhart bought her own airplane in which she set an altitude record for women at 14,000 feet. When she moved to Boston as a social worker, Earhart kept on flying.

The year after Charles A. Lindbergh flew alone across the Atlantic, Earhart got her chance to fly across the ocean. Publisher George Putnam helped set up the flight of the *Friendship.* Earhart was just a passenger aboard the three-motored gold-colored airplane. Equipped with pontoons in case of an emergency landing on water, the airplane flew from Boston to Newfoundland.

Bad weather held up the flight for several days. Meanwhile, another airplane also waited for better weather. It, too, had a woman on board. Both wished to be the first to fly a woman across the ocean.

On June 17, 1928, the *Friendship* took off in bad weather. The radio failed. Fuel was low. The fliers attempted to ask a ship for directions but failed. With little fuel left, they reached Burrey Port, Wales, in Great Britain.

Earhart wrote a book called *20 Hrs. 40 Min.,* which was the story of her flight. George Putnam published the book. Earhart was on her way to becoming famous.

Earhart flew alone across the United States. Once she had to land on the main street of a town when she ran out of fuel. As her skills improved, she learned instrument flying.

When George Putnam proposed, Earhart accepted and they were married. With her husband's help, Amelia planned new flights. In 1932, she flew alone across the Atlantic.

Earhart was invited to the White House. She and Eleanor Roosevelt flew with reporters above Washington, DC. Earhart piloted the plane in her evening gown and slippers.

Her dream was to fly around the world. In March 1937, she and navigator Fred J. Noonan took off from California. They landed in Hawaii, but crashed when taking off again. The two returned to California on a ship to have their plane repaired.

On their next attempt, they flew east to Florida. From there they flew to South America and across the ocean to Africa and on to India. When they left the island of New Guinea, their goal was tiny Howland Island in the Pacific. They never reached it.

Amelia Earhart's fate has never been known. Did she crash in the ocean? Did she and Noonan land on an island and become Japanese prisoners? Did the Japanese execute her as a spy? The final end to the story of America's greatest female flier has never been discovered.

The government began to take an interest in managing natural resources. Irrigation and power projects were started. Dams were built to control floods, generate power, and store water for irrigation. The largest of these projects was the *Tennessee Valley Authority*. The *TVA* is still helping people along the Tennessee River and its branches. By itself, the TVA has raised the living standards of thousands of people by giving them electric power for things like refrigerators, lights, radios, and other appliances.

The *Social Security Act* was passed. It is still in force today. Under this law, workers and employers pay a part of the wages of a worker to Social Security. When the worker reaches retirement age, he or she can then begin to receive monthly payments from Social Security. In this way a retired worker is sure of having some income for the rest of his or her life. If a worker is injured and can no longer work, he or she may begin drawing Social Security at an earlier age. If a worker dies, his or her spouse and young children will be paid money to live on from the fund.

### Think About It:

When the Social Security Act became law, the average life expectancy of male American workers was about 59 years. Why did Social Security payments not begin until a much later age?

Banking laws were changed to make banks safer. Many businesses came under government regulation. Some people said the government was gaining too much power under the New Deal. Others said the New Deal had saved the nation. Both sides had good reasons for what they said.

By the time the United States was getting back on its feet, great changes had taken place in the rest of the world.

## The United States in the 1930's

**Directions:** Use the clues to help fill in the blanks. Each answer has something to do with America in the 1930's.

1. _ _ _ _ _ _ _ N
2. _ E _ _ _ _ _ _
3. _ W _
4. D _ _ _ _ _ _ _ _ _ _
5. _ _ E _ _ _ _ _
6. _ A _ _ _
7. _ _ L _ _ _

1. The CCC was the _____ Conservation Corps.
2. Social _____ provided income for retired or injured workers.
3. Initials for Public Works Administration.
4. President Roosevelt worked hard to end the Great _____ in America.
5. Workers were to get time and a half for _____ after the Wages and Hours Act was passed.

6. American workers got more protection when the National _____ Relations Act became law.

7. The Tennessee _____ Authority was called TVA.

## Dictators and Warlords Threaten World Freedom

Changes in the rest of the world were important to the future of the United States. In 1922, **Benito Mussolini** became the leader of Italy. He promised to make Italy as great as the Roman Empire. So he had roads built, swamps drained for farmland, and the army made much bigger. Italy even took over two more colonies. But even for Italians, things started getting worse. Mussolini's **Fascist party** used fear to keep the people in line. As **dictator**, Mussolini's word was law. His secret police made sure everyone obeyed that law. Jail, beatings, and death waited for anyone who went against the dictator.

North of Italy, another nation came under the power of a ruthless dictator. **Adolf Hitler**, leader of the **Nazi party**, took charge of Germany in 1933. The German people had been in a depression even worse than the one in the United States. They, too, turned to a new leader who promised to help them. Hitler also promised to recapture the land taken from Germany at the end of World War I.

Once Hitler had gained control of the government, the secret police, or **Gestapo**, used prison, torture, and death to make sure the dictator's orders were followed. In Germany, the life of the **Jewish** people became one of constant fear. Hitler blamed the Jews for Germany's depression. Jews lost their homes, their businesses, and their lives.

Adolf Hitler

On the other side of the world, the island nation of **Japan** was governed by an **emperor**. This emperor was being influenced by **warlords**. These men were looking for lands to conquer. In 1931, the Japanese army marched into **Manchuria**, in northern **China**.

In 1935, Mussolini's Italian army invaded the free African nation of **Ethiopia**. Ethiopia's spears were useless against Italy's tanks. Italy took over Ethiopia by mid-1936. Ethiopia's ruler, **Haile Selassie**, went to the League of Nations to beg for help. The League could not give military help, although it did ask that nations refuse to trade with Italy. This did not help Ethiopia very much. Selassie's nation was lost, and the League collapsed.

In 1936, German armies invaded the **Rhineland** between Germany and France. In 1937, Japan marched into China. In 1938, Germany took over **Austria** without a fight. Also in that year, German armies captured **Czechoslovakia**.

## Jesse Owens

J.C. Owens was born James Cleveland Owens but is remembered by his nickname Jesse. He worked hard to earn money to attend Ohio State. On May 25, 1935, Jesse Owens broke three world records and tied a fourth in a track meet. He was America's hope in the 1936 Olympic Games to be held in Germany.

Jesse Owens was black. He did not fit Adolf Hitler's idea of a member of the Master Race. During the Olympics, Owens won four gold medals in track and field events. Hitler refused to give him these awards in person. Owens became a hero to the American people.

The rest of the world was not prepared for war. It was easier to let the dictators continue than to fight them. This is called *appeasement.* Many Americans insisted that what happened in Europe and Asia was not America's business.

In August 1939, Germany and the Soviet Union signed an agreement to remain friends. On September 1, Hitler's troops invaded *Poland.*

Two days later, Great Britain and France declared war on Germany. The Soviet Union invaded Poland to help Germany and get land for itself. Europe was again at war!

Entire nations were conquered by Germany in a few days or weeks. Countries such as Denmark, Norway, Belgium, Holland, and France were captured by German forces. British and French troops were pushed back into the sea at Dunkirk. British boats and ships, from warships to rowboats, crossed the English Channel to save their soldiers. A third of a million trapped soldiers were taken to England.

Almost at once the **Battle of Britain** began. As many as a thousand German planes a day flew over Great Britain, bombing and killing. British pilots, outnumbered as much as 20 to 1, attacked the Germans again and again. German losses became so great that the bombing of Britain ended.

Meanwhile, China was suffering from Japanese attacks. The only thing that saved the Chinese army from complete defeat was the great size of the Chinese nation. Japan had only so many soldiers; they could not be everywhere at once in that huge country. Other nations in **Southeast Asia** watched Japan in fear. Their turn was coming soon.

In 1941, Germany attacked the Soviet Union. Treaties and promises did not mean much to Hitler. Europe and Asia became one huge battleground.

What was the United States doing at this time? Americans were once again remaining neutral. Congress even passed **neutrality laws** saying the U.S. would have nothing to do with any nation at war.

Finally, when it was almost too late, the United States did begin to build its army and navy a little. The **Lend-Lease Act** was passed, which let the president sell or loan war materials to nations whose safety was important to us.

### Think About It:

Americans hated the thought of fighting another war. Why did they not realize that what happened in the rest of the world affected the United States?

## Training Soldiers Without Equipment

Long before the United States entered World War II, the government had begun to call up, or draft, men between the ages of 21 and 35. Many problems were involved in preparing a military force on short notice. One was the lack of equipment with which to train the new troops.

Soldiers drilled with broomsticks instead of rifles. Big pipes had the word "cannon" written on them. Airplanes dropped sacks of flour that were supposed to represent bombs. Old cars and trucks carried signs calling themselves tanks.

The amazing thing is that these men learned to be soldiers even without the equipment needed for proper training.

## War!

On December 7, 1941, the American naval base at *Pearl Harbor, Hawaii*, was attacked by Japanese airplanes. When the surprise attack was over that Sunday morning, America's Pacific fleet was in ruins. Eight battleships were sunk or seriously damaged. Many smaller ships were also sunk or badly hurt. Over 3,000 Americans were killed or missing, and more than 1,000 were wounded. The next day, the United States declared war on Japan. On December 11, Germany and Italy declared war on the United States.

The war that followed brought great suffering for many Americans. Millions of men and women went to war.

## Rationing and Price Controls

Many items were needed for the war effort. In order to make certain the military got the material it needed to fight the war, the government imposed *rationing*. This was a means of restricting the amount of certain items any one person or family could purchase.

Food, clothing, tires, and gasoline were rationed to American citizens. Sugar, meat, and shoes were in limited supply and came under the rationing program.

Citizens were issued ration books containing coupons for scarce items. At certain times, the government told the citizens which coupons were good for which items. Customers found the item they needed, presented their ration coupon, and then paid for the item, such as a pair of shoes, a pound of coffee, or five pounds of sugar. If customers could not locate the items, then their coupons did not help. At times some things just could not be found.

In order to keep merchants from raising prices so high that only the rich could have scarce items, the government established price controls. Tires and shoes weren't the only things that came under these controls. So did rents. Without rent controls, many people could not have afforded a place to live.

In 1942, United States and British troops landed in **North Africa** and began a hot, bloody battle with the German tank corps there. When the terrible fighting ended, most of the Germans had been killed or captured. North Africa was freed.

In 1943, the U.S. and its allies invaded the island of **Sicily** and defeated the enemy. Beginning with a terrible battle at **Anzio**, Allied troops fought their way up the country of Italy. The Italians forced Mussolini out in July 1943, and their troops stopped fighting. As the Allied forces moved on through Italy, they continued to fight German troops.

The Soviet Union, meanwhile, had lost millions of soldiers fighting German troops. Finally, the great German army was stopped at **Stalingrad**. The bitter cold winter of 1942–1943 ruined much of the invading German army and forced a large part of it to surrender in February 1943. Now the Soviets began to attack the remaining German troops. Soon the Germans were being driven back as they lost battle after battle. In one three-month period, the Soviets killed or captured half a million Germans.

On June 6, 1944, the **D-Day** invasion of France began. Troops from the United States, Canada, and Great Britain landed at Normandy in France and attacked the German armies. For the next eleven months, they fought their way closer and closer to the heart of Germany. American warplanes bombed German cities and targets by day, and the British bombed by night. Soviet armies moved forward from the east. Germany was doomed!

## Codetalkers

Talking on the telephone or radio was a great way to pass messages during wartime. However, the telephone and radio were not safe to use. Spies could learn where American forces would be from overheard messages.

The United States began to use Native Americans to send messages in their own language. Enemy spies could not understand what was being said.

Most of the Codetalkers in combat were Navajo. Their tribe was large enough to furnish many speakers. The sound of the Navajo language was impossible to counterfeit. At the end of World War II, 420 Codetalkers were helping the U.S. win the war.

On May 8, 1945, Germany surrendered. Hitler was dead. Mussolini was dead. Much of Europe was in ruins. Only 1 building out of every 20 was left standing in Berlin, Germany's capital. Millions of soldiers and civilians were dead. The Germans had killed over 6 million Jewish men, women, and children. The terrible war in Europe was over.

If anything, the war with Japan was worse than the war in Europe. Battles were fought at sea and on hot, wet, jungle islands. Every island the Japanese had captured had to be invaded and taken back. Thousands of American soldiers died on each island. When islands were captured, air bases were built so American planes could bomb other islands held by the Japanese. In late 1944, the United States invaded the Philippine Islands, which Japan had taken in December 1941.

As American forces got closer and closer to Japan, military leaders hoped for a miracle. If the United States had to invade Japan itself, a million soldiers might die.

President Harry S. Truman

Then, President *Harry S. Truman* received word that the *atomic bomb* was ready for use. On August 6, 1945, the first atomic bomb was dropped on the Japanese city of *Hiroshima*. The bomb totally destroyed about five square miles of the city. Between 70,000 and 100,000 people died in the explosion. Thousands more died later from *radiation sickness*. On August 9, a second atomic bomb hit *Nagasaki*. Shortly thereafter, the Japanese surrendered. The war with Japan was over!

**Think About It:**

Armed forces from many nations fought Germany and Japan. What things besides troops did the United States have that made a major difference in the war effort?

### World War II Was Total War

The Second World War was the nation's first total war. It was a war that involved the entire world. This terrible war was fought not just by armed forces but also by the people at home. Citizens donated war material, such as metals and paper. They did without many things they were used to.

More than any other war, World War II made use of scientific discoveries. Radar, guided missiles, and rockets were new aids to fighting the war. Ships were threatened by magnetic mines. Eventually, the atomic bomb brought the war to an end.

New medical discoveries helped save lives. Treatment with penicillin brought antibiotics into use. Sulfa drugs were responsible for saving many more lives.

For the first time, people knew what total war actually meant.

# World War II

**Directions:** Following are five groups of events related to World War II. The events in each group are out of order. Renumber the happenings in each group in correct order. Do each group separately.

I.   1. The Nazi party took control of Germany.
     2. The Fascist party took control of Italy.
     3. Japan invaded Manchuria.
     4. Italy invaded Ethiopia.

II.  1. Japan invaded China.
     2. Germany invaded Poland.
     3. Germany took Austria.
     4. Czechoslovakia was taken by Germany.

III. 1. The Battle of Britain was fought.
     2. France was defeated.
     3. Great Britain and France declared war on Germany.
     4. The Japanese bombed Pearl Harbor.

IV.  1. U.S. and British troops invaded North Africa.
     2. The Italians got rid of Mussolini.
     3. The United States declared war on Japan.
     4. Germany and Italy declared war on the United States.

V.   1. The atomic bomb was dropped on Hiroshima.
     2. The Germans were defeated at Stalingrad.
     3. Germany surrendered.
     4. The D-Day invasion started.

# Europe in World War II

Use the map on page 150 to help you answer the following questions

1. Name the two European Axis nations during World War II.

   _____ and _____

2. Five Allied nations were not taken over by the Axis powers. Name these five.

   _____, _____, _____,

   _____, and _____

3. "D-Day," the Allied invasion to free Europe, took place in this country.

   _____

4. What new countries can you find on this map next to the Soviet Union that are not on the World War I map?

_____, _____, _____,

_____, and _____

5. What is the name of the new country between Germany and Rumania?

_____

6. What new country lies south of Austria and Hungary and north of Albania?

_____

## Japanese Territory in World War II

Use the map on page 151 as well as the pages you have just read in order to answer the following questions.

1. What United States naval base was attacked by the Japanese in 1941?

_____

2. What two European nations declared war on the United States four days after the Japanese raid on the U.S. naval base?

_____ and _____

3. Which seven nations or islands did the Japanese control at least a part of during World War II?

_____, _____, _____,

_____, _____, _____, and

_____

4. What two cities in Japan were hit by the atomic bombs that ended World War II?

_____ and _____

5. What English-speaking country was on the edge of Japanese-held territory during World War II?

_____

## Europe: 1939–1941

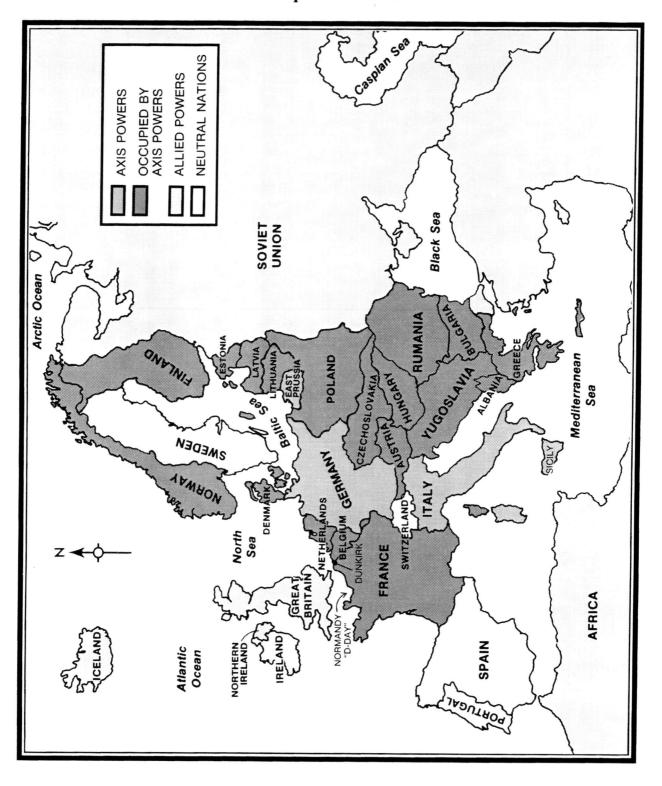

# Japanese Territory in World War II: 1931–1945

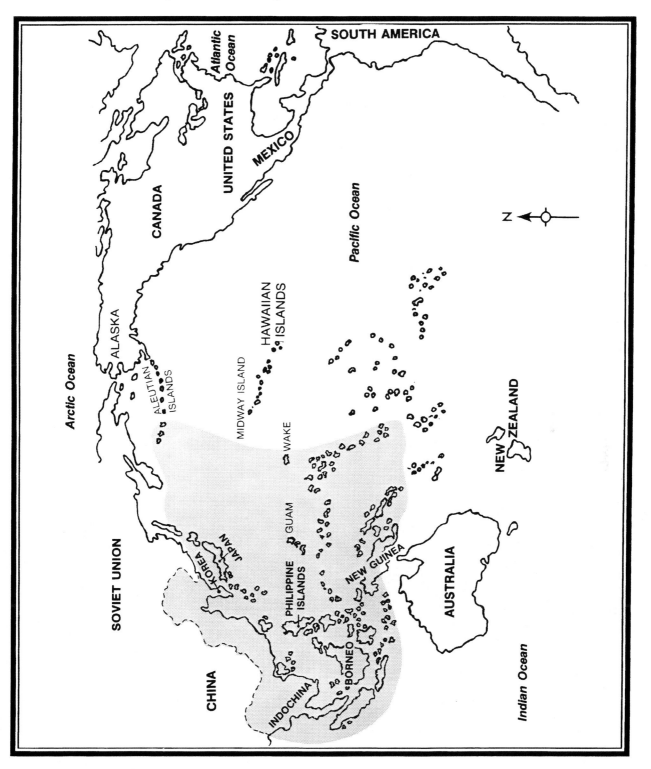

## Peaceful Alliances

In 1941, President Roosevelt and English Prime Minister **Winston Churchill** met and agreed on the **Atlantic Charter**. In April 1945, representatives from nearly 50 nations met in San Francisco. They added to the ideas in the Atlantic Charter. The result of their work was the **United Nations**.

### Ralph Bunche (1904–1971)

**Ralph Bunche** was born in Detroit, Michigan, and worked to get a college education. During his school years, he won many awards. He wanted to help black people throughout the world to improve their lives. Ralph Bunche became an authority on colonialism in Africa.

Bunche worked in the United Nations. He wanted to find peaceful ways to settle problems. He labored to find a settlement in the Arab-Israeli dispute. In 1949, he arranged an armistice in this struggle. For this work Ralph Bunche became the first black American awarded the Nobel Peace Prize.

He was also honored with the Presidential Medal of Freedom in 1963.

United Nations buildings

In addition to keeping the peace, the United Nations did many other things. It gathered food and supplies for needy nations. New homes were found for **refugees** who had lost their homes in the war. **Third World** nations were given help with problems of health, farming, and education.

The United Nations has not always been successful in what it does, but it has done many good things.

The United States signed agreements in 1947 with many Latin American nations. These agreements or alliances promised that the nations would help each other if any of them was attacked. In 1949, the **North Atlantic Treaty Organization (NATO)** was formed. Then alliances such as **SEATO** were signed with Southeast Asia and **ANZUS** with Australia and New Zealand.

The idea behind these alliances is that a nation is not likely to attack a country whose friends are ready to help.

The United States also helped in other ways. In 1947, the **Marshall Plan** provided great amounts of money to help Europe rebuild factories and farms destroyed in the war. By 1950, the **Point Four** program was giving help to developing nations.

## Europe After World War II

The map on page 154 shows how Europe looked after World War II. Communism spread from the Soviet Union to include eight other nations. Most of this spread occurred right after World War II. The six countries closest to the Soviet Union on the west—East Germany, Poland, Czechoslovakia, Hungary, Rumania, and Bulgaria—were called satellite countries. They had Communist governments and were controlled by the Soviet Union. Yugoslavia and Albania were Communist too, but they did not take their orders from the Soviet Union. These nations were not included as satellite countries.

1. Name the countries in Europe that had Communist governments.

   _____   _____   _____

   _____   _____   _____

   _____   _____   _____

2. Name six nations that declared themselves neutral.

   _____   _____   _____

   _____   _____   _____

3. List twelve nations allied with the Free World.

   _____   _____   _____

   _____   _____   _____

   _____   _____   _____

   _____   _____

## Problems with Communism

When the fighting stopped at the end of World War II, one big question was what was to be done with Germany. The Soviet Union, Great Britain, France, and the United States each took a part of Germany to govern. In the same way, they divided the city of Berlin, which was inside the Soviet Union's zone or area. It was not long before **West Germany** was made up of the parts governed by all nations except the Soviet Union. **East Germany** was that part of Germany controlled by the Soviet Union. West Germany became a democracy much like the United States. East Germany became Communist.

A **cold war** between the Soviet Union and the nations of the West began after World War II. This was fought with words and ideas instead of guns. For example, on July 24, 1948, the Soviets refused to let food and supplies cross their zone to get to West Berlin. Western troops and the people living there were in danger of starving. For over a year the West had to fly all supplies into Berlin. The **Berlin Airlift** flew 277,274 planeloads of supplies into Berlin during that time. A plane landed every three minutes night and day in Berlin. Finally, the Soviets again opened up the roads to Berlin. The West had won a "battle" in the cold war.

## Europe After World War II: 1945–1950

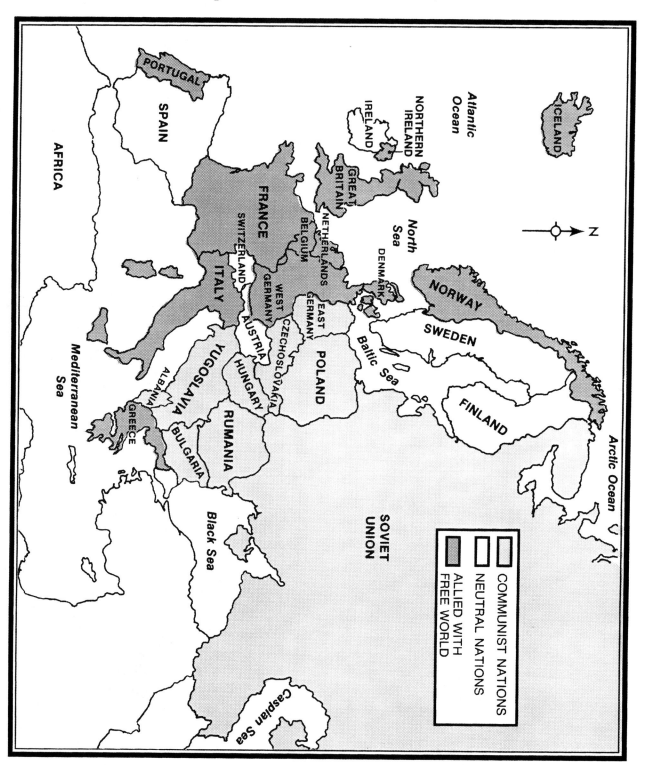

In June 1950, the cold war became a hot war in **Korea**. North Korea attacked South Korea. Communist China helped the North Koreans. The United Nations came to the aid of South Korea. Even though this was called a police action, not a war, thousands of Americans died in Korea. When the fighting stopped in 1953, South Korea was still a free nation. American and United Nations troops are still in South Korea protecting that country more than 40 years after the war.

While battles raged in South Korea, the cold war went on in Europe. Winston Churchill said an **"iron curtain"** had been dropped between the free world and the Communist nations. The Communists had gone so far as to put up barbed-wire fences and mine fields between their land and the free nations. Finally, they built the **Berlin Wall** to divide East and West Berlin. The Communists were tired of people escaping to freedom in West Berlin.

But not all of our troubles with communism took place in Europe and Asia. Just about a hundred miles from Florida is the island nation of Cuba. After Cuba became independent in 1934, a man named **Fulgencio Batista** became important in its government and ruled with an iron hand. In 1959, **Fidel Castro** took control of Cuba. The United States was glad to see Batista out but soon decided that Castro was worse.

Castro took over land belonging to American companies. He asked the Soviet Union for help. People began leaving Cuba to come to the United States. These **exiles** told how bad life had become for them in Cuba. In 1962, some of these people went back to invade Cuba, with U.S. support. They landed at the **Bay of Pigs**. Their plan failed and many were captured. Cuba blamed the United States for the invasion. Relations between the two nations grew worse.

Fidel Castro

In 1962, American planes flying high over Cuba took pictures of Soviet missile sites being constructed. The missiles were aimed at the United States. President **John F. Kennedy** set up a naval blockade around Cuba. Then he ordered the Soviet Union to take its missiles home. War with the Soviet Union was possible, but the Communists backed down. The missiles left Cuba.

Cuba is still Communist. Some Americans are still bothered that a Communist nation is so close to United States soil. Even so, the two nations have begun to try to get along with each other.

Almost from the end of World War II, a struggle had been going on in Southeast Asia. French Indochina had been divided into **Laos**, **Cambodia**, and **Vietnam**. From 1946 until 1954, the French fought with Vietnam. When **Ho Chi Minh** and his followers drove the French out, they set up a Communist government in northern Vietnam. The nation became divided into North and South Vietnam, and civil war broke out. The United States began sending aid to South Vietnam. Americans started training soldiers for South Vietnam. Then U.S. **advisers** went into battle. By 1963, about 15,000 American troops were in Vietnam. In 1964, two United States ships were supposedly attacked in the **Gulf of**

*Tonkin.* In 1964, American planes began bombing North Vietnam. By 1968, over half a million Americans were in Vietnam. The war was costing over $2 billion a month.

Soldiers in air-mobile assault training

### Think About It:

A civil war began between North and South Vietnam. Presidents Kennedy and Johnson said the United States helped South Vietnam in order to stop the spread of Communism. Why was the government willing to fight Communism in Vietnam but not in Cuba?

In order to try to halt the war, the United States quit bombing North Vietnam. President **Richard M. Nixon** started bringing American troops home. Peace talks began in Paris, but the war dragged on. It became the longest war in United States history.

In April 1970, American forces invaded *Cambodia* and destroyed many Communist supplies. By June 30, 1970, the American troops had left Cambodia but still sent supplies to the Cambodian and South Vietnamese troops there.

*Laos* began its struggle with the Communists. Once again American supplies were needed.

Americans were tired of a war many of them did not believe in.

## Letter Maze

**Directions:** One word is left out of each sentence below. Fill in the missing word. Then find that word in the letter maze and circle it. The words in the letter maze are written across, up and down, and backwards. Many words cross other words, so look carefully.

1. The greatest peace-keeping organization in the world is the United _____.
2. The Marshall _____ helped Europe get on its feet after World War II.
3. The North Atlantic Treaty Organization is better known by its initials as _____.
4. The Soviet Union and the United States were involved in a _____ war for years.
5. When the West flew supplies into Berlin, it was called the Berlin _____.
6. Fighting broke out in 1950 in _____.
7. Winston Churchill called the division between Communist nations and the free world an iron _____.
8. Fidel _____ turned Cuba into a Communist country.
9. French Indochina was divided into three new nations. They were _____, _____, and _____.
10. President Richard M. _____ began bringing American soldiers home from Vietnam.

| | | | | | | | | |
|---|---|---|---|---|---|---|---|---|
| N | A | L | P | L | A | O | S | V |
| A | I | R | L | I | F | T | C | I |
| T | N | A | T | O | V | O | R | E |
| I | I | O | R | T | S | A | C | T |
| O | X | C | U | R | T | A | I | N |
| N | O | A | K | O | R | E | A | A |
| S | N | S | K | C | O | L | D | M |
| C | A | M | B | O | D | I | A | D |

# THE UNITED STATES MEETS NEW CHALLENGES (1955–1982)

## Time Line

| EVENTS ELSEWHERE | DATE | EVENTS IN AMERICA |
|---|---|---|
| | 1954 | *Brown v. Board of Education* ended legal school segregation |
| | 1955 | Montgomery bus boycott |
| | 1961 | Shepard was first American in space |
| | 1962 | Rachel Carson's *Silent Spring* began environmental movement; Glenn was first American to orbit Earth |
| | 1963 | Kennedy assassinated; Civil Rights march on Washington; King's "I Have a Dream" speech |
| | 1964 | Civil Rights Act |
| | 1965 | Watts riots; Voting Rights Act outlawed discrimination at the polls; Malcolm X assassinated |
| | 1967 | Thurgood Marshall appointed Supreme Court Chief Justice |
| | 1968 | King assassinated; Robert Kennedy assassinated |
| | 1969 | Armstrong walked on the moon |
| | 1970 | Kent State students killed |
| | 1972 | Nixon visited China |
| *Arabs at war with Israel* | 1973 | Cease-fire in Vietnam; Watergate scandal; *Roe v. Wade* legalized abortion |
| | 1974 | Nixon resigned |
| | 1977 | Social Security tax increased |
| *Camp David Accord signed* | 1978 | |
| *Soviet troops invaded Afghanistan* | 1979 | U.S. began diplomatic relations with China; Salt II signed; U.S. embassy in Tehran seized; Three Mile Island nuclear accident |
| *Egypt's President Sadat assassinated* | 1981 | U.S. hostages in Iran released; space shuttle *Columbia* launched; Sandra Day O'Connor first female on U.S. Supreme Court |

## Introduction

When President Kennedy was elected in 1960, he said the United States was entering a *"New Frontier."* In the following years, we entered the Space Age. Great advances were made in science. Computers became more common and useful.

Important things happened outside the United States, too. Americans entered a war that they did not win. Relations with other nations became more and more important.

## From the Earth to the Moon

Human beings first went into space in the 1960's. Russian astronauts were the first to see Earth from space. But Americans were not far behind. In 1961, Alan Shepard was the first American to go up into space—and come straight back down. The next year, John Glenn was the first American to orbit the earth. He later became a U.S. senator for many years. Then, on July 20, 1969, *Neil Armstrong* took a "giant step for mankind." He was the first person in human history to walk on the moon.

Pictures from outer space helped people to realize that Earth is like a spaceship. *Resources*, such as oil and minerals—even air and water—are limited. People became concerned with *ecology*, which means that everything in the world is related. Americans realized that *polluting* the *environment* threatens our health and the quality of our lives. The government passed laws to reduce pollution from cars and factories and clean up our air and water. A growing population makes this harder and more expensive. At some point, choices may have to be made between some kinds of economic development and environmental health.

## From Civil War to Civil Rights

Even though the Thirteenth Amendment ended slavery, African American people were still *discriminated* against. They did not have equal rights or equal opportunities. Peaceful demonstrations, many led by Reverend *Martin Luther King, Jr.*, made Americans aware of this.

The Black Power movement was not based on the nonviolence taught by Dr. King. It said that self-defense was a proper answer to violence from white people. The Black Power movement spoke to many younger black people about the need for them to be proud of who they were. It introduced the Afro hair-style and colorful African clothing to the United States. It also sparked many colleges and universities to offer black studies. Black Muslims were important in this movement. Malcolm X was a well-known leader of this group. The famous boxing champion, Cassius Clay, became a Black Muslim and changed his name to Muhammad Ali.

By 1965, Congress had passed far-reaching *civil rights* and voting rights bills. These built on an important court case, *Brown v. Board of Education*. In 1954, that case had made school segregation illegal. In 1967, *Thurgood Marshall* became the first African American Supreme Court justice.

## The Montgomery Bus Boycott

In many cities in the South, African American riders were forced to ride in the rear seats of the bus. In 1955, in Montgomery, Alabama, Mrs. Rosa Parks refused to take a seat at the back of the bus. She was arrested.

The arrest of Mrs. Parks was the beginning of the **Montgomery bus boycott** by African American riders. They refused to ride the city buses until African American riders had the same rights and treatment as did white American riders. Civil rights leaders from other cities and states came to Montgomery to call attention to the boycott.

Dr. Martin Luther King, Jr., was a boycott leader. Dr. King gained support for his peaceful but effective means of protest against segregation.

The Supreme Court ruled that segregation of public means of transportation was unconstitutional. The Montgomery bus boycott ended. It had proven that peaceful protest can work.

Other *minorities* learned from the example of African American people and organized to promote their rights. They included the poor, the aged, women, *Hispanics* (people of Spanish descent), and Native Americans.

President *Lyndon Johnson* declared a "War on Poverty." Congress passed bills on health care for the elderly and to give better educational opportunities to all Americans.

## *Shirley Chisholm*

Although she was born in the United States, Shirley Chisholm was raised by her grandmother in Barbados. She learned pride, courage, and faith from her grandmother.

When she returned to the United States, Chisholm continued her education. She debated well and studied sociology. She became a teacher and learned Spanish so she could talk to her students' parents. Shirley Chisholm worked for better conditions for children.

Chisholm entered politics. She was the first black woman to serve in the New York State Assembly. She wanted state-supported day care centers. She worked on ways for poor people to go to college.

Chisholm ran for the House of Representatives. Her slogan was "Unbought and Unbossed." In 1968, she became the first black woman ever elected to Congress. A liberal, Chisholm was a leader in getting help for underprivileged minority city dwellers. In 1982, she retired from Congress to become a college professor.

## Cesar Chávez

On March 31, 1927, *Cesar Chávez* was born in the Gila River Valley near Yuma, Arizona. Cesar spent his first 10 years on the 160-acre farm where his parents and grandfather lived. Cesar's parents and grandfather were born in Mexico.

During the Depression, Cesar's grandfather died. The farm was sold for taxes. In 1937, the family packed up and moved to California. They traveled from one labor camp to another as they worked to harvest crops.

By the time he was in seventh grade, Cesar Chávez had attended 30 schools. He read and wrote poorly.

During World War II, Chávez served in the navy. When the war ended, he returned to work as a migrant farm worker. He married Helen Fabela, and together they joined his family in San Jose, California. There, the family picked strawberries on shares. The owner and the pickers each got part of the crop. After two and a half years of such work, Chávez figured the entire family averaged 23¢ per hour for their work!

Major labor unions were not interested in migrant farm workers. They moved a lot and were often unable to read or write. However, in 1952, Saul Alinsky met Chávez and got him to join the Community Service Organization, which worked to improve life in poor communities.

Chávez studied and considered an organization for farm workers. In 1962, he moved to Delano, California. There, he began organizing farm workers. He worked 18-hour days to get the National Farm Workers Association going.

The Agricultural Workers Organizing Committee of the AFL-CIO called a grape strike in 1965. Chávez's group joined in. The *huelga*, or great strike, began.

Chávez led a march from Delano to the state capital in March 1966 to call attention to the strike. By that time, one company was willing to negotiate. It agreed to pay farm workers $1.75 per hour. The *United Farm Workers* Organizing Committee was born, and controlled by Chávez.

The workers' contract was with wine growers, not growers of table grapes. These owners got permission to bring in *braceros*, or workers from Mexico. Chávez sent workers across the nation to call attention to the strike. Many people refused to buy California table grapes.

Some workers wanted to resort to violence, but Chávez opposed it. He called attention to the strike when he went on a hunger strike of his own.

Finally, in July 1969, the last of the big grape growers signed with the new union. The five-year strike ended.

Chávez went on to organize the lettuce workers in the Salinas Valley. He continued to work for the betterment of farm workers. The lives of migrant farm workers are still not good, but they are better because of Cesar Chávez.

## Violence and Threats of Violence

All of this change did not come peacefully. President Kennedy was assassinated in Dallas, Texas, on November 22, 1963. In 1965, Malcolm X was assassinated. Reverend King was killed in Memphis, Tennessee, on April 4, 1968.

*Urban riots* by black and poor citizens swept the country. Thirty-four people were killed in six days of rioting in the Watts area of Los Angeles in August 1965.

> **Think About It:**
>
> Urban riots result from frustration, fear, and anger. Why do rioters often destroy homes and businesses in their own neighborhoods.

---

### Nonviolent Marches

Civil rights workers found that boycotts, sit-ins, and marches were all effective in calling attention to situations that violated the civil rights of some people.

In 1963, African American leaders organized a peaceful march in Washington, DC, to protest the slow progress of civil rights laws. Nearly a quarter of a million people attended, both black and white.

This gathering doubtless helped influence the national government. The following year the **Civil Rights Act** became law. It says that it is illegal to treat people in the United States differently in voting, use of public facilities, education, and jobs because of their race or color.

In March 1965, another noted march took place. This time it began at **Selma**, Alabama. The protesters marched to the state capital to demand equal voting rights for African American voters in Alabama.

News pictures of law officers turning fire hoses on marchers, attacking them with clubs, and doing other illegal acts did a lot to gain public support for the march.

That same year, partly because of the Selma march, no doubt, Congress passed the **Voting Rights Act**. This legislation made it easier for African American voters, especially in the South, to exercise their right to vote.

---

When Richard Nixon was elected President in 1969, the United States was a divided and sometimes violent society. *Terrorists* were *hijacking* airliners. The planes and passengers were held as *hostages* by the hijackers. Often the hijackers demanded that terrorists already in prison be released. The United States tightened its airport security. Hijackings in the United States all but ended.

Terrorists attracted attention in other ways. *Bombs* were set off in crowded buildings. Many Americans were injured in such blasts.

Other Americans were protesting against our long involvement in the war in Vietnam. In the spring of 1970, students at *Kent State* University in Ohio staged a protest against the war in Vietnam. The *National Guard* was called in to break up the demonstration. During the protest, some troops fired at students. Four students were killed and ten wounded.

In many parts of the nation, Americans held *peace marches*. Some marches got out of hand. In May 1971, over 12,000 people protesting the war were arrested in Washington, DC.

By the end of 1972, peace talks had been going on for three months. And in January 1973, the *cease-fire* came at last. More than 46,000 Americans had died in Vietnam. Soon after American troops left Vietnam, the Communists took control of the entire nation.

---

### Guerrilla Wars

The world has seen many wars since the end of World War II. Most of these have been **guerrilla wars**. A guerrilla war usually begins when a small group of people oppose the government. They assemble and train in remote areas and attack villages or small government outposts.

Terror is one weapon in guerrilla wars. Another is the speed with which small groups attack and then fade away to hide. Quite often guerrilla wars are to **revolt** against an unpopular government.

If guerrilla forces achieve victories, more people are willing to join the group or at least help the guerrilla fighters. Eventually, the guerrillas are able to build a small army, especially if outside nations aid them with money and supplies. Once they are strong enough, the guerrillas will meet the government in open battle.

Communist forces long believed that guerrilla war is the best way to take over a nation. It worked in China. It also worked in Vietnam, where guerrilla forces drove out the French and were never defeated by the United States military.

Guerrilla warfare has worked well in nations in Africa, South America, and Central America. Guerrilla fighters in Afghanistan were able to hold their own when the Soviet Union invaded that nation. Just like the United States in Vietnam, the Soviets finally withdrew from Afghanistan in the face of unrelenting guerrilla warfare.

---

## Working for World Peace

Not everything in the 1970's was violent. Several major attempts were made to promote world peace.

In February 1972, President *Nixon* visited *China*. Because of Nixon's visit, the two nations began to trade with each other. At last, the United States had admitted that the People's Republic of China did exist.

Throughout the 1970's, American and Soviet leaders talked about peace. In November 1974, President *Gerald Ford* visited the *Soviet Union*. He and the Soviet leaders agreed to limit the *arms race* between the two nations.

Since 1903, the United States had controlled the **Canal Zone** in **Panama**. In 1977, the United States and Panama signed a new *treaty*. This agreement said the United States would gradually turn the running of the canal over to Panama. Panama began taking over the Panama Canal in 1979. This process was to be completed by 2000.

A major step toward world peace began in 1978 when President **Jimmy Carter** invited Egypt's President **Sadat** and Israel's Prime Minister **Begin** to talk about peace. The three leaders met at **Camp David** in the United States. They worked out a peace *accord* that they signed in September 1978.

## Political Surprises in the 1970's

Just as the nation was beginning to relax from Vietnam, another problem came to light. *Watergate* became a household word in 1973. Some of President Nixon's *aides* had been involved in a break-in at the Watergate building. They wanted to steal information from the Democratic party's headquarters to help Nixon win a televised election debate. The president said he was not involved. His aides were forced to *resign*.

In October, Vice President Spiro Agnew resigned for other reasons. In December, **Gerald Ford** became the first *appointed* vice president in American history.

The Watergate problem went on. A federal *prosecutor* held hearings. President Nixon was involved. Some of Nixon's former aides were found guilty of criminal acts. But it wasn't only because the acts were criminal that people were angry. It was because they tried to influence the outcome of a presidential election in a criminal way. Congress decided to hold hearings about the president to decide whether or not he should be *impeached*.

In August 1974, President Nixon resigned. He was the first president to do so. Gerald Ford became the new president on August 9. Ford was the first American president who had been appointed instead of elected. A month later, President Ford pardoned Richard Nixon.

## Oil and Inflation

In 1973, the **Arabs** were again at war with Israel. The United States was friendly with Israel. In late October 1973, the Arabs ordered a halt of oil *exports* to the United States. This *embargo* stayed in effect until March 1974.

As a result of the embargo, an oil shortage developed in the United States. Prices of gas and oil rose, allowing major American oil companies to make huge *profits*. Americans began to worry about the cost of gasoline and fuel to heat homes, schools, and factories.

When oil again began to flow from the Arabs, it was priced higher. Americans were spending billions of dollars for *imported* oil. A group of private oil companies began construction of the **Alaska pipeline**, approved by Congress in 1973. This huge 789-mile long pipeline carries oil from northern Alaska to the southern part of the state. From there it is shipped to the rest of the nation. By 1978, the pipeline was carrying close to a million barrels of oil each day.

> **Think About It:**
> The price of oil influences the entire economy of the United States. How does oil's price affect almost everything in your life?

The rising cost of imported oil forced American *consumers* to pay more for many products. When prices keep going up, it is known as *inflation*. Inflation was destroying the will of the people to work and save.

With the economy weak, the number of workers entering the country illegally became an issue. Many Americans felt illegal *aliens* took jobs and money from American workers. Others argued that they took underpaid jobs most Americans did not want.

## Changing Times

**Directions:** Fill in the blanks below with the correct word or words.

1. President Kennedy said the United States was entering a New _____.

2. _____ was the first person to walk on the moon.

3. _____ means everything in the world is related.

4. Reverend _____ led peaceful demonstrations against racial discrimination.

5. Urban _____ were common in the 1960's.

6. _____ became president in 1969.

## The United States in the 1970's

**Directions:** Match each clue below with a word used in discussing the United States in the 1970's. Be sure each answer you choose fits the puzzle spaces exactly.

**Across**

1. Taking an airplane and its passengers by force
2. When two or more nations make and store large numbers of weapons, the nations are having an _____ _____.
4. This nation met with Egypt and the United States for peace talks in 1978.
6. An agreement between two nations
7. When a U.S. president has been ordered to stand trial, he has been _____.
8. A refusal to ship goods to a nation
10. When rising prices cause money to drop in value, it is called _____.
12. Nation visited by President Nixon in 1972
13. Nation that agreed to take over the Panama Canal

**Down**

1. People held by hijackers or by terrorists
2. People in a nation who are citizens of another nation
3. Name of a building that became associated with President Nixon and his aides
5. Guerrilla wars are often a _____ against an unpopular government.
9. State crossed by a huge oil pipeline
11. The first American president to resign from office

*(continued)*

## Relations with Other Nations

Peace between Israel and Egypt was an important part of world peace. The Camp David Accord of 1978 helped to promote that peace. Then, in October 1981, Egypt's President Sadat was assassinated. Egypt's new president continued to support the peace with Israel.

President Carter continued the policy President Nixon had started with China. He, too, felt that a strong *China* was good for U.S. interests. Plans were made to sell scientific and military goods to the Chinese. On January 1, 1979, the United States again began *diplomatic* relations with China. This meant that the United States could no longer officially recognize Taiwan as an independent nation.

In June 1979, President Carter signed the *SALT II* (Strategic Arms Limitation Treaty) with the Soviet Union. But the treaty was never ratified by the Senate. Before that could happen, the Soviets invaded *Afghanistan.*

In response to this invasion, President Carter halted the shipment of *grain* to the U.S.S.R. He also said if the Soviets did not leave Afghanistan, the United States would not attend the Summer *Olympics* in Moscow. And he withdrew the SALT II Treaty from the Senate.

In January 1979, the *Shah* of Iran was forced to leave his nation. A month later, a fundamentalist *Muslim* religious leader returned to *Iran* after 15 years in *exile.* The *Ayatollah Khomeini* quickly took over Iran.

On November 4, Iranians seized the U.S. *embassy* in *Tehran,* the capital of Iran. About 90 Americans were taken *hostage.* The Iranians wanted to trade the Americans for the Shah. The hostage *crisis* dragged on. Some women and African Americans were released. Fifty-three other Americans were still held captive. An attempt to rescue the hostages in April 1980 failed.

Finally, in January 1981, the Americans were released. They had spent 444 days as captives. Diplomats from *Algeria* helped obtain their release. Many Americans thought the Iranians were afraid the newly elected U.S. president, **Ronald Reagan.**

Central America continued to be a problem area. Haitians and especially Cubans left their island homes in great numbers. In **Cuba** criminals were released from prison early to be among the 125,000 who came to the U.S. during six months in 1980.

In **El Salvador** growing unrest was becoming a civil war. The Soviet Union sent weapons to the rebels. The United States provided weapons and advisors for government forces. Americans feared another Vietnam.

---

### Think About It:

American authorities quickly realized Cuba was sending criminals to the United States along with real refugees. Why didn't President Carter stop the program immediately?

---

## Problems at Home

Not all of America's difficulties involved other nations.

In December 1977, Congress voted a massive increase in the **Social Security** tax. It was the biggest tax increase during peacetime in the history of our nation. Even with this increase, however, finding enough money to pay Social Security benefits was a problem still facing the United States in the year 2000.

In 1978, the U.S. Supreme Court said police could search newsrooms to look for evidence and the names of sources of information.

Veterans of the Vietnam War began to demand more help. Soldiers sprayed with **Agent Orange** during the war said the chemical used to kill trees in the war was making them sick years later.

---

### Urban Renewal

Beginning in the 1960's, the federal government tried to improve urban housing, especially for the poor of the inner cities. Slums and decaying houses and apartments were torn down to make way for new dwellings. This was called **urban renewal**.

The federal government financed many such projects. Others were paid for by private investors with federal aid. The plan was to provide adequate, low-cost housing for the nation's poor city residents.

Two things went wrong. One was that many huge projects immediately began to turn into new slums with a lot of vandalism. Residents, especially young children and elderly people, lived in terror as gangs took control of entire housing projects.

A second thing also went wrong. In some cases, once the old buildings were torn down, they were replaced by high-rise apartments with expensive rents. In these cases, the poor were priced out of the new housing. Middle-class renters came in and lived in the new buildings. This helped the neighborhood but hurt the poor the projects were supposed to help.

---

The *economy* was probably the biggest problem. In 1979, **inflation** reached a yearly rate of 13.3 percent. That was the worst rate of inflation since 1946. The increase in oil prices fueled some of it. Imported Arab oil had become much more expensive earlier in the 1970's. Then, in 1979, price controls were lifted on oil produced in the United States. This caused another round of price increases.

People began to get scared. They bought things they didn't need right away. They worried that waiting would mean even higher prices. But this increased the **demand** for things and made the prices continue to rise.

Congress tried to help poor people by raising the minimum wage, the lowest pay an employer can give a worker. It also tied the amount Social Security paid retired people to the cost of living. This helped the income of older people keep up with inflation. But it also resulted in more demand for things. And this further fueled the rise in prices.

Inflation hurt people at tax time as well as in the stores. Income taxes in the United States were **progressive**. This means that as people earned more, they had to pay a higher **percent** of their income to the government. Inflation made it look as if people earned more, even if their bigger paychecks didn't buy more because prices were higher. They still had to pay more taxes. Inflation also increased the value of their homes, whether they planned to move or not. So property taxes rose too.

Taxpayers began to revolt against high taxes. In June 1978, the people of California voted to slash property taxes in their state.

Inflation also hurt the government, which had to pay more to provide services. The federal **deficit**, the amount the government owed to others, began to rise faster and faster. Because the federal government was borrowing more and more money, **interest rates** went up. These are the rates banks charge borrowers to lend them money. High interest rates hurt everyone—individuals, businesses, and the government.

Some businesses began to have problems so big that they needed government help. In 1980, Congress voted to guarantee $2 billion in loans to the Chrysler Corporation (an automaker) to keep it from going broke. This time the results were good. Chrysler regained its health and came up with new ideas for improving cars. But some have questioned

the example this government action provided. Other government help to individual businesses has not always been so successful.

Environmental problems were another area of concern. As early as the spring of 1970, the first celebration of Earth Day took place. U.S. Senator Gaylord Nelson organized this as a teach-in on the environment. Twenty million people observed, or went to, the first Earth Day. This included many thousands of students in schools and colleges. About 1,000 communities took part. Earth Day was still being observed across the United States 30 years later.

In 1979, the first major nuclear power accident in the United States happened. For 13 days, radiation leaked at the **Three Mile Island** plant in Pennsylvania. A dangerous disaster was avoided, but the accident frightened Americans. Although many people still supported nuclear power, more and more protested against it.

Nuclear power plant

Another big problem that surfaced will take many years to solve. **Toxic wastes** were discovered hurting people in such places as **Love Canal** in New York. Many by-products from manufacturing are toxic, or poisonous.

Hundreds of dangerous toxic waste dumps were found all around the nation. In 1980, Congress created the Superfund to use tax dollars to clean up the worst dumps. Slowly, the toxic wastes are being moved to special dumps where they can be handled properly. But all too often, the ground and water at a site have also been poisoned. Cleaning them up too increases the cost of many Superfund projects.

---

## Urbanization and Strip Cities

As more and more people lived in cities rather than in rural areas and on farms, it was said America was becoming **urbanized**. Over half of our population is now living in huge **metropolitan** centers: a big city surrounded by suburbs. This is urbanization.

One by-product of urbanization is the **strip city**. A strip city develops when two cities expand toward one another until they meet. In this way a solid strip of buildings and people is formed. Such a strip city may extend for dozens or even hundreds of miles.

Today a person driving from Los Angeles to San Diego, California, drives through what has become a strip city. The same thing is true of those traveling from Boston, Massachusetts, south to Washington, D.C.

Urbanized strip cities are the result of people living in huge metropolitan areas because of employment, cultural activities, educational facilities, and public transportation.

---

There were some bright spots.

Space shuttle

In 1979, *Voyager I* passed Jupiter in space. Later in the year, *Pioneer II* reached Saturn. In April 1981, the *Columbia*, the first space shuttle, went into space and returned. The shuttle repeated its trip in November. Its sister shuttle, *Challenger*, was launched in April 1983.

In 1979, an American pedaled his aircraft across the English Channel. A year or so later, an airplane flew that was powered only by solar energy.

## *Jesse Jackson (1941–    )*

A man who was to become one of the nation's civil rights leaders was born in Greenville, South Carolina, in 1941.

After college, *Jesse Jackson* enrolled in the Chicago Theological Seminary. In 1968, he became a Baptist minister. Jackson's concern for the civil rights and economic well-being of African Americans caused him to spend more time working in that area than as a minister.

Jackson knew what it was like to be poor. As a boy he worked at a variety of jobs. He was active in church work and was a fine athlete. In college he was a football star, an honor student, and student body president. Jesse Jackson spent much of his life working for success.

After graduating from college, Jackson helped organize clubs for young Democrats. He worked for Martin Luther King, Jr., and Dr. King's Southern Christian Leadership Conference, or SCLC. Dr. King chose Jackson to head the Chicago branch of Operation Breadbasket, which used boycotts and picketing to get more jobs for African Americans.

In 1967, Jackson became a field director for the Congress of Racial Equality, or CORE. The next year he was with Dr. King's group when Martin Luther King, Jr., was assassinated. Jackson stayed with the SCLC until 1971. Then he started Operation PUSH, which was planned to gain more economic and political power for poor people.

For 10 years, Jesse Jackson traveled through the United States. He spoke to students and challenged them to work hard and aim high.

By 1979, Jackson was a national figure. President Carter helped get permission for Jackson to visit South Africa. Soon Jackson was involved with Mideast politics and Yasir Arafat, who led the Palestine Liberation Organization, or PLO. Conservative Arabs resented Jackson's visits with Israel. Some Jews felt Jackson was too pro-Arab.

By 1983, Jackson was deeply involved with voter registration of African Americans. He traveled to Europe and spoke with African American soldiers about the problems of world hunger. It did not surprise anyone when Jackson announced in 1984 he was running for the Democratic nomination for president.

Jackson is a gifted speaker. He also knows how to capture the attention of people. In order to provide himself with a solid political base, he organized his Rainbow Coalition. The group was made up of poor and minority people. With their support and the support of others both black and white, Jackson did well in the primary elections. But Jackson did not get the Democratic nomination.

In the 1988 presidential campaign, Jackson again did well. But he did not do well enough to get the Democratic nomination.

Jackson's trips to Africa, the Middle East, and Latin America continue to gain media attention. Jackson continues to work for civil rights in the United States and remains a political leader.

The fact that Jesse Jackson has received more than 35 honorary degrees says a lot about his work and ability.

## Issues in the 1980's

*Ronald Reagan* took over as president in January 1981. Republicans outnumbered Democrats in the Senate for the first time in many years. The problems facing the new president were many.

- Nearly every month the United States paid more for goods *imported* from other nations than it received for things it *exported.*

- Inflation had reached the highest levels in a quarter of a century.

- *Interest rates* were high and going higher. The high cost of borrowing money cut down on the number of homes and autos people could buy. This caused people to lose their jobs in the *construction* and auto industries.

- Unemployment increased government costs and lowered the amount of money people could spend.

- Each year the federal *budget* got bigger. Every year the federal government was spending more than it took in.

- The *national debt* was growing every year. By early 1982, the American government owed over $1 trillion.

President Reagan asked Congress to cut government spending to save money. He asked for income tax cuts so people would have more of their own money to spend.

Congress granted the budget and tax cuts. Then some people began to complain. They didn't want any spending cuts that would affect them. They wanted only cuts that affected someone else.

President Reagan nominated *Sandra Day O'Connor* to become the first woman on the U.S. Supreme Court.

### Letter Maze

**Directions:** Use an important name or term from the material you just read to fill in each blank in the statements that follow. Locate each answer you fill in and circle it in the puzzle. Answers in the puzzle are written backwards, forwards, horizontally, vertically, and diagonally.

```
R  O  D  A  V  L  A  S  L  E  S
T  C  H  I  N  A  A  E  E  A  A
S  O  U  U  N  L  I  C  G  I  D
E  N  U  B  T  A  R  U  N  B  A
R  N  E  U  A  N  R  R  A  M  T
E  O  D  N  A  L  S  I  R  U  O
T  R  T  F  A  R  D  T  O  L  X
N  X  S  C  I  P  M  Y  L  O  I
I  T  O  N  A  G  A  E  R  C  C
```

1. Egyptian President _____ signed the Camp David peace accord.

2. In 1979, President Carter began diplomatic relations with _____.

3. President Carter and the Soviet Union signed the Strategic Arms Limitation Treaty called _____ II in 1979.

4. President Carter ordered American athletes to stay home from the 1980 Summer _____.

5. The nation of _____ held American hostages for 444 days.

6. In 1980, the United States accepted about 125,000 refugees from _____.

7. Many Americans in the early 1980's were afraid our involvement in _____ would turn into another Vietnam.

8. The massive tax increase voted in 1977 was included to make Social _____ financially sound and safe.

9. Agent _____, a chemical sprayed on trees in Vietnam, has caused health problems for American soldiers.

10. The nation's first major nuclear accident came at Three Mile _____ power plant in 1979.

11. At places such as Love Canal in New York, _____ waste dumps have been proved dangerous to people living in the area.

12. In 1981, Ronald _____ became the new president of the United States.

13. The construction and auto industries were badly hurt by high _____ rates in the early 1980's.

14. The first woman justice on the U.S. Supreme Court was Sandra Day _____, who was nominated by President Reagan.

15. The nation's first reusable space shuttle was the _____, which first flew in 1981.

# THE UNITED STATES WORKS TO REMAIN A WORLD LEADER (1981–1991)

## Time Line

| EVENTS ELSEWHERE | DATE | EVENTS IN AMERICA |
|---|---|---|
| | 1981 | Deregulation of the airlines |
| | 1983 | U.S. embassy bombed in Lebanon; U.S. invaded Grenada |
| *Iran-Iraq war* | 1984 | U.S. left Lebanon |
| *"Glasnost" began when Gorbachev became Soviet premier* | 1985 | |
| *Explosion of Chernobyl nuclear power plant in Russia* | 1986 | Tax Reform Act; Iran-Contra affair |
| | 1987 | U.S. hostages in Lebanon; *U.S.S. Stark* hit by Iraqi missile |
| | 1988 | Pan American passenger plane blown up over Lockerbie, Scotland |
| *Poland held free elections; Tiananmen Square protest in China; Berlin Wall down* | 1989 | |
| *Iraq invaded Kuwait; East and West Germany reunited* | 1990 | Deficit Reduction package |
| *USSR dissolved* | 1991 | Gulf War |

## Introduction

During the 1980's, the question was whether or not the United States could continue to lead the rest of the world and care for its own people at the same time.

In order to lead the world, the United States had to look for a way for its own people to live at peace with one another. Americans needed to discover how to protect the rights of everyone without harming some people.

## Politics, Government, and Crime

People began to doubt the ability of government to cope with growing national problems. Crime was a major problem. Other big problems included the growing number of poor and homeless citizens and the ever-increasing **national debt**.

Illegal **drugs** are an international problem. Often produced abroad, drugs are smuggled into U.S. cities. There, drug dealers battle each other for control of territory. Law officers are all too often outnumbered and outgunned by the dealers.

The U.S. government declared a *war on drugs*. Billions of dollars were spent trying to stop the flow of illegal drugs into the nation. In 1990, in Washington, D.C., 83 percent of women arrested tested positive for drugs. In New York City, 79 percent of the men arrested were drug users.

In major cities a new term came into use: *drive-by shootings*. People on the street were gunned down from passing cars. Some drive-by shootings were the result of members of one gang shooting and killing members of rival gangs. Sometimes the wrong person was shot at. Other times, stray bullets ended innocent lives.

In 1989, Congress banned the import of automatic *assault rifles*. However, U.S. gun-makers were allowed to continue to make and sell these weapons.

The 1980's were a time when the actions of many elected officials set a bad example.

In 1980, the FBI told us the results of *Abscam*. This was a bribery investigation involving public officials. Among those the FBI trapped were a U.S. senator and seven members of the House of Representatives.

---

**Think About It:**

Abscam was only one of many times members of Congress have been caught breaking the law. Should Americans have the right to expect elected officials to be honest and obey all laws? Why or why not?

---

In 1986, the Republican administration stood accused in the *Iran-Contra affair*. Top administration officials were selling weapons to Iran in return for the release of some U.S. hostages. Some of the money from these sales was then used to arm the Contra rebels fighting the Communist government of Nicaragua. But there were two big problems with this deal. First, the United States government and President Reagan had said that no one should bargain with such terrorists as hostage takers. Second, in 1984, Congress had passed a law banning the U.S. government from giving further military aid to the Contras. A special prosecutor was appointed to look into the matter. No evidence was found linking the president to the affair, but several of his aides were eventually tried.

---

## Ben Nighthorse Campbell

Ben Campbell, a Native American, did not have an easy early life. His mother had tuberculosis and often had to have treatment in a sanatorium. His father was a chronic alcoholic who was unable to find work. Ben and his sister were put in an orphanage. Terrified at the time, he later said the orphanage was for the best. His stay there made him believe in himself and be independent.

Campbell learned to make Native American jewelry. He studied judo for four years at a Japanese University. He won a gold medal at the 1963 Pan American Games and was on the Olympic team in 1964.

Campbell entered politics by serving in the Colorado State Legislature. Later he was elected to the U.S. Senate. Ben Nighthorse Campbell was the first Native American to serve as a senator in more than 60 years.

# Sandra Day O'Connor

*Sandra Day O'Connor*, the first woman to become a justice of the Supreme Court, was born in 1930 in El Paso, Texas. After attending private and public schools, she went to Stanford University, where she got her college degree in 1950. Two years later she received her law degree and graduated third in her class.

Soon after graduation, Sandra Day married John O'Connor, who had also been in law school. She found it difficult to get a job as a lawyer because few women were in law firms. For a short time she served as a deputy county attorney in California. Soon she and her husband moved to West Germany, where he was a military lawyer and she worked as a civilian lawyer for the army.

In 1957, the O'Connors moved to Phoenix, Arizona. Two years later Sandra O'Connor opened her own law firm. In addition, she took care of her three sons and served in many civic organizations. She was on a board of appeals, served on a Committee on Marriage and Family, volunteered in a school for minorities, helped the Salvation Army, and was active in politics.

By 1965, O'Connor was an assistant attorney general for Arizona. In 1969, she was a member of the state senate. In 1972, she became the first woman ever to be majority leader in the Arizona Senate or any other state senate.

Her first judgeship came in 1974, when O'Connor became judge of Maricopa County Superior Court. After five years, she was appointed to the Arizona Court of Appeals. She was especially concerned with issues such as workers' compensation, divorce, economic issues, and criminal appeals.

As early as 1974, O'Connor had spoken out about abortion. She wanted birth control information made easy to obtain. She felt it would be wrong to have an anti-abortion amendment added to the Constitution. However, she had voted against spending money for abortions and supported the right of hospital workers to refuse to take part in abortions.

President Reagan made O'Connor the first woman named to the Supreme Court in 1981. Some of the first questions asked about the nomination focused on O'Connor's feelings concerning abortion.

She said abortion offended her but she had to accept the fact that others had different views. Both senators who approved of abortion and those who did not voted for her. In September 1981, Sandra Day O'Connor became the first female member of the U.S. Supreme Court.

When she was confirmed as a member of the Court, O'Connor was asked how she hoped to be remembered. She replied she hoped her tombstone might say, "Here lies a good judge."

Those words seem to sum up the life and work of our first female Supreme Court justice.

By 1990, the savings and loan crisis had become one of the worst financial scandals in U.S. history. Hundreds of savings and loan companies failed. Many failed because company officials had acted improperly. Some company officers simply stole depositors' money.

*The Keating Five* was a term everyone knew in 1990. It referred to five U.S. senators who were linked with one of the huge savings and loan failures.

The government *bailout* saved the people who deposited money in failed savings and loan companies. But American taxpayers faced a bill of at least $500 billion.

*Wall Street* was the focus of financial fraud. Some stockbrokers were found guilty of *insider trading.* This was illegal use of information learned from company officials to make billions of dollars in profits while cheating customers.

Another financial problem came from the sale of *junk bonds.* They paid high interest but were not very safe. Countless investors lost money when the bonds they bought became nearly worthless.

---

**Think About It:**

The savings and loan crisis and many investment frauds took place in areas the government was supposed to oversee. What do you think this indicates about government supervision?

---

## An Unsteady Economy

During the 1980's, our nation spent more than it took in year after year. This *federal deficit* ran into hundreds of billions of dollars yearly. Each year our *national debt* rose because of the deficit.

Congress did not want to cut spending for such domestic programs as education, help for the poor, and environmental protection. President Reagan did not want to cut spending for defense so the country would stay strong. In the end, the *rate of increase* in many programs was cut, but this was not enough to *balance the budget.*

Buying foreign oil has long contributed to our *foreign trade deficit.* After the Arab oil embargo in the 1970's, Americans worked to conserve energy. By 1982, the effects of world conservation paid off. The resulting oil *glut* caused prices to drop.

In 1989, the United States still depended on other nations for more than half of its petroleum needs. When, in August 1990, *Iraq* invaded *Kuwait*, the cost of a gallon of gasoline quickly rose. This happened even though Saudi Arabia and other nations increased their oil production to make sure no one went without oil.

Other things also added to the foreign trade deficit. The United States continued to buy more foreign goods than it sold American products to other nations. American consumers bought foreign goods for two reasons. Some were cheaper than U.S. products. Many were considered better than U.S. goods.

Americans struggled to make a living. The number of women who worked outside the home increased rapidly as families tried to get ahead. In 1990, at least 7.2 million U.S. workers were holding two or more jobs in order to have enough income to live.

Before President Carter left office in January 1981, his government approved two major changed in important industries. These changes *deregulated* the airlines and the telephone company. The new laws ended most government control of airlines and broke the huge telephone company into smaller companies.

Deregulation of airlines was seen as a way to encourage competition and bring down the cost of flying. Ticket prices did drop for a time but rose to all-time highs by 1990. Over 200 airlines went out of business or were merged with larger companies. For a while, instead of more competition, there was very little. But during the 1990's, competition picked up and prices again began to drop.

Breaking AT&T—the big phone company—into smaller companies did nothing to lower local telephone rates. Customers complained of less service than before at much higher costs. Deregulation did allow other telephone companies to compete with AT&T. And toward the end of the century, long-distance rates did begin to come down.

President Reagan insisted the national economy would improve if people paid less in taxes and had more left to spend. In 1986, the *Tax Reform Act* became law. President Reagan wanted to simplify the income tax system. So the new law set only two rates for taxpayers. He also wanted every company that made a profit to have to pay income tax.

Tax rates were lowered. About six million lower-income taxpayers no longer had to pay income tax. However, lawmakers took away many tax benefits that helped middle-income and higher-income workers. Millions of middle-income workers discovered they were actually paying more income tax after the tax reform than before. And families that made $30,000 were paying the same rate as families that earned $30 million.

Four years later, in 1990, Congress passed the *Deficit Reduction Package*, which included some income tax increases and higher taxes on gasoline, tobacco, and alcohol.

Our government must collect taxes in order to pay for necessary programs. Once taxes are taken away from consumers, the consumers have less money to spend, so they buy fewer products and save less money.

Some lawmakers believe our economy is better off with lower taxes and more consumer spending. They feel this helps everyone by making the economy stronger. Others want higher taxes, which allow the government to provide more services and make sure health, safety, and environmental laws are enforced.

---

### Literacy and Jobs

Business leaders in the late 1980's and early 1990's reported that more and more people applying for jobs were unable to read and do basic math at a level that allows them to hold a job.

More and more tasks require the ability to read and operate a computer. So workers have to come to the job better prepared.

Business leaders have called on the nation's schools to prepare students better for future jobs. To help, many businesses are donating money and material to help improve educational opportunities. Some businesses even send their workers into the schools to help teach.

Students must be able to read, write, understand basic math, and have computer skills in order to get and keep jobs. Yet great numbers are leaving high school without the ability to cope with the modern world.

Unless and until this problem is solved, millions of students are leaving school with little hope for the future.

---

### Think About It:

A 1990 study showed that Congress spends more than is collected each time taxes are increased. Why does Congress do this, and what may happen if this continues?

## The United States and International Problems

There were some great successes during the 1980's. The ending of the *cold war* with the Soviet Union gave hope for the future.

The 1980's and early 1990's were a time when the United States found itself trying to help nations of *Latin America* and at the same time having problems because of those nations.

*Mexico* produces lots of oil. It is also a nation with a rapidly growing population and terrible poverty. The United States has been accused of exploiting Mexico because Americans want to buy its oil and have it buy our products. On the other hand, Mexico's poverty drives people from that nation to this. It also encourages some Mexicans to take part in the illegal drug trade that harms the United States.

South of Mexico in some Central American nations, danger and death were everywhere. The 1980's became the turning point in a long struggle for power. For many years, right-wing dictators had allowed power and wealth to belong to very few people in their countries. Because these dictators were not communists, the United States often backed them. Sometimes the U.S. backed them even when it did not approve of everything they did.

When poor people saw the U.S. support for these dictators, some of them turned to the Soviet Union and Cuba for help. Sometimes they were successful in their revolutions, like in *Nicaragua*. Sometimes they were not, like in *El Salvador*. But in all cases the wars brought death and terror. Right-wing death squads and left-wing guerrillas both killed many people.

Fortunately, during the 1990's, the worst acts of both sides seemed to be ending. A balance was being found to allow everyone a fairer chance to create a good life. In 1996, even the 36-year-old civil war in *Guatemala* finally ended.

The nation of *Colombia* still supplied much of the illegal *cocaine* that ended up in the United States. The Medellin drug cartel there has so much power that even with American aid, the Colombian government cannot seem to stop it.

In October 1983, U.S. troops invaded the island nation of *Grenada*, where engineers and troops from Cuba were building an airstrip. President Reagan said the airstrip was part of Cuba's plan to export communism throughout Latin America.

To the west of Grenada, *Panama* was ruled by a powerful military dictator named *Noriega*. He was making millions of dollars for his part in the drug trade. President Bush ordered U.S. troops to invade Panama and capture Noriega in 1990. They succeeded and Noriega was taken to Florida. There he was convicted of drug charges in 1992.

Nations such as Mexico, Brazil, and Argentina owed the United States vast amounts of money for loans given to help their economies. These and other countries have been unable to repay the loans.

Though it is under Communist rule, *China* has begun to get along better with the United States. However, that relationship was threatened in 1989. In April 1989, students began a protest in *Beijing*. They gathered in the central square known as *Tiananmen Square* and called for democracy. Workers cheered the students and demanded more freedom. In early June, the military crushed the demonstration in two terrible days. Arrests were made and executions followed.

---

## Amy Tan

*Amy Tan* is an American-born daughter of Chinese immigrants. Her father, John Tan, was an electrical engineer in China. Her mother followed John Tan to California and worked as a nurse at night to help raise Amy and her two brothers. The family stressed hard work in school.

Amy became a business writer. A workaholic, she was driven to succeed. She wrote a fictional book, *The Joy Luck Club,* which became a bestseller. She wrote the book to better understand the tensions between herself and her mother. These tensions were because of the difference in generations and culture. Amy was young and American. Her mother was older and Chinese. Amy Tan's writings helped everyone to understand better what it was like to be a Chinese immigrant in America.

---

But all was not bad in the world. President Reagan and Soviet leader *Mikhail Gorbachev* met in Geneva for a summit conference in 1985. They met again in Iceland the next year. In 1988, Reagan flew to *Moscow* for more talks. The Soviet people welcomed Reagan. There seemed to be a chance the *cold war* might end.

Gorbachev was trying to make the Soviet economy better. He could not do this and continue to spend so much for weapons and the military. Neither could the Soviet Union continue to help support the nations it controlled. The Soviets announced they were going to allow those nations to manage their own affairs.

Change came quickly. In April 1989, *Poland* held free elections. In *Czechoslovakia*, a playwright, Vaclav Havel, was released from prison and elected president.

People left *East Germany* by the thousands when travel restrictions were lifted for the first time in 20 years. In *Hungary, Rumania*, and *Bulgaria*, the Communist governments were overthrown.

On November 9, 1989, the first holes were made in the *Berlin Wall.* The *iron curtain* was coming down.

The next year, the two Germanies became one again. Before 1990 ended, the Soviets signed an arms treaty with NATO members in Paris that put a limit on conventional arms.

In Eastern Europe and the Soviet Union, people expected a better way of life at once. When this did not happen, citizens became angry.

In1991, the Soviet Union collapsed. The former Soviet states formed 15 independent states. In 1992, 11 of these states formed the Commonwealth of Independent States, or CIS.

---

### Think About It:

Why is the economic health of Russia so important to the United States?

---

The *Middle East* remained a tinderbox, an area where violence could easily erupt.

*Lebanon* had been fighting a bloody civil war for years. In the early 1980's, peacekeeping forces from the United States, France, and Italy were sent there to try to stop the fighting. In the spring of 1983, the U.S. embassy was bombed by pro-Iranian *Muslim* terrorists. Sixty-three people died.

That fall, 241 U.S. marines were killed in *Beirut* when a truck full of explosives was driven into their post. In 1984, the marines left Lebanon.

In Lebanon, *hostages* were taken by Muslims who supported Iran, which hated the United States. In January 1987, CIA agent *William F. Buckley* was hanged by the Muslims who held him captive. Others remained captive with no hope of being freed.

*Iran* and *Iraq* fought a terrible war for eight years in which over a million soldiers died. In 1984, that war spread to the *Persian Gulf*, where Iran attacked oil tankers. British and U.S. warships were sent to protect the unarmed tankers.

Just as relations between the United States and the Soviet Union were the best in half a century, *Saddam Hussein* of Iraq brought the world again to the brink of war. Hussein needed money to pay for the war just ended with Iran. He threatened to invade *Kuwait* to gain control of its oil fields.

President Mubarak of Egypt met with Hussein, who promised to leave Kuwait alone. A few days later, on August 2, 1990, Iraq invaded Kuwait. It looked as though Iraq would also attack neighboring *Saudi Arabia*.

The United States sent troops to protect Saudi Arabia in an operation called *Desert Shield*. For the first time, female troops among the U.S. forces were near the front lines. Though they were not supposed to take part in combat, everyone knew that if they were attacked, the female soldiers would be involved in battle.

On November 29, 1990, the United Nations voted to allow the use of force if Iraq did not leave Kuwait by January 15, 1991. The January 15 deadline passed, and Iraqi troops remained in Kuwait. Two days later an air war, *Operation Desert Storm*, began. On February 23, the ground war began. Forces from the United States and 29 other nations advanced into Kuwait and southern Iraq. In 100 hours the ground war ended. Iraq's forces were in retreat after suffering terrible losses.

Stealth bomber

Once the fighting ended, the world saw what terrible destruction Iraq had caused. Most of Kuwait's oil wells were on fire. Five million barrels of oil burned daily.

United States experts began the long task of putting out all the oil-well fires. Kuwait began to rebuild its shattered nation.

Meanwhile, in Iraq, civil war raged as Muslims in the south and Kurds in the north fought with Saddam Hussein's military forces.

**Think About It:**

Most of the world sees the United States as a world peacekeeper. How did Americans get this role and why?

Troops from the United States and other nations began returning home, even though it was obvious many military troops would have to stay in the area for a long time. Winning the war turned out to be easier than trying to keep the peace in a part of the world where conflict was more common than peace.

## Looking Back

Read each statement carefully. If a statement is true, write a "T" in the space provided. Write an "F" in that space if the statement is false.

1. _____ Illegal drugs are only a U.S. problem and not an international problem.

2. _____ The Keating Five involved in the savings and loan failures were all members of organized crime groups.

3. _____ Insider trading and junk bonds involved Wall Street during the 1980's.

4. _____ When we buy more foreign goods and services than we sell abroad, it causes a foreign trade deficit.

5. _____ President Carter was in office when plans were made to deregulate the U.S. airline industry.

6. _____ The Tax Reform Act of 1986 cut income taxes for all American taxpayers.

7. _____ Both sides of the armed struggle in Central America were responsible for many deaths.

8. _____ U.S. troops invaded the island nation of Grenada in 1983.

9. _____ The Chinese student demonstrations in Tiananmen Square were crushed by the military.

10. _____ Mikhail Gorbachev was the Soviet leader when the cold war ended.

11. _____ The Berlin Wall used to divide West and East Poland.

12. _____ U.S. marines were killed by a bomb in Beirut, Lebanon, in 1983.

13. _____ U.S. naval ships protected oil tankers in the Atlantic Ocean during the war between Iraq and Iran.

14. _____ In August 1990, Iraq invaded Kuwait.

15. _____ In the fall of 1990, Operation Desert Shield kept Saudi Arabia from invading Iran.

# THE END OF THE SECOND MILLENNIUM

## Time Line

| EVENTS ELSEWHERE | DATE | EVENTS IN AMERICA |
|---|---|---|
| *Gulf War fought; Yugoslav republics declared independence; war in Balkans* | 1991 | Thurgood Marshall resigned |
| | 1992 | Haitian refugees returned to Haiti; Rodney King police officers tried; U.S. troops to Somalia |
| | 1993 | Motor voter bill passed; World Trade Center bombing; women combat pilots approved |
| | 1994 | North American Free Trade Agreement became law; U.S. troops left Somalia |
| | 1995 | Million Man March; Oklahoma City bombing; U.S. planes bombed Serb positions; 20,000 U.S. troops sent to Bosnia |
| *War in Bosnia, Serbia, Croatia ended; China threatened Taiwan* | 1996 | Madeleine Albright first female Secretary of State; Welfare Reform bill |
| *China got control of Hong Kong* | 1997 | |
| *India and Pakistan tested nuclear weapons; Japan's economy in recession; Serbs threatened province of Kosovo* | 1998 | President Clinton impeached by the U.S. House of Representatives |
| *NATO launched air strikes against Yugoslavia; Serb troops withdrew from Kosovo* | 1999 | U.S. returned Panama Canal to Panama; President Clinton acquitted by the U.S. Senate |

## Introduction

The final years of the twentieth century provided an idea of what the future might hold. In the United States violence and the threat of violence were close to home. On the world scene the United States was involved in peacekeeping that was not always successful.

The economy of the U.S. improved greatly. Millions of citizens invested in the stock market for the first time. Congress and the president agreed on a plan to balance the budget.

The United States was the world's major superpower.

Financial problems in Japan and Southeast Asia were a potential problem. China's growing economic strength was both good and bad. India and Pakistan both tested nuclear weapons.

The nation's president was popular with a majority of Americans. But scandals dogged the White House. As a man, Bill Clinton failed his family and his country. As a president, Clinton advanced a popular agenda, or plan for the country. Trying to weigh the relative importance of these facts was a major struggle for the nation.

## International Relations

The island nation of *Haiti* is close to the United States. It is in the Caribbean Sea. The people of Haiti suffered from poverty and bad government. Many living in Haiti fled to the U.S.

In May 1992, President Bush told the Coast Guard to send boatloads of Haitians back to Haiti. The United States feared accepting too many immigrants. After his election President *Bill Clinton* also ordered Haitians sent back home when they tried to come to America.

President Bill Clinton

Eventually, the United States sent troops to Haiti to help Haitians gain a democratic government. UN troops soon replaced the U.S. troops. Changes were made in Haiti's government. Although elections are now held, the government in Haiti is far from good for all citizens.

*Somalia* is a nation in eastern Africa. Its economy is poor. Bad weather and poor harvests cause starvation. Many nations sent food and medicine to Somalia, but little of the food and few medicines reached the people. Warlords controlled the nation. They stole the food and supplies for their followers. This helped the warlords remain powerful.

In December 1992, the United States sent troops into Somalia. Their mission was to protect the hungry people from the warlords. UN forces soon followed. By the middle of the next year, these forces felt they had to attack the warlords.

The mission was not successful. Too many people followed the warlords. Old tribal hatreds kept the people from uniting. One group fought another group. Some turned on the foreign soldiers.

By March 1994, the last American troops left Somalia. The final UN forces soon followed. The good intentions of the United States and the UN failed to bring change.

Yugoslavia was a nation formed from several smaller regions after World War I. Under the Communist leadership of President Tito, it was a stable country. When Communist rule ended in Yugoslavia, the smaller regions began to fight among themselves. Several new countries were formed.

The biggest country kept the name *Yugoslavia*. It is made up of *Serbia* and Montenegro. The other countries are *Slovenia*, *Macedonia*, *Croatia*, and *Bosnia and Herzegovina*. Although the last country really does have a double name, it will be called Bosnia from here on.

Two of the countries, Slovenia and Macedonia, managed to get self-rule with very little fighting. They became nations in 1992. After some fighting, Croatia, too, became a nation in 1992.

Bosnia was not so lucky. Three ethnic groups live in Bosnia: Serbs, Croats, and Muslims. Each ethnic group has its own background and culture.

From 1992 until 1996, Bosnia suffered a bloodbath. All over Bosnia, Serbs drove Muslims from their homes in a campaign of *ethnic cleansing*. By the end of the fighting, at least 24,000 Muslims were missing. Many of the Muslims were later found in mass graves.

Finally, in 1996, the fighting stopped. Bosnia was divided into two parts—the Bosnian Serb Republic and the Muslim-Croat federation. But it took the United Nations, NATO, and the United States to end it. NATO had to bomb Serb positions several times to make the peace possible. The UN and the U.S. provided peacekeeping troops to make sure the peace was kept.

---

**Think About It:**

Bosnia is not close to the United States. Why did the U.S. government get involved in bombing the Serbs and in later peacekeeping efforts?

---

There were also problems in a Yugoslavian province called *Kosovo*. Many of the people in this province are ethnic Albanians. They wanted freedom from Yugoslavia and closer ties with the neighboring country of Albania. Yugoslav president *Slobodan Milosevic* wanted to keep Kosovo.

Yugoslavian Serbs used ethnic cleansing and terror to keep hold of a people who

didn't want them to rule. Once again, NATO, including the United States, stepped in.

In March 1999, NATO began bombing Yugoslavia. Within days, thousands of ethnic Albanians left Kosovo. They told of murders by Serb forces in Kosovo. Soon, hundreds of thousands of refugees were living in camps in nearby nations.

After 79 days of NATO air strikes, a peace agreement was signed. Serbian troops began to leave Kosovo. Serbian civilians left Kosovo, too. Some Serbian civilians were killed by ethnic Albanians. Serb houses and churches were burned. Many Serbs feared staying in Kosovo. An independent Kosovo began to seem more likely.

Montenegro, the smaller Yugoslav republic, was also moving toward independence. People in Montenegro did not support President Milosevic. They wanted to make their own decisions.

There were some bright spots in international relations. Cuba and the United States were more friendly by the end of the century.

The United States and other nations met during the years to discuss world problems.

One such meeting ended with the 121 nations agreeing to a treaty about chemical weapons. Iraq did not sign the treaty, however.

At another world meeting representatives talked about global warming. Pollution and destruction of the ozone layer were topics at a third global meeting.

## Crime and Violence at Home

When Los Angeles police officers beat *Rodney King*, a black motorist, it was filmed on video. Scenes of the beating were seen around the world. In April 1992, the officers were tried and found not guilty. Riots broke out in Los Angeles. Businesses were looted and destroyed. Fires raged out of control. At least 50 people were killed. The National Guard was called in to restore order.

On February 26, 1993, a huge bomb went off in the parking garage of the *World Trade Center* in New York City. The explosives were hidden in a rented truck. Six died in the blast.

In an effort to cut down on violence in the nation, Congress passed the *Brady Bill* in 1993. This was named for the man who was paralyzed during an attack on President Reagan years before. The Brady Bill required a background check on all persons who wish to buy a handgun. It also provided for a five-day waiting period before handguns may be sold.

Congress also approved a crime bill in August 1994. The death penalty was possible for 60 types of crime. Nineteen kinds of semi-automatic assault weapons were banned. All 19 were made by foreign gun makers. American gun makers were allowed to continue to manufacture and sell such weapons.

All previous acts of terror and violence were forgotten in April 1995. A tremendous bomb made of diesel fuel and fertilizer exploded in *Oklahoma City*. The bomb was in a truck parked in front of the federal building. In all, 169 people died in the terrible blast.

Some militant antiabortion protestors used violence to try to end abortion. They bombed abortion clinics in several cities, such as Tulsa, Oklahoma.

On March 10, 1993, a doctor was killed at an abortion center in Florida. That was just the beginning. Before the end of the 1990's,

two more people were killed by protestors at Florida abortion clinics. A guard died in a bombing in Georgia. Several workers at abortion clinics in Boston were killed. And a doctor who provided abortions was shot to death in his own home in upstate New York.

> **Think About It:**
>
> Why do people who call themselves "pro-life" think it is ever all right to kill someone?

Violence in school classrooms was common. Teachers and students were threatened and assaulted. In some cases, students came to school with guns and opened fire, killing students and teachers.

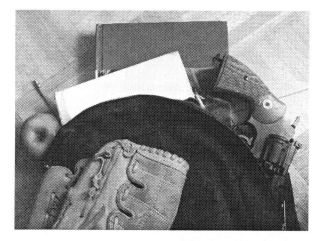

> **Think About It:**
>
> Terror and the threat of terrorist attacks became more common during the 1990's than before. What changes and frustrations in the United States and the rest of the world contributed to the growing use of terror?

The century ended on an encouraging note. The crime rate was dropping for much of the nation. Violent crime dropped 21 percent between 1993 and 1999.

## Changing Human Relations

The final years of the twentieth century were a time of changes in human relations. Homosexual men and women were more widely accepted in society. More attention was paid to the needs of those with mental or physical disabilities.

In April 1993, the government decided that women were eligible for aerial combat. This meant female pilots could fly combat planes. Previously, they flew many aircraft even in battle areas. Now they could engage in combat.

The Navy followed with its own rule change. Female sailors were allowed as crew members on warships that engaged in combat.

In a related area, the courts ruled that women were to be admitted to **The Citadel**. Before the 1994 ruling, only men attended this military college in South Carolina.

In a surprise action, the **California Board of Regents** made a major change in 1995. The Board decided that the admission policy for California colleges would change. No longer would students be given special consideration because of race. This ended *affirmative action* in California college admissions.

Many people of all races protested this change. The courts reminded them that the Civil Rights Act of 1964 made it illegal to discriminate against anyone because of race. This applied to white students as well as minority students.

### *Tiger Woods*

Eldrick (Tiger) Woods became a household name in 1996. He won the Masters golf tournament that year. Woods shattered the old course record. He had the lowest score in tournament history! Tiger Woods was also the youngest player ever to win the Masters.

Woods is of mixed heritage. His father is black, and his mother is from Thailand. Tiger represents the best of the twentieth century and the strength of the twenty-first. He shows love and respect to his parents and tries to be a role model for minority youth.

One of the most interesting changes in U.S. human relations came in December 1996. *Madeleine Albright* became the nation's first female Secretary of State. Secretary Albright dealt with male leaders from all over the world. Some of these leaders represented nations in which women had no rights and were given no respect.

Madeleine Albright

## America's Economy Booms

A nation's economy depends, in part, on trade with other nations. In 1992, the United States, Canada, and Mexico agreed to a major change. All three nations agreed to make it easier to trade with one another.

This was called the North American Free Trade Agreement. It is better known as *NAFTA*. The agreement was signed in 1993 and became law on January 1, 1994.

Under NAFTA, products can be shipped among the three nations easily. One nation can build manufacturing plants in another nation without lots of red tape.

Critics of the plan felt U.S. workers would lose their jobs. This was because workers in Mexico make so much less money than American employees. Also, environmental standards are lower in Mexico. Those who supported NAFTA said trade would increase. This would mean more profits for Americans.

Many U.S. manufacturing companies built new plants in Mexico. Many U.S. products are now made there using cheap labor. Trade did increase. But mostly it was the United States buying more products from Mexico.

Still, U.S. companies were making record profits. And foreign trade was vital. In 1994 the U.S. approved the General Agreement on Tariffs and Trades. *GATT* was an agreement with the world's nations concerning how trade is regulated. It seemed a good idea for countries to cooperate.

There were some things about GATT most citizens were not told. The nations in GATT can make rules about interest rates. They can decide on trade policies. As a part of GATT, the United States has to accept these rules.

In spite of some problems, the American economy improved year after year. In March 1993, the *Dow Jones Average* closed at 3478.34. This was an all-time high for the U.S. stock market. A year later, the market closed above 4000. In October 1996, it reached 6000. By August of the next year, the Dow reached 8000. It passed 9000 in 1998, and 10,000 in 1999.

As the economy of the United States improved, the *jobless rate* went down. Beginning in early 1995, this rate dropped year after year. By June 1998, only 4.3 percent of those wanting to work were out of work. The *unemployment* rate was the lowest in almost 30 years.

At the same time the jobless rate improved, the *trade deficit* got worse. In 1995, it was over $100 billion for the first time in six years. This meant the U.S. bought $100 billion more in foreign goods than it sold to other nations.

A year later the trade deficit dropped slightly for several months. This did not continue. In 1998 the U.S. trade deficit reached $168 billion. This was the worst in history. The poor economies of Japan, Russia, Southeast Asia, and much of South America hurt U.S. trade. The U.S. continued to buy products from these nations. The people in these countries could not afford to buy U.S. products.

Increased trade was a goal of the nation. *China* had a growing economy. Capitalism became more acceptable in that huge nation. The Chinese people wanted U.S. products. Companies from the United States opened in China. Manufacturing there grew rapidly. So did our trade deficit with China. By the end of 1996, the United States was spending billions of dollars more for China's products than China spent for ours.

Then in 1998, *Japan* and other nations in Southeast Asia had economic troubles. Japan's economy was the second largest in the world. When Japan, Indonesia, and South Korea had problems, it affected the entire world.

Stock markets all over the world began to react. Huge banks and international companies in Japan, South Korea, and other nations suffered losses. Some went bankrupt. Economists placed much of the blame on fraud and lack of sound economic policies.

The fact that the United States was part of the *global economy* was obvious. The United States and other nations would have to help Japan and its neighbors.

Closer to home the "greying of America" was becoming a challenge. Americans were living longer. Older citizens need more services such as health care than do younger ones.

*Baby Boomers*, the large generation born right after World War II, were close to retirement age. They will put another strain on the nation's resources, especially *Social Security*. When they retire, there will not be enough workers paying Social Security taxes to pay for Baby Boomer retirement benefits.

The *National Debt* was over $5 trillion. Most of this had built up in the 1980's. This amounted to about $20,000 for every child and adult living in the United States. Just paying the interest on this debt each year had become a major item in the budget.

In 1997, Congress and the President reached agreement on a *balanced budget*. According to their plan, the United States would stop spending more than it collected in taxes and fees. The *annual budget deficit* (debt) would end. The excellent economy at the time seemed to make this possible. There might even be a budget *surplus*.

In 1998, due to a good economy, the United States did have its first budget surplus in years. Both Congress and the president began suggesting ways to spend this money even before it was received. The only thing everyone agreed on was that more than half of the surplus would be used to help Social Security.

---

**Think About It:**

If the economy is good and the budget is balanced, surplus money becomes available. What are some of the best ways this money can be used, and why are these uses better than others?

---

One major concern, however, is the way the budget is calculated. The federal government counts all payments into the Social Security fund as yearly income. The problem is that these Social Security payments one day have to be repaid.

In 1998 and 1999 Congress and the president began talking about Social Security. It, and Medicare, were in danger of going broke early in the new century. Plans to "rescue" these vital programs were discussed. President Clinton wanted to use much of the budget surplus to aid Social Security. But what will happen when there is no surplus?

Some in Congress wanted to let people invest some of their Social Security money in the stock market. But what happens if the market crashes?

There are no easy answers. Social Security and Medicare cannot be allowed to fail those who depend on them. As Americans live longer, more people need these programs. Fewer workers must support more retirees. No matter what changes are made more changes will be needed fairly soon.

## The Nation's Government

In June 1991, Supreme Court justice **Thurgood Marshall** resigned. Justice Marshall was the first black judge on the nation's highest court.

Thurgood Marshall

Eventually, Clarence Thomas, another African American, was approved as Marshall's replacement.

Two years later **Ruth Bader Ginsburg** replaced another retiring Supreme Court judge. For the first time in history, there were two women on the Supreme Court.

**Welfare reform** became a reality during the 1990's. In 1996, a bill became law. It set a two-year limit to the amount of time people able to work could stay on welfare. It also gave the states more say in how to run welfare programs. The bill provided such help as more spending for child care and job training. It gave people on welfare incentives, or reasons, for going to work.

The government also offered tax incentives to businesses to hire people off welfare.

Setting up Empowerment Zones to lure businesses to areas of high unemployment also created more jobs where they were needed.

The only down side of the welfare reform legislation was that it was too harsh on legal immigrants. But by 1998, changes were made making it fairer for these people.

It seemed to have worked. The end of 1998 found the lowest percentage of people on welfare in 30 years.

Congress and the president had to work hard to agree on a budget for the next year. Clinton vetoed the first budget bill before Christmas. This meant that the government was shut down in January. Without a budget bill, there were no funds available to pay federal employees. Eventually, a budget bill passed. Congress blamed the president for the government shutdown. The president blamed Congress.

In 1997, the federal budget for the year was 1.69 billion dollars. Even with agreement on a balanced budget bill, the nation was spending a lot of money each year. And too much of it was still pork-barrel spending.

There is another longstanding problem between presidents and congresses of the opposite party. This is the fact that Congress sometimes attaches ideas the president does not support to completely different laws that he or she does support.

The **disaster aid** bill that Congress passed during the summer of 1997 is a good example. States in the north central part of the nation had suffered terrible damage from blizzards and then from floods. The bill also included a provision to supply money to keep the government open in the future even if a budget bill was not agreed on.

President Clinton vetoed the disaster aid bill because of the part that prevented future government shutdowns. Congress removed the provision to end shutdowns so the disaster victims could receive aid.

## The Clinton Presidency

During the 1992 presidential campaign, other Democratic candidates raised questions about Bill Clinton's morals. Yet, Clinton was elected and became president. Within months, news items appeared concerning questionable activities. Throughout Clinton's presidency, troubling questions kept coming up about him, his wife, and some of his business partners and friends.

It started with investigations into business dealings involving the *Whitewater* scheme. This was an unsuccessful land development plan he had been part of in Arkansas years before. It ended with his impeachment in the House and acquittal in the Senate on two charges. These were lying about his sexual life and obstructing justice in the sexual harassment case brought by Paula Jones. Her case was dismissed even after his lies were uncovered.

In the meantime, several of his business partners in the Whitewater scheme were convicted. And the Paula Jones case made into household words the names of some of the women he had approached sexually, like Monica Lewinsky. Kenneth Starr, the special prosecutor, spent over $40 million of taxpayer money without finding enough evidence of specific wrongdoing to remove the president from office.

In the final analysis, some people felt the pattern of Clinton's behavior was bad enough that he should not remain president. But many people felt that the policies he supported as president were more important than his personal failings.

In every public opinion poll, President Clinton's popularity remained high. People did not like what he had done. But they also did not feel his actions threatened the government enough to be called "high crimes and misdemeanors." These are the only reasons the Constitution of the United States gives for removing someone from office. And, as the economy remained strong, the people trusted Clinton to run the country well.

## Recalling the 1990's

Read each statement and decide whether it is true or false. Write "T" or "F" in the space provided to indicate your answer.

_____    1. After Clinton was elected president, the United States always welcomed refugees from Haiti.

_____    2. U.S. military forces were sent to Somalia to stop an invasion from Sudan.

_____    3. Macedonia and Bosnia were formed out of what was once the nation of Czechoslovakia.

_____    4. Ethnic cleansing killed many Serbs.

_____    5. The World Trade Center bombing was in Chicago.

_____    6. The Brady Bill stopped the sale of all semiautomatic weapons.

_____    7. In the Oklahoma City bombing, 169 people died.

_____    8. Madeleine Albright was the first female Secretary of State for the United States.

_____    9. NAFTA was set up to improve trade between the United States and Japan.

_____    10. Clarence Thomas became the first black Supreme Court justice.

_____    11. When Congress and the president agreed to a balanced budget, it ended the national debt.

# THE INFORMATION AGE ARRIVES (1959–    )

**13**

## Time Line

| Events Elsewhere | Date | Events in America |
|---|---|---|
| | 1959 | Computer chip patented by American scientists |
| | 1975 | Microsoft Corporation founded |
| | 1977 | First mass market personal computers appeared |
| *Louise Brown, first healthy test-tube baby, born* | 1978 | |
| | 1981 | Space shuttle *Columbia* launched; AIDS identified |
| | 1982 | First artificial heart implanted |
| | 1983 | Sally Ride became first American woman in space |
| | 1986 | Space shuttle *Challenger* exploded |
| | 1989 | Stealth bomber introduced; World Wide Web introduced |
| | 1992 | New food labels appeared |
| *Ebola outbreak in Zaire* | 1995 | |
| | 1996 | Class action lawsuit against tobacco companies started |
| *Scottish scientists cloned a sheep, Dolly* | 1997 | |

## Introduction

The Industrial Revolution began at about the same time as the American Revolution. Close to 200 years later, a new age seemed to be in the making, the Information Age.

The seeds of this new age were planted earlier. Sprouts began to appear in the 1970's. But by the 1980's and 1990's, the Information Age was in full flower. Much of it was linked to the growing use of the computer.

Great advances were made in health care and technology. At the same time, the nation's infant death rate was worse than that of a dozen other nations. Computers brought the ability to do things faster and more accurately than ever before. Meanwhile, the nation struggled to find ways to keep air, water, and land clean enough to support life. The big challenge will be for Americans to work with people around the world to find ways to use the new technology for the good of all. It will not be an easy task.

## Computers and Artificial Intelligence

*Computers* made many of the other advances of the 1980's and 1990's possible. They do in seconds what used to take hours or even years. People use computers for things as basic as record keeping or as complex as designing spaceships. The world's financial system is computerized. Stock markets could no longer function without computers. Government would be at a standstill without them. *Artificial intelligence* is no longer something just for science fiction writers to dream about.

Computerized *robots* are used in manufacturing and industry for dangerous jobs and for tasks that require the same motions over and over. Though robots do many jobs quickly and safely, some people argue that they replace human workers.

Another problem with computers is that they do sometimes *crash*, or stop working. When people depend too much on computers, mistakes can occur when computers are down.

Computers can also get viruses. A *computer virus* is a command programmed into a computer to destroy or change a program. In 1988, a college student introduced a virus into a computer network as a prank. Thousands of government and scientific computers had to be shut down until the virus was cleared up. Even private computer owners found that their computers could pick up viruses. And with the introduction of the World Wide Web in 1989, viruses could be spread by downloading or taking programs from the Web.

The World Wide Web did much more than spread computer viruses, however. This vast computer network linked computers around the world. Anyone with a modem and a telephone line could join. Suddenly, people had more information than ever before at their fingertips. People could also use the World Wide Web to meet new friends. They could even use it to shop. Some companies formed that did not have physical stores, just *virtual* stores. People could buy what they wanted with the click of a button and have it mailed to them.

There were some problems. Not all the people on the Web were trustworthy. Privacy became a real issue. *Hackers* were clever computer programmers who used their knowledge to steal information such as medical or financial records. And not everyone could afford the technology. This made it even harder for some poor people to get ahead. However, there is no doubt that computers have permanently changed the way people live and work.

**Think About It:**

Advances in science, medicine, and technology are often related. Why do advances in these areas often cause so many people to become upset and fearful about the future?

## The Space Program

In the beginning, the Soviet Union led the space race. But by the 1980's and 1990's, the American space program led the world. The development of *space shuttles* was one of the reasons.

In April 1981, the first space shuttle, **Columbia**, orbited the Earth 36 times and landed in California. Two years later, in June of 1983, *Sally K. Ride* became the first American woman in space. She was a member of the crew of the space shuttle **Challenger**. That shuttle exploded in 1986 in one of the worst space disasters in American history. All seven astronauts on board died.

Space shuttles also helped with some great successes. A huge space telescope, the ***Hubble telescope***, was launched. It was supposed to send back the best photos ever taken of space. But a flaw in its mirror caused the photos to blur. Then, in December 1993, the crew of the shuttle *Endeavor* repaired the telescope in space.

During the following years, the Hubble photographed things undreamed of. It sent back to Earth photos of events many millions of light-years away. For the first time ever, evidence of planets in outer space could be seen. Massive stars were photographed. Astronomers were delighted. Other citizens were fascinated.

Hubble Space Telescope over Earth

Astronauts from the United States and Russia worked together. In 1994, a Russian astronaut flew aboard the shuttle *Discovery*. A year later, the *Atlantis* shuttle docked with the Russian **Mir** space station.

During the next four years, American astronauts spent time aboard *Mir.* After a series of problems with oxygen generators,

computer failures, and fires, this program ended. *Mir* was wearing out. A new ***international space station*** was planned to replace it.

On a smaller scale, satellites had a big role to play. The ability to communicate fast was increasingly vital. Communications satellites made this possible. Better weather forecasting came because of orbiting weather satellites. Spy satellites helped keep an eye on what happened in other parts of the world.

Meanwhile, space exploration moved forward. In September 1992, the United States launched a spacecraft to study Mars. It was the first time in 17 years such a space probe had been launched. Then, during 1997, Mars **Pathfinder** sent back photos of the surface of Mars. Later space probes discovered evidence of frozen water on Mars. And Jupiter's moons were studied.

Some of America's most advanced technology, however, was reserved for war and defense. The ***B-2 Stealth bomber*** flew in 1989. It was designed to be difficult to detect on radar. Thus, it could avoid enemy antiaircraft guns. Earlier in the decade, some research had been conducted on a *"Star Wars"* plan. Part of the plan was to use laser beams fired from satellites to bring down enemy rockets.

But perhaps one of the most important contributions of the space program has been to let people all over the world take a look at our own Earth from space.

## Environmental Issues

Everyone needs clean air and water. ***Emissions*** from vehicles and factories foul the air. ***Acid rain*** is created by factory smokestacks. When the acid rain falls on lakes and forests, they are poisoned. Runoff water from fertilized farm fields, city streets, and industrial sites further poisons lakes and oceans.

Scientists warn that people are destroying the *ozone layer* in the atmosphere. It protects all of life from damaging rays from the sun. *Chlorofluorocarbons*, or gases made by people for air conditioners, insulation, and some spray cans, may be causing the ozone layer to become thinner. Use of these gases was ended during the 1990's.

Another threat comes from emissions from cars and industry. These form a barrier in the atmosphere that holds heat in rather than letting it escape into space. Called the *greenhouse effect*, this slow heating may change much of life on Earth. Even a few degrees of warming may change farmland into desert. It could also cause melting polar icecaps to raise the sea level and flood many important cities.

One of the solutions is to use less oil as fuel. However, replacing oil is difficult. Burning coal also causes pollution. Solar and wind power are not always available. Many people fear nuclear power.

---

**Think About It:**

Another way to cut down on the use of oil is by conservation. So, why are Americans buying bigger vehicles and building energy-consuming homes?

---

In December 1997, many of the world's nations, including the United States, met in Kyoto, Japan, to start working on a way to reduce greenhouse gases. The following year, they met again in Buenos Aires, Argentina. Many issues still remained to be resolved, but progress was made. The next meeting was scheduled for the year 2000.

One of the things that became ever clearer is that human health is linked to the health of our Earth.

## Progress and Failure in Health and Medicine

The 1980's and 1990's were a time of many medical advances. But new and terrifying diseases also appeared. A great debate took place about the right to health care for all Americans. At the same time, there were debates over a person's right to die with dignity.

*Dr. Jack Kevorkian's* name appeared in the news. This retired doctor believed that a person in pain who would die soon from an incurable disease had the right to ask for help in dying. This help is called *assisted suicide.* Kevorkian came up with several ways of bringing a painless death to those who wished for it. This offended many people. In 1999, Dr. Kevorkian was convicted of murder for helping a sick man die. Many people were glad. They believed doctors should save people, not kill them. Other people disagreed with the verdict. They felt that very ill people who wanted to die should have a doctor's help.

More doctors searched for ways to save lives than to end them. One of the ways they could do this was with *organ transplants.* In 1982, Barney Clark received the first *artificial heart.* He did not live long, but his heart worked. Transplanting real organs became more successful because antirejection drugs helped one person's body accept another's donated organ.

In a major health move, the government began requiring new food labels in 1992. These labels stated the amount of fat, cholesterol, and other nutrients in a product. With these labels as guides, consumers could buy healthier foods.

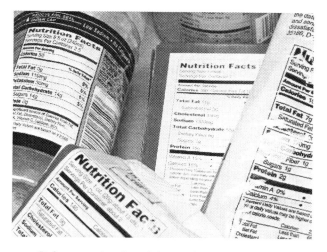

Other major health problems are also related to diet. In the last decades of the twentieth century, *anorexia* claimed several famous people. This is a disease where people can starve to death because they are afraid to eat. They think they are too fat. It happens especially to young women.

On the opposite end of things, the problem of overweight and *obesity* was becoming worse each year. According to figures available at the end of the century, nearly half of all American adults are overweight. Perhaps more important, about one quarter of American children are as well.

Doctors continue to identify health problems related to being overweight. The lifestyle of many Americans encourages them to eat too much and exercise too little. This may well become a major medical problem of the twenty-first century.

Another lifestyle choice related to health issues is smoking. Smoking had long been viewed as a cause of some health problems like lung cancer. In January 1993, the Environmental Protection Agency began warning of the dangers of *secondhand smoke*. In the following years, evidence grew concerning this danger. Children of smokers, employees in smoky workplaces, and others near smok-

## Our Changing Population

The United States of the twenty-first century is going to be different from the nation of today in many respects. One of these involves the changing population.

Ours is an aging population. By the 1990's, one of the fastest growing parts of our population is elderly people. Over 30 million people are drawing Social Security. Every day more people reach age 65. People are living longer due to better health care and the fact that more and more people are learning how to care for themselves in order to prolong life. Changed diets and living habits all help increase life span.

We are faced now and will be in the future with finding ways to allow our elderly people to live in safety and with dignity. This must be done as a steadily smaller percentage of the population is of working age.

A second major change in our population is the ethnic makeup of the people of the United States. Anglo population growth has slowed while minority population growth is continuing.

In 1990, a government study indicated that during the period studied in the 1980's, the Anglo population had increased 2%. During the same time period, the African American population grew 21% and the Hispanic population increased just over 40%.

Just as the "baby boom" of the 1950's and 1960's changed the way Americans lived, the current changes in age and ethnic makeup will affect us in the years to come.

ers were likely to have a number of serious health problems.

In the 1990's, tobacco companies began to have some expensive problems. For years, individual smokers had tried unsuccessfully to force tobacco companies to pay them damages. By 1996, some states began taking a new approach. They sued tobacco companies for the cost of health care for smokers.

The first big *class action* lawsuit ended in March 1996. One tobacco firm agreed to pay up to $50 million yearly for programs to help people stop smoking.

The following year a tobacco company finally admitted that smoking is addictive. It even admitted that tobacco companies had known smoking was addictive for quite some time.

The next year proved the most expensive yet for tobacco companies. In November 1998, they settled a big lawsuit with the states. They agreed to pay 46 states, the District of Columbia, and 4 territories $206 billion over the next 25 years. They agreed to pay $1.5 billion for research and advertising against underage tobacco use. The settlement did not include government regulation of nicotine, the main addictive drug in tobacco. And it did not force the companies to raise the price of cigarettes. But the settlement did leave open the door for further lawsuits. Only the states involved in the settlement would not be able to sue tobacco companies again.

Meanwhile, thousands of children and teens continued to begin smoking every day. Each day, older smokers continued to die of diseases related to tobacco use.

Another health problem began to make big headlines in the 1980's. In 1981, people started to learn about *AIDS*, or Acquired Immune Deficiency Syndrome. This disease is spread from person to person through blood and other body fluids.

A few people got AIDS through blood transfusions. This led to better screening of blood donors. But most people got AIDS through unprotected sex or drug abuse using shared hypodermic needles. Education seemed the best protection against AIDS and HIV, the Human Immunovirus that often leads to AIDS.

The AIDS virus was isolated in 1986. People hoped this would quickly lead to a cure for this deadly disease. It wasn't until the mid-1990's, however, that real progress started being made in helping people with AIDS to live. New drugs were discovered. Combinations of drugs kept HIV infections from turning into AIDS. Old drugs were found to be effective in slowing the advance of AIDS toward death.

In 1996, major progress was made in AIDS research. A protein was found that lets the AIDS virus enter a person's system. If this protein can be controlled or blocked, it is possible that AIDS can be avoided.

Some old diseases also started to cause problems. Diseases like *tuberculosis* were once almost gone from the United States. By the end of the century, they were reappearing. Some of these diseases resisted the antibiotics that once cured them. Some germs can change so that old drugs no longer work. New, powerful antibiotics were developed. But unless they are used carefully, germs may soon be able to resist them too. The return of old killers may be one of the big health problems of the next century.

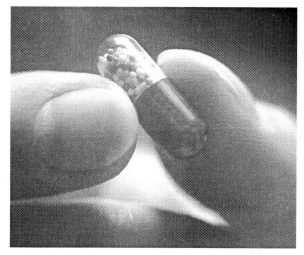

*Bubonic plague* is another one of these old killers. It is common for cases of this disease to occur in the Southwest every year. If treated promptly with antibiotics, it can now be cured. Still, it is amazing that medicine has not yet conquered the plague that killed one third of Europe's people in the fourteenth century.

The warm, dry area of the Southwest is ideal for keeping some germs alive. During the summer of 1993, a new germ made the news there. *Hantavirus* killed 19 people. This almost unknown virus was carried in the droppings of rodents.

In 1995, another disease most Americans had never heard of caused great fear. *Ebola* causes massive bleeding that almost always results in death. UN doctors were eventually able to stop the ebola outbreak in Zaire.

This outbreak and other disease outbreaks in different countries caused great concern. What happens when medicines cannot control a disease? Just as important, with modern air travel, how can the spread of disease from nation to nation be stopped? An exposed passenger may be far from where he or she caught the disease before becoming ill.

Another medical mystery is *Gulf War Syndrome*. Some soldiers who fought in the Gulf War complained of strange symptoms. They suffered from fatigue, nausea, head-aches, joint pain, and even memory loss. As the year 2000 approached, research was still being done into the cause of these symptoms.

In a very different area of research, doctors found a link between cockroaches and *asthma*. This may help to explain why so many children in poor urban areas suffer from this condition. It is not the whole story, however, as asthma continued to become more and more of a problem for children around the country at the end of the twenti-eth century.

At the other end of the life cycle is *Alzhei-mer's disease*. This loss of memory and the

ability for self-care is a devastating disease. It afflicts millions of the elderly and the families who must take care of them. President Reagan was diagnosed with Alzheimer's a few years after he left the presidency. Because Americans are living longer, more people suffer from Alzheimer's than ever before. With the older population growing, there is a real need to find ways to prevent or treat this disease.

Perhaps the most controversial area of research at the close of the twentieth century is research involving genes. These are the basic units of heredity. They determine what each living being becomes—from the hair color of a person to the number of arms on an octopus. When something goes wrong with some genes, disease or disability can result. When genes determine that a certain plant or animal is the best possible, *cloning*, or copying that set of genes exactly, can result in an identical plant or animal.

In March 1997, some Scottish scientists did clone a sheep from another adult sheep. At once, people asked whether humans could also be cloned. The idea of reproducing an exact replica of any human being was not popular. But being able to copy the best of what a farmer produces would be a big help in agriculture.

Scientists have also learned how to move genes around. This is one way new medicines are being developed. Not only may they be more powerful, but these medicines may be more targeted, more able to affect just the problem they are meant to attack.

Since 1990, scientists have been working on the **Human Genome Project**. This 15-year project will try to identify all 80,000 or so human genes. In addition to providing basic information, scientists hope this project will lead to new ways to diagnose, treat, and possibly prevent disease and disability. They will learn which genes to target with the new medicines!

Even more controversial is research using human fetal tissue or stem cells. Both of these include cells that have not yet been told by their genes what to become. Therefore, working with them can open up many new areas of research. It is possible that some day, scientists may be able to grow new organs like hearts and livers from a single stem cell. Then organ transplants would have far fewer problems. Needed organs would be quickly available, and recipients would not have to worry about their bodies rejecting the new organ.

---

**Think About It:**

There are ethical problems involved with this kind of research. What are some of the issues you would like to see addressed before further research in this area is done?

---

## Checking Your Own Information Age

The clues below will help you fill out the blanks on the right. When you have completed these sentences, use the letters over the numbered blanks to complete the last sentence.

1. _____ companies will pay $206 billion over 25 years to settle a class action lawsuit.

   _ _ _ _ _ _ _
   1

2. _____ is a disease linked to cockroaches.

   _ _ _ _ _
    2

3. The _____ effect is the warming of the Earth caused by trapped heat.

   _ _ _ _ _ _ _ _ _
    3

4. _____ do in seconds what used to take hours or even longer.

   _ _ _ _ _ _ _ _ _
       4

5. The _____ was the space shuttle that exploded, killing all seven astronauts on board.

   _ _ _ _ _ _ _ _ _ _ _
       5

6. _____ rain poisons lakes and forests.

   _ _ _ _
    6

You have now reached   _ _ _   _ _ _   of this book.
                        1 2 3   4 5 6

# ANSWERS

## Maps Help Us Understand United States History

### A Quick Review, page 4
1. true
2. false
3. true
4. false
5. false
6. true
7. false
8. true
9. true
10. false

## A New Land Is Reached and Settled

### Exploration Puzzle Quiz, page 10
1. Da Gama
2. Vikings
3. Northwest Passage
4. Cabot
5. de Soto
6. Coronado
7. Hudson
8. Cartier
9. Marquette
10. La Salle

### Exploration, page 11
1. Spain
2. England
3. France
4. Spain
5. England
6. France
7. Spain
8. Hudson
9. Coronado
10. de Soto
11. Hudson
12. Cabot
13. Atlantic
14. Cabot
15. La Salle

### New World Settlements, page 18
1. the Atlantic Ocean
2. New York
3. Rhode Island
4. New York
5. North Carolina
6. Virginia
7. Delaware
8. St. Augustine
9. Spain
10. Massachusetts
11. Montreal
12. Potomac
13. five
14. France
15. Georgia

### Settlers, page 20
#### Across
1. St. Augustine
7. Williams
8. Rolfe
9. Penn
12. Quebec
14. Dutch
16. Delaware
17. French
18. slave
19. Jamestown

#### Down
1. Santa Fe
2. New York
3. Pilgrims
4. Quaker
5. Massachusetts Bay
6. Georgia
8. Roanoke
10. Dare
11. Rhode
13. Calvert
15. Hooker

## Thirteen Colonies Become a Nation

### Colonial Life, page 26
1. clearing
2. tobacco
3. religion
4. stocks
5. Native Americans
6. Bible
7. branding
8. Salem
9. plantation
10. rivers
11. French
12. education

### Colonial Land Claims, page 29
1. France
2. England
3. Spain
4. France
5. France
6. Spain
7. Appalachian Mountains
8. Cumberland Gap
9. Boonesborough

### American Revolution, page 38
1. Fort Vincennes
2. Northwest Territory
3. Fort Pitt
4. Cowpens
5. Valley Forge
6. Yorktown
7. West Point
8. Saratoga
9. New York City
10. New Jersey

### *Where Am I?, page 39*

1. Boston
2. Salem
3. Lexington
4. Plymouth
5. Saratoga
6. Long Island Sound
7. Connecticut
8. Lake Champlain
9. Boston
10. Hudson River

## The New Nation

### *A New Government, page 46*

1. Articles
2. George
3. compromise
4. House
5. Senate
6. Constitution
7. amendments
8. Bill of Rights
9. branches
10. checks; balances
11. four; senators; two
12. cabinet
13. Hamilton
14. tariff
15. excise

GEORGE WASHINGTON

### *The United States in 1783, page 48*

1. Atlantic Ocean
2. Lake Erie
3. British
4. Vermont
5. North Carolina
6. Massachusetts
7. Maryland
8. Kentucky
9. Ohio River
10. Spanish
11. Tennessee
12. Maryland
13. New York
14. Cumberland Gap
15. Mississippi River

### *Louisiana Purchase, page 55*

1. Mississippi River
2. thirteen
3. Lewis and Clark
4. Pike
5. Pike
6. St. Louis
7. Columbia River
8. Gulf of Mexico
9. Missouri River; Mississippi River

### *War of 1812, page 59*

**Across**

1. New Orleans
4. Toronto
7. Washington
8. New Jersey
9. Chesapeake Bay
11. blockade
15. Louisiana
17. Indiana
18. Carolina
19. Baltimore
20. Spanish Florida

**Down**

2. Erie
3. New York
5. Tennessee
6. Ohio
9. Champlain
10. Atlantic
12. Detroit
13. British
14. Champlain
16. Canada

## The Nation Keeps Growing

### *Puzzle Quiz, page 65*

1. toll
2. Erie Canal
3. James Watt
4. *Clermont*
5. *Tom Thumb*
6. National Road
7. turnpike
8. Samuel Morse
9. Peter Cooper
10. Robert Fulton

### *North and South, page 68*

1. 1
2. 1
3. 2
4. 2
5. 3
6. 2
7. 2
8. 2
9. 1
10. 2

### *Westward Ho!, page 76*

1. Santa Fe Trail
2. Oregon Trail
3. Santa Fe Trail
4. California Trail
5. Pony Express
6. Butterfield Southern Overland Mail
7. Rocky Mountains
8. Mormons
9. Independence
10. Old Spanish Trail

### *Western Expansion, page 78*

1. Whitman
2. Kearny
3. Scott
4. Forty-niners
5. Mexican Cession
6. Oregon
7. Lone Star
8. secedes
9. annex
10. spoils
11. Jackson
12. San Jacinto
13. Sutter
14. California
15. gold
16. Santa Anna

## Brother Against Brother

### *The United States in 1820, page 84*

1. true
2. true
3. false
4. false
5. false
6. false
7. true
8. true
9. false
10. true

### The United States in 1850, page 86

| | |
|---|---|
| 1. false | 8. false |
| 2. false | 9. true |
| 3. true | 10. false |
| 4. true | 11. true |
| 5. true | 12. true |
| 6. false | 13. true |
| 7. false | |

### Civil War Sites, page 94

| | |
|---|---|
| 1. Missouri, Kentucky Maryland, Delaware | 8. West Virginia |
| | 9. Bull Run |
| 2. Georgia | 10. Shiloh |
| 3. Atlanta | 11. Vicksburg |
| 4. Maryland | 12. South Carolina |
| 5. Maryland | 13. Union Blockade |
| 6. Virginia | 14. Pennsylvania |
| 7. Gettysburg | 15. Virginia |

### Civil War, pages 96–98

| | |
|---|---|
| 1. Calhoun | 15. West |
| 2. Compromise | 16. *Alabama* |
| 3. Slave | 17. Sherman |
| 4. Railroad | 18. Gettysburg |
| 5. Harriet | 19. Grant |
| 6. Brown | 20. Lee |
| 7. Douglas | 21. Antietam |
| 8. Lincoln | 22. Stuart |
| 9. Civil War | 23. Days' |
| 10. Vicksburg | 24. slaves |
| 11. *Merrimac* | 25. Barton |
| 12. Davis | 26. truce |
| 13. *Monitor* | 27. draft |
| 14. Bull Run | 28. George |

### Matching, page 101

| | |
|---|---|
| 1. g | 6. b |
| 2. j | 7. i |
| 3. a | 8. c |
| 4. d | 9. f |
| 5. h | 10. e |

## Years of Growth and Change    7

### Building America, page 109

| | |
|---|---|
| 1. reaper | 9. airplane |
| 2. irrigation | 10. petroleum |
| 3. demand | 11. Ward |
| 4. Field | 12. corporations |
| 5. telephone | 13. monopoly |
| 6. system | 14. Oil |
| 7. Ford | 15. steel |
| 8. line | 16. Hill |

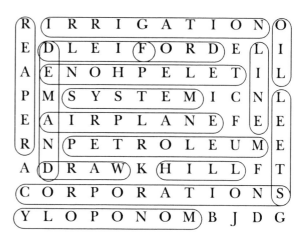

### Problems, page 116

1. American Federation of Labor, Knights of Labor, Congress of Industrial Organizations, A.F.L.-C.I.O.
2. strike, collective bargaining, arbitration, cooling-off period, wages
3. immigrate, quota, citizens
4. Hull House, Chicago slums
5. Wyoming, suffrage, Nineteenth Amendment
6. Prohibition, repeal, Eighteenth Amendment, Twenty-first Amendment

## The United States Becomes a World Power    8

### Alaska and Hawaii, pages 122–123
**Across**

| | |
|---|---|
| 1. Alaska | 12. Nome |
| 2. Kodiak | 16. Molokai |
| 5. Juneau | 18. Pearl Harbor |
| 6. Hilo | 19. Honolulu |
| 8. Bering Strait | 21. Anchorage |
| 11. Niihau | 22. St. Lawrence |

### Alaska and Hawaii (continued)
**Down**

| | | | |
|---|---|---|---|
| 1. | Aleutian | 10. | Mauna Kea |
| 2. | Kahoolawe | 13. | Mauna Loa |
| 3. | Kauai | 14. | Diamond Head |
| 4. | Point Barrow | 15. | Brooks Range |
| 7. | Maui | 17. | Pacific |
| 8. | Big Diomede | 20. | Oahu |
| 9. | Seward | | |

### Matching and Ordering, page 128

I.
1. 1867
2. 1898
3. 1917

II.
1. Seward's Folly
2. Manila Bay
3. Rough Riders

III.
1. Cuba
2. Philippines
3. Havana Harbor

IV.
1. $7.2 million
2. $25 million
3. $10 million

V.
1. Yellow fever
2. Panama Canal builder
3. The Big Ditch

### Protectorates and Territories, page 130
1. Cuba, Haiti, Dominican Republic, Panama, Nicaragua
2. Puerto Rico, Virgin Islands
3. Northwest to southeast

### World War I, page 133

| | | | |
|---|---|---|---|
| 1. | Nicaragua | 6. | neutral |
| 2. | Pancho Villa | 7. | *Lusitania* |
| 3. | Allies | 8. | Alfred Zimmerman |
| 4. | Triple Alliance | 9. | submarine |
| 5. | Francis Ferdinand | 10. | armistice |

### Europe in 1914, page 135

| | | | |
|---|---|---|---|
| 1. | Russia | 6. | Great Britain |
| 2. | France | 7. | Bulgaris |
| 3. | Central Powers | 8. | Norway, Sweden |
| 4. | neutral | | |
| 5. | Russia | | |

WORLD WAR ONE

### Review Exercise, page 138

| | | | |
|---|---|---|---|
| 1. | Fourteen | 6. | Speakeasies |
| 2. | Nations | 7. | Bootleggers |
| 3. | Treaty | 8. | stock |
| 4. | Court | 9. | Depression |
| 5. | Roaring | 10. | Bowl |

## An Uneasy World

### United States in the 1930's, pages 142–143

| | | | |
|---|---|---|---|
| 1. | Civilian | 5. | overtime |
| 2. | Security | 6. | Labor |
| 3. | PWA | 7. | Valley |
| 4. | Depression | | |

### World War II, page 148

| | | |
|---|---|---|
| I. | 2, 3, 1, 4 | IV. 3, 4, 1, 2 |
| II. | 1, 3, 4, 2 | V. 2, 4, 3, 1 |
| III. | 3, 2, 1, 4 | |

### Europe in World War II, pages 148–149
1. Germany, Italy
2. Iceland, Great Britain, Northern Ireland, Turkey, Soviet Union
3. France
4. Finland, Estonia, Latvia, Lithuania, Poland
5. Czechoslovakia
6. Yugoslavia

### Japanese Territory in World War II, page 149
1. Pearl Harbor
2. Germany, Italy
3. Philippine Islands, Korea, Indochina, Guam, Wake, New Guinea, Borneo
4. Nagasaki, Hiroshima
5. Australia

### Europe After World War II, page 153
1. Soviet Union, East Germany, Poland, Czechoslovakia, Hungary, Rumania, Yugoslavia, Bulgaria, Albania
2. Finland, Sweden, Ireland, Spain, Austria, Switzerland
3. Iceland, Denmark, West Germany, Greece, Norway, Belgium, France, Portugal, Great Britain, Netherlands, Italy, Northern Ireland

**Letter Maze, page 157**

1. Nations
2. Plan
3. NATO
4. cold
5. Airlift
6. Korea
7. curtain
8. Castro
9. Laos, Cambodia, Vietnam
10. Nixon

## The United States Meets New Challenges

**Changing Times, page 165**

1. Frontier
2. Neil Armstrong
3. Ecology
4. Martin Luther King, Jr.
5. riots
6. Richard Nixon

**The United States in the 1970's, page 165**

**Across**

1. hijacking
2. arms race
4. Israel
6. treaty
7. impeached
8. embargo
10. inflation
12. China
13. Panama

**Down**

1. hostages
2. aliens
3. Watergate
5. revolt
9. Alaska
11. Nixon

**Letter Maze, pages 171–172**

1. Sadat
2. China
3. SALT
4. Olympics
5. Iran
6. Cuba
7. El Salvador
8. Security
9. Orange
10. Island
11. toxic
12. Reagan
13. interest
14. O'Connor
15. *Columbia*

## The United States Works to Remain a World Leader

**Looking Back, page 181**

1. F
2. F
3. T
4. T
5. T
6. F
7. T
8. T
9. T
10. T
11. F
12. T
13. F
14. T
15. F

## The End of the Second Millennium

**Recalling the 1990's, page 191**

1. F
2. F
3. F
4. F
5. F
6. F
7. T
8. T
9. F
10. F
11. F

## The Information Age Arrives

**Checking Your Own Information Age, page 199**

1. Tobacco
2. asthma
3. greenhouse
4. computers
5. *Challenger*
6. Acid

Last sentence: THE END